The
Northern Pacific Railroad
and the
Selling of the West

The
Northern Pacific Railroad
and the
Selling of the West

●

A Nineteenth-century Public Relations Venture

by Sig Mickelson

The Center for Western Studies

© 1993 The Center for Western Studies
All rights reserved

The Prairie Plains Series

Published by The Center for Western Studies
Box 727, Augustana College
Sioux Falls, South Dakota 57197

The Center for Western Studies is an archives, library, museum, and publishing house concerned principally with collecting, preserving, and interpreting prehistoric, historic, and contemporary materials that document native and immigrant cultures of the northern prairie plains. The Center promotes understanding of the region through exhibits, publications, art shows, conferences, and academic programs. It is committed, ultimately, to defining the contribution of the region to American civilization.

Library of Congress Cataloging-in-Publication Data:

Mickelson, Sig.
    The Northern Pacific Railroad and the selling of the West : a nineteenth-century public relations venture / by Sig Mickelson.
      p. cm. – (The Prairie plains series)
      Includes bibliographical references and index.
      ISBN 0-931170-54-0
      1. Northern Pacific Railroad Company – History. 2. Advertising – Real estate business – History – 19th century. 3. Land settlement – West (U.S.) – History – 19th century. I. Title. II. Series.
HE2791.N855M53 1993
385'-.06'579 – dc20   92-47038
                                                                                                   CIP

Cover illustration: From a reproduction of a painting based on photographs by F. J. Haynes, showing the completion of the Northern Pacific's main line between the Great Lakes and the Northern Pacific Coast. Among the dignitaries shown at this "Last Spike" ceremony, held at Gold Creek, Montana Territory, September 8, 1883, are Gen. Ulysses S. Grant, holding the spike mall, and, at his left, Henry Villard, then president of the Northern Pacific.

Cover design by Bob Child Graphics

Printed in United States of America

PINE HILL PRESS, INC.
Freeman, S. Dak. 57029

For Elena

Table of Contents

Chapter		Page
	List of Tables	ix
	Preface	xi
	Foreword	xv
I.	Background of the Drive for Settlers	1
	Status of Western Lands in 1872	3
	Factors Influencing Emigration and Migration	5
	Relationship of the Northern Pacific Program to Other Emigration Agencies	7
II.	The Northern Pacific Program Gets Underway, 1870-1873	9
	Distribution of Printed Matter	11
	Getting Publicity into the Press	14
	Public Speakers, Excursions, and Miscellaneous Devices	16
	Advertising in the Newspapers	18
	Arousing Interest Through Exhibits	20
	Employing Agents and Forming Colonies	22
	Forerunners of the Public Relations Counsels	24
III.	The Period of the Big Boom, 1876-1884	27
	The Flow of Printed Publicity Resumed	31
	Advertising in the Newspaper	39
	Keeping Up an Agitation in the Press	40
	Use of Miscellaneous Publicity Techniques	41
IV.	The Period of Drought, Crop Failures, and Large-Scale Land Sales, 1886-1893	45
	Advertising During the Adverse Years	48

V. Newspapers Becoming the Dominant Medium,
      1897-1902 51
   Paying for Advertising in Transportation 52
   Advertising in the West 53
   Inspiring Favorable Letters in the Press 58
   Publicity Techniques with Source Unconcealed 62
   The Job of the Land Solicitor 68
   1897 to 1902 in Review 71

VI. The Campaign in Europe 73
    The Land Department Chooses Its Prospects 82
    Printed Promotional Material Flows to Europe.... 85
    Placing Advertising in European Newspapers 88
    Exhibiting Products of the Northwest 90
    The Promotional Devices Summarized 93

VII. An Analysis of the Pressures Exerted 95
     The Contents of the Advertising Arguments
        Analyzed 99
     An Analysis of Individual Articles 109
     Conclusion on the Worth of the Promotional
        Material 112

VIII. Results of the Campaigns 124
      Sales of Northern Pacific Lands 126
      The Growth of the Northwest's Population 131
      The Direction of the Migratory Movement 143
      Conclusions on the Effectiveness of
         Northern Pacific Promotion 153

      Appendix 155

      Notes and References 177

      Bibliography 213

      Acknowledgments 226

      Index 227

List of Tables

Table		Page
I.	Advertising Expenditures by Years, 1888 to 1893..	49
II.	Advertising Contracts for the Years 1897, 1898, and 1899	54
III.	Advertising Contracts Made up to and Including April 30, 1897	55
IV.	Number of Solicitors at Work, 1896 to 1900	70
V.	An Analysis of the Frequency of Mention of Various Appeals to Readers in Northern Pacific Advertisements	98
VI.	An Analysis of Land Sales by Periods of Promotional Activity	126
VII.	Land Sales by Years from 1875 to 1907	129
VIII.	Populations of the Northwestern States, 1870 to 1920	132
IX.	Populations of Counties in Minnesota Along the Northern Pacific Line	133
X.	Population of North Dakota Counties Through Which the Northern Pacific Passed	136
XI.	Population of Montana Counties Through Which the Northern Pacific Passed	137

XII. Populations of Minnesota Towns and Cities
Along the Northern Pacific Line........................138

XIII. Estimated Populations of Minnesota Cities
in 1882 Compared with 1880 Census................140

XIV. Estimated Populations of Minnesota Counties
in 1882 Compared with 1880 Census................141

XV. Estimated Populations of Dakota Towns
in 1882 Compared with 1880 Census................142

XVI. Estimated Populations of Dakota Counties
in 1882 Compared with 1880 Census................142

XVII. Population According to State, Territory,
or County of Birth..148

Preface

The editor of the *Alta Californian* in the August 9, 1866, issue of that newspaper declared that completion of a railroad to San Francisco would, in its wake, increase intelligence, liberalize intercourse, improve industry, and drive out casual adventurers. In the same year, well to the east in central Iowa, another editor had written more soberly in the *Eldora Ledger* for January 16 that "the successful development of the vast resources of this state, and its subsequent prosperity and wealth, are largely dependent upon facilities offered by railroad communication." These two editors, separated by half a continent and surely strangers, reflected a powerful and prevailing theme among journalists and writers from the dawn of the railroad era in the 1830s through the grandest hours of the steamcar civilization.

Early promoters along the eastern seaboard of the country saw railroad technology as a means to hold hinterlands subservient to the commercial interests of specific cities—a means to implement a policy of urban economic imperialism. Thus was born, for example, the Baltimore & Ohio—to connect Baltimore with the vast valley of the Ohio River and in that way deliver finished goods to a burgeoning market with return of raw materials to Baltimore manufacturers. Not surprisingly, there was little interest in connecting lines, in systemizing, since that would give options to otherwise captive customers. But there was no forestalling such systemization. Indeed, the Baltimore & Ohio eventually brought other roads, added construction for its own account, and forged a through route from Atlantic tidewater to Lake Michigan and the Mississippi River. So did the New York Central, the Pennsylvania, and other companies follow a similar path of expansion to serve a variety of cities in a broad geographic expanse.

"Railroad fever" affected all persons in all regions and certainly could not be divorced from strong feelings of "manifest destiny" that characterized American thinking at mid-century. Even before the Mexican War, Asa Whitney, a New York merchant, proposed a line stretching across a broad country uninhabited for the most part by other than aborigines from Milwaukee to the Columbia River. Nothing came of Whitney's plan, but the concept of a transcontinental rail route soon gained general acceptance. There was no agreement, however, as to the eastern terminus of such a line. Southerners favored New Orleans, Vicksburg, or Memphis; northerners urged St. Louis or Chicago among other aspiring cities. Visionaries and practical men alike understood that any line to the Pacific would be built ahead of demand and that to complete it would require the blended assets of the federal government and private enterprise. But the "Pacific railroad matter" was subordinated during the volatile 1850s to the overarching national issue – the potential expansion of slavery to the West – and no decision was forthcoming.

With Southern states absent during the Civil War, however, Congress passed and President Abraham Lincoln signed into law acts that provided for the establishment of and support for a central route and then a northern route. The first, reaching from Council Bluffs and Omaha on the Missouri River to Sacramento and eventually San Francisco, was completed by the Union Pacific and the Central Pacific in 1869. The second, the Northern Pacific, was to connect the head of the lakes with Puget Sound and finally, in 1883, placed in service a through line between Duluth/Superior and Portland (eventually to Tacoma and Seattle).

The idea of a northern transcontinental line was not new. Indeed, Whitney's scheme of 1844 represented that view. A few years later some New Englanders dreamed of a true transcontinental – from Boston through New England, Quebec, and Ontario and then westward via Chicago or Sault Ste. Marie to Pacific salt water. Such a grand scheme was not prosecuted, but the Northern Pacific held an abiding interest for many New Englanders, who invested heavily in it and who were for many years involved in its management.

In any event, the Northern Pacific project was planned as a solitary enterprise and proved to be the single greatest

American corporate undertaking of the nineteenth century. The road captured the fancy of Jay Cooke, but not even the great financier could survive the Panic of 1873 and NP's failure during those troublesome times. The road pitched into the courts again a decade later just after the golden spike was driven in Montana. The reasons for such distress were many and varied, but even more than the central route (which had its own difficulties), the northern line had been built ahead – well ahead – of demand. NP suffered accordingly. There was little through business, and local volumes increased only as the land became occupied. It was to that end that NP executives pledged prodigious resources.

They were not naive. NP held a land grant of admittedly monumental proportion, its route passed through huge preserves of commercially valuable timber, minerals were sure to be sprinkled about, and the Red River Valley and much of the northern Great Plains featured productive soils bound to produce wonderful crops. On the other hand, this was – in the minds of many if not most Americans and Europeans – a land savage and untamed. Moreover, the reputation of the region's fierce weather was deeply etched in the public mind. "Selling" NP's service area would be challenging in the extreme.

The company employed several well-known publicists for work in advertising the Northern Pacific and the territory of its route. These men focused early on New England, on the Middle States, and on Germany, Norway, Sweden, and the United Kingdom. Later efforts of recruitment turned toward states nearby, Iowa and Wisconsin as examples. Efforts ebbed and flowed, predictably, according to business cycles, with great energies and resources expended whenever the economy was strong.

All of it reflected a common wisdom in the executive suite: NP would prosper only if its constituents prospered. The land had to be populated with a diligent and productive people – and as quickly as possible. This benign selfishness was, we should remember, perfectly compatible with national goals of the time. Indeed, "settle up the West" and maximize use of its resources was the nearly universal goal of Americans in the last four decades of the nineteenth century.

Northern Pacific's campaigns to populate and make productive the "Great Northwest" were not unique. Other railroads — the Great Northern and the Milwaukee Road among others — were similarly active from the upper Mississippi to the Pacific, as were most state governments in the area. NP's efforts, though, were important because they were early, because they were so wide ranging, because they were so innovative, and because they were demonstrably successful.

This is not a matter of conjecture. The Northern Pacific chose to retain its records in astonishing volume and completeness and — long before it passed many of its holdings to the custodianship of the Minnesota Historical Society — generously allowed scholars access. One of those scholars was Sig Mickelson, whose thesis of 1940 has stood the test of time and remains well respected by students of the American West and railroad history. After more than a half century it finally gets the broader exposure it so richly deserves.

Don L. Hofsommer
Department of History
St. Cloud State University
St. Cloud, Minnesota

Foreword

Much has been written about the history of propaganda and promotional activities. Particularly since the end of World War I, when "propaganda" became a phenomenon of absorbing interest, research students have discovered much evidence concerning the use of propaganda techniques by political pressure groups and business interests.

Case studies of commercial propaganda have been undertaken in recent years, and their results have been recorded in numerous books and articles, but these investigations have accented either the work of public relations counsel on behalf of business organizations,[1] or they have described the public relations activities of modern business institutions.[2] In short, research students, to this point, have focused attention primarily on public relations and promotional policies of business since the close of World War I. Not a single notable case study has analyzed business promotion and propaganda, in all its ramifications, in the era of expanding business dating back from World War I to the Civil War.

It is the purpose of this writer to present such a case study. The subject of analysis will be the propaganda and promotional activities of the Northern Pacific Railroad. A subordinate part of this study will portray the promotional work of Jay Cooke & Co., which acted as the Northern Pacific's banking house until 1873, but the reader should bear in mind that the major investigation throughout relates to the promotional enterprises of the railroad, not those of the Cooke firm. The Northern Pacific was faced with the dual problems of selling lands from a grant which comprised about 50,000,000 acres and of attracting enough settlers to the region of its grant to provide for profitable freight traffic. It was the task of Jay Cooke & Co. to sell sufficient bonds to finance the building of the railroad.

The media used by the railroad and its banking house to induce persons to leave their established homes and migrate to the unsettled section of the West through which the railroad ran provide the material for this analysis.

Northern Pacific land-sales promotion divides itself into four periods of heaviest concentration. The first opens with the beginning of construction of the railroad line in 1870 and continues until the crash of the Cooke banking house in 1873; the second begins with the reestablishment of financial stability in 1876 and extends to the weakened financial position of Villard management in 1884; the third runs from about 1886 until the receivership of 1893; and the fourth starts with reorganization in 1897 and continues until most of the good land had been sold in 1902.

A chapter will be devoted to each of these periods and another to the background that precedes the first period. Pressures exerted in Europe will be given a separate chapter. In an effort to establish definitely the effectiveness of the entire promotional campaign, additional chapters will analyze the contents of the publications used and the results of the program as reflected in land sales and population shifts. The study will be limited to the lands lying east of the Belt mountains in Montana.

While no study of the promotional media has been undertaken, other writers have analyzed Northern Pacific land sales policies. Dr. James B. Hedges has written two monographs on the subject and included some material in a book.[3] Harold F. Peterson submitted a master's thesis on the problem to the Graduate School of the University of Minnesota.[4]

With the exception of Dr. Hedges' monograph, "The Colonization Work of the Northern Pacific Railroad," these studies embrace a much broader scope than is proposed for this thesis. Mr. Peterson's thesis describes promotional efforts, prior to 1880, of all railroads operating in Minnesota; Dr. Hedges' monograph, "Promotion of Immigration to the Pacific Northwest," includes Northern Pacific activities only as they supplemented the work of Henry Villard's transportation companies in the Pacific Northwest; and his volume on Henry Villard devotes only one chapter to Villard's connection with Northern Pacific land-sales efforts in its broader account of Villard's railroad career.

"The Colonization Work of the Northern Pacific Railroad" was of great value to this writer. It simplified the task of rooting

FOREWORD

out the organization of the Land Committee and the Bureau of Immigration of the Northern Pacific. It also provided the writer with a skeleton outline of promotional activities. This article, however, goes no further than 1888.

Dr. Hedges devoted much space to a description of the early organization of the Land Committee. This writer will treat that subject only briefly and concentrate on the nature of the work done by that committee. Mr. Peterson has very adequately pictured the colonization program carried on by the Bureau of Immigration. This writer will only mention that project as one feature of the entire campaign.

Those features of Northern Pacific promotion which have been stressed by Dr. Hedges and Mr. Peterson will be discussed by this writer only as they relate to the specific objective of this thesis. It must be remembered that both these men pictured the Northern Pacific as a force in inducing settlement of the Northwest. They did not analyze its efforts as a gigantic commercial propaganda campaign. Their aim was to prove that the Northern Pacific was a major force in populating the Northwest. The aim of this thesis is to dissect railroad promotion to discover the methods by which it populated that territory.

A thorough analysis of a propaganda campaign entails three distinct functions: an effort to discover the pre-existing attitudes of the persons on whom pressures are to be exerted, a study of the nature of the suggestion applied to bring about an integration of those pre-existing attitudes, and finally, a survey of the results accruing from the new dominant attitude which the application of suggestion has brought about.

The first and third of these functions belong rightly in the field of the student of migration. The authority in that field is conversant with the causes of discontent which make men susceptible to pressures urging migration and with the population trends which result from migration. Emphasis in this thesis will be placed on the second function: the study of the pressures themselves. It will, of course, be necessary before arriving at any conclusions concerning the effectiveness of the propaganda, to know in general the pre-existing attitudes toward which the pressures had to be designed and the results which came about as a consequence of those pressures. These subjects will be developed only in sufficient detail to give the promotional campaign adequate perspective.

Basic materials used in the preparation of this thesis were forty-nine volumes and three boxes of letters of the Land and Emigration Departments of the railroad and the Annual Reports of the company from 1876 to 1905. All these documents were discovered by the writer in the archives of the Northern Pacific in St. Paul. With very few exceptions the letters are handwritten duplicate copies bound in leather covers. Only the volumes of the later years were typewritten. Scores more, in addition to the forty-nine used, were paged through and then discarded when it was discovered that they contained no pertinent information.

Dr. Hedges and Mr. Peterson both used some of the earlier volumes, particularly those relating to colonies and foreign emigration. The writer has been unable to discover evidence that any of the volumes, including correspondence after 1888, have ever been used for any research purpose. It is very probable that their covers have never been opened since the documents were stored away.

This material was supplemented by pamphlets, folders, and newspaper articles in the Minnesota Historical Library, by census reports, and by accounts of railroad and immigration activity in secondary sources.

Necessarily the writer encountered many difficulties. It was necessary to browse in dust-laden shelves and over-filled cabinets in the Northern Pacific storage building in an effort to discover volumes that related to the problem. Once found, the articles were difficult to read because of their fading handwriting. There is no way of knowing whether the archives are complete nor how much material may have been lost by the railroad over the years. It is necessary in many cases to generalize on the nature of promotional ventures from the few samples discovered. In constructing the unified account of the entire promotional program that appears in this thesis, it was necessary to piece together isolated bits from various volumes, making organization of this study a knotty problem.

But whatever the problems, the study was an interesting one. It is the hope of the writer that the findings presented

FOREWORD

here will open up an entirely new vista in the study of commercial and industrial promotion; that General A. B. Nettleton, George Sheppard, George B. Hibbard, F. W. Wilsey, and others of the Northern Pacific's Land Department staff will be given their rightful places as nineteenth-century forerunners of the present-day public relations counsels and advertising and promotion specialists; and that this study of promotion will shed additional light on reasons underlying the great American frontier movement.

For their help in making this study possible, the writer is indebted to L. L. Perrin, advertising manager of the Northern Pacific Railway Company, who started him out on his search through the archives; to L. L. Schwarm of the Land Department and A. M. Gottschald, assistant secretary of the company, who gave him access to the archives; to Walter Hunt of the Emigration Department, who gave him many valuable clues; and to J. J. Lesneski, custodian of the storage building, who helped him search through shelf after shelf of dusty files.

For the inspiration they provided and for their expert counsel in the preparation of this manuscript, the writer is deeply grateful to Dr. Ralph D. Casey, chairman of the Department of Journalism, and Ralph O. Nafziger, professor of journalism, at the University of Minnesota.

To the members of the staff of the Department of History, particularly Lester B. Shippee, chairman, and Ernest S. Osgood, assistant professor, the writer is indebted for aid in familiarizing him with the historical background against which this thesis was written.

Chapter I
Background of the Drive for Settlers

When Jay Cooke & Co. signed a contract to handle the financing of the Northern Pacific Railroad Company in 1869, the firm was faced by a three-fold problem. It was necessary, first, to sell enough bonds to begin construction, second, to construct the railroad itself, and, third, to dispose of the largest land grant that had ever been given to a railroad. We are interested in the first two of the problems only as they relate to the third, which is the topic under consideration in this study.

In a law entitled "A Bill granting lands to aid in the construction of a railroad and telegraph line from Lake Superior to Puget Sound, on the Pacific coast, by the Northern Route," signed by President Lincoln July 2, 1864,[1] provision was included for a grant of twenty sections to the mile in the states of Minnesota and Oregon and forty sections to the mile in the territories of Dakota, Montana, Idaho, and Washington.[2] That meant that the railroad should have 12,800 acres to the mile of track in the states and 25,600 acres in the territories.

In describing this huge gift of land, a Jay Cooke brochure published in 1871 states: "The amount of land granted to the Northern Pacific by its charter, original and as amended, exceeds 50,000,000 acres. This superb estate is larger by 10,000 square miles than the six New England states, or as large as Ohio and Indiana combined. There is room in it for ten states as large as Massachusetts, each of them with a soil and climate, and resources of coal, timber, ores of metals and perpetual water power, altogether superior to those upon which Massachusetts has become populous, rich, refined and politically powerful. The grant is nearly seven times as large as Belgium and more than three-and-one-half times as large as Holland."[3]

The brochure was overly optimistic in its estimate that the grant would total 50,000,000 acres, but title to 46,824,960 acres had been earned by 1892.[4] The magnitude of the task of selling that much land is obvious.

The scope of the undertaking was greatly increased by the fact that the country from Lake Superior to Puget Sound, over which the track was to be laid, was practically uninhabited, except by Indians, in 1870. There were no whites in northern Minnesota, not a single farm nor settlement along the line of the road in Dakota, and nothing in Montana east of the Belt mountains. The towns of Butte, Boseman, and Helena, in Montana, had been established and there was some mining in this vicinity, but Idaho and eastern Washington were almost devoid of population.[5] Thus the sale of lands of the Northern Pacific had a dual purpose: to realize the income necessary for building and maintenance, and to populate the countryside so that the new road might have enough business to make it a profitable investment.

There were three possibilities for the disposition of the land. It might be held for speculation, it might be sold to large Eastern land companies for grazing or speculation, or it might be sold in small tracts to actual settlers.[6] The first and second alternatives were ruled out because there was a crying need for the benefits produced by the third, settlers and population.[7] For freight revenue it was necessary to have farmers on the land, shipping their produce back to the East. Through traffic would not be enough to justify the building of a 2,000-mile railroad spanning an unsettled wasteland. With that theory in mind the railroad officials and the Cooke organization set out to advertise their land grant, and to sell it in small parcels to actual settlers.

Specific details of the organization of the Land and Emigration Departments and the methods they used will be discussed in later chapters, but it is necessary to mention here that Jay Cooke & Co. had established a framework for advertising and publicity work that served as a precedent and model when work was undertaken in earnest. In fact, even before Cooke signed the contract with the Northern Pacific officials, those officials had cast envious eyes at Cooke's promotional organization.[8]

BACKGROUND OF THE DRIVE FOR SETTLERS

The famous financier had popularized government loans during the Civil War "by means of profuse advertising in the newspapers, supplemented by editorial articles, and by a lavish distribution of pamphlets and circulars. No man in his day could equal him in the effective use of printer's ink."[9]

As soon as Cooke took over the Northern Pacific contract, this promotional machinery went to work to "popularize" the so-called 7-30 bonds.[10] Eugene Smalley writes that "Advertisements were published in the newspapers far and wide, including the country weeklies, and city dailies. Liberal payments for advertising secured favorable editorial comments on the loan and the railroad enterprise generally. For many months it was almost impossible to take up a newspaper in any part of the United States without finding in it something concerning the Northern Pacific. Prominent statesmen and army officers wrote letters describing the merits of the country the road was to traverse."[11]

This advertising served a second purpose equally as important as that of providing a model for the organization of the publicity divisions for the Land and Emigration Departments; it served to focus the attention of the nation on the railroad. It created an interest in the enterprise that made the public more receptive to the land advertising that was to come later.

By the opening of 1870, then, the Northern Pacific had the prospect of receiving approximately 50,000,000 acres of land, and had the framework of an advertising organization that could sell that land. Before putting machinery in operation to sell the land, however, it was necessary to complete the financing and to begin building the road.

Status of Western Lands in 1872

It is impossible here to investigate thoroughly the amount of good farm land that was still available in the West at the time of the beginning of the Northern Pacific project, but we may safely draw the conclusion that more unsettled fertile land was included in the Northern Pacific grant than in any other section of the country. True, there was much land still belonging to the government in various sections of the country, but most of it was of inferior quality.

W. J. Barney, a Chicago real-estate agent, described to A. B. Nettleton, trustees' agent for Jay Cooke & Co., the land situation in the fall of 1872 as follows: In Iowa, Barney said, "There is none to be had unless an isolated forty-acre tract here and there not worth the trouble of looking up." Of Kansas, he reported, "East of the 106th Meridian...is all entered...West of the Meridian is well picked over...There are no large tracts for colonies." Nebraska, he said, was like Kansas: "No selections of value can be made. There is government land in the west but not of good quality." Barney concluded his letter with the statement, "I feel very sure that no colonies could be settled in any of these states...The Northern Pacific grant affords, and from its vast size will continue for many years to afford, the best field for colonies."[12]

Even allowing for a certain degree of exaggeration in Barney's statement, it is obvious that the Northern Pacific was about to build into the last remaining large area suitable for farming. Railroads already criss-crossed the states to the east. Iowa, Nebraska, and Kansas had been crossed by the Union Pacific and the Kansas Pacific. Missouri had been settled decades earlier.[13] Southern Minnesota lands, too, had been partly taken up, and some settlers had moved into what is now South Dakota.[14] But the Northern Pacific was planning to build into a vast and unpopulated area, much of which was later to prove itself high-grade agricultural land.[15]

It should not be surmised from the foregoing that the Northern Pacific was to have no competition. It did have competition, serious competition, but that competition was not to last for long. The most potent adversary was the Kansas Pacific Land Company, but the Kansas Land Company's grant was all sold out by 1882. All of the land belonging to the St. Paul and Pacific was gone in 1880, the Chicago, Milwaukee and St. Paul had sold all of its land by 1882, the Santa Fe by 1883, and Little Rock and Fort Smith by 1886.[16]

At this point we may conclude that the fates had conspired to give the Northern Pacific a huge land grant, had put the

BACKGROUND OF THE DRIVE FOR SETTLERS   5

selling of the grant in the hands of a company that was experienced in advertising, and had seen to it that most of the land that would be in direct competition with the Northern Pacific's had been taken up. Only one essential remained. If there was any widespread feeling of unrest or discontent, which the Northern Pacific could take advantage of in its propaganda featuring the advantages of the Northwest, then it was entirely probable that the project should succeed.

Factors Influencing Emigration and Migration

Before we begin a thorough analysis of the techniques used to influence people to leave their old homes in established territories and take up new ones in an entirely new country, we must know why those people would be willing to take so uncertain, and in some of their minds, so desperate a chance; why they would leave the environment with which they were familiar and begin life in a new one devoid of many of the advantages to which they were accustomed. Knowing the pre-existing attitudes of these persons will make it easier for us to determine the effectiveness of the various promotional techniques used and to analyze more adequately the reactions to those techniques.

Subsequent chapters will prove that the Northern Pacific was more greatly interested in inducing residents of the United States to migrate than in influencing natives of foreign countries to emigrate. It is still true, however, that a high percentage of those who settled on Northern Pacific lands were foreign born, as many of them stopped briefly in states farther east before going on to Minnesota, Dakota, and Montana.[17]

This being the case, if we study the reasons and motives for emigration from European countries, we will have gone a long way toward knowing the basic attitudes on which the propagandists played.

In regard to this topic, George M. Stephenson makes the statement that

Students of immigration are in agreement that the great bulk of immigrants to America were impelled by the desire to get a better living; that economic causes overshadowed all others ... Economic discontent in England, Ireland, Germany, Scandinavia, and Netherlands was fanned at times by religious and political dissatisfaction.[18]

Professor Stephenson in several instances reiterates the importance of the economic motive. "In general, punishment and oppression have had little to do with the migration movement," he writes, "the desire for material betterment being the main reason."[19] Later he summarizes the motives in the following statement:

In general the underlying causes are similar. Hard times, crop failures, difficulty of securing loans, money stringency, low wages, men out of work, the demand for laborers and house maids in America, a certain dissatisfaction with church and state, the propaganda of states and emigration agencies, letters from enthusiastic immigrants, an unfair social system — all concentrated to the same end.[20]

It is obvious that the economic factor leads all other motives for migration by a wide margin, and historians of the American West are in agreement that the same is true of the westward movement in the United States. Underlying the entire frontier push is the desire for free or for cheap land.[21] Harold Briggs applies this theory specifically to North Dakota in a discussion of the factors producing the great boom of 1879 to 1886 in that state. He points out that a major factor causing the tremendous influx of settlers at that time was the earlier occupation of land farther east and the gradual increase in the price of the land. After the price increase came a tax increase.[22]

If the foregoing is true, we may expect to see a Northern Pacific promotional program emphasizing the low prices and desirability of Northern Pacific lands. That such is the case will be borne out in later chapters.

BACKGROUND OF THE DRIVE FOR SETTLERS 7

Relationship of the Northern Pacific Program to Other Emigration Agencies

There is no space here to present a detailed report of the work of the state emigration agencies of Dakota and Minnesota, other than to mention the fact that such agencies did exist, and to a certain degree they cooperated with the officials of the railroad.[23]

These boards had been set up long before the Northern Pacific machinery started to function, and they functioned in much the same way as the railroad was to do later. The Minnesota agency had representatives in the Scandinavian countries and published pamphlets and circulars exhorting prospective settlers to come to Minnesota. One of the most famous of Minnesota's emigration agents, Colonel Hans Mattson, who had been Minnesota's secretary of state, left the Minnesota Emigration Bureau in 1873 to work for the Northern Pacific.[24] There is evidence of much further cooperation between the state and railroad agencies.

That the states were much interested in the problem is indicated by the fact that a convention was called by the governors of various states. This convention met at Indianapolis in 1870 and considered means by which immigration to the United States could best be promoted. The body went on record as favoring the establishment by the federal government of a Federal Bureau of Immigration to protect immigrants en route to the United States and on their arrival.[25]

The federal government, too, cooperated to a certain degree with the railroads and the states by publishing a *Special Report on Immigration* in 1871. The report was prepared by Edward Young, chief of the Bureau of Statistics. The booklet included 231 pages of information on prices and rentals of land, staple products, facilities for marketing goods, and kinds of labor in demand. Several hundred copies were distributed in Europe.[26]

A detailed report of the work of state and federal agencies is outside the scope of this thesis, but it must be noted that the Northern Pacific was, in 1870, about to enter a well-exploited field as it prepared to sell its nearly 50,000,000 acres of land. As this writer has already pointed out, it had much good land to sell, its land was superior to most then on the market, its banking house was experienced in promotional methods, and it had the cooperation of interested state governments. Now it devolves upon us to examine the methods used by the railroad as it went about its monumental task.

Chapter II
The Northern Pacific Program Gets Underway

The first actual step in the marketing of the Northern Pacific's land grant was taken in 1869 when a Land Committee was set up with offices in New York. Frederick Billings was its chairman, and John S. Loomis was chosen Land Commissioner. A supplemental office under the direction of a general agent was established at St. Paul. Closely affiliated with the Land Committee was a Bureau of Immigration, with George B. Hibbard as its superintendent. This Bureau of Immigration in turn organized the European land sales campaign. George Sheppard was in charge of the European division with headquarters at London, and branch agencies were set up at Liverpool and in Germany, Holland, and the Scandinavian countries.[1]

A five-fold plan embracing the following provisions was recommended for the Land Committee: maps and documents for the railroad and the land along the line were to be published in the languages of all peoples and all nationalities; this material was to be distributed by general and special agencies throughout the United States and Europe, and by consular officers and agents of the United States in foreign countries; cordial business relations were to be established with steamship lines and with railway and other transportation agencies in the United States with a view to cooperation in the interests of the Northern Pacific and to obtaining favorable rates; friendly relations were to be established with the American and European press; and finally, every effort was to be made to enlist the support of professional and public men, humane and benevolent societies, and religious societies.[2]

In one of its publicity pamphlets the Jay Cooke company explained that its aim was "to employ as its land and emigration agents, at home and abroad, only men of the highest character; to permit no representations to be made by its authority which the facts will not fully warrant; to promote, as far as possible, the formation of colonies, both in Europe and the older states of our own country, so that neighbors in the old home may be neighbors in the new, so that friends may settle near each other, form communities, establish schools, and, in short, avoid most of the traditional hardships which have usually attended pioneer life; and to exercise over emigrants, en route, whatever supervision their best interest may require."[3] How closely the Land Committee followed this policy will be noted as the story of the land sales unfolds. It must be noted at this point, however, that the railroad embarked on its effort with a well-planned program.

In addition to his direction of the foreign department of the Emigration Bureau, Major Hibbard also prepared to stage a strong campaign to bring Civil War veterans to the Northern Pacific lands. A New England Military and Naval Bureau of Migration was set up in Boston to colonize veterans along the line of the railroad. Work was carried on in western New York and New England, most of it through G.A.R. posts.[4]

Terms for the purchase of land were so set as to make it possible for a pioneer to move to the West with a minimum of capital, and the costs of transportation were kept as low as possible for the same purpose. To purchase a tract of land at prices varying from $2.50 to $8.00 an acre, the buyer made a down payment of 10 per cent and then paid 10 per cent each year for three years and, beginning with the fourth year, 15 per cent each year for four years. This plan allowed seven years for full payment.[5]

The person who desired to see the land before he purchased was to pay full fare to the point where he contemplated buying. Then, if he bought forty acres or more within sixty days, the cost of transportation was to be deducted from his purchase price. Free transportation was to be provided for settlers and their families while en route to take up new homes, and reception houses were provided at Brainerd, Duluth, and Glyndon where the migrants could stay until their new homes were ready for occupancy.[6] A one-third deduction was allowed on all freight for settlers.[7]

THE NORTHERN PACIFIC PROGRAM GETS UNDERWAY 11

By the end of March, 1871, the program was functioning.[8] But it was not until 1872 that any results were evident, the public apparently being apathetic before that time. Maps, pamphlets, and documents were flowing freely to prospective settlers through 1872 and 1873, but in 1873 the Cooke banking house crashed and expenses of promotion had to be curtailed. In 1874, the European agency was withdrawn and not much was left of the domestic organization.[9]

Distribution of Printed Matter

Although the Land Committee did not get its land-sales program into full swing until 1872, it is evident that many pamphlets descriptive of the lands along the road were distributed during 1871. The bulkiest of these was one entitled *The Northern Pacific Railroad, Its Route, Resources, Progress and Business.* This publication consisted of forty-eight pages, divided into eight chapters. It was published by Jay Cooke in Philadelphia. It was used primarily to stimulate the sale of bonds, but it is evident from a perusal of chapter headings that it would also be of value in promoting land sales. The booklet included chapters on "The New Northwest, Its Mildness and Fertility"; "The Railroad's Land Grant, Its Extent and Value"; "The Future Business of the Road"; "Progress of Construction," and other topics.[10]

Cooke's agents, during the latter part of the year, were distributing widely a pamphlet entitled "The Red River Country and Northwest Minnesota," which was made up of letters from Bayard Taylor, Charles A. Dana, Clark M. Bryan, Samuel Bowles, and others. The Cooke firm was willing to sell these publications to the Northern Pacific Land Department at their cost of $5.00 a thousand.[11] The writers had been guests of Cooke and the railroad on an excursion to the Red River country early in 1871.[12]

During December Hibbard was writing to his officer friends in New England and New York, sending them copies of soldiers' and sailors' pamphlets in the hope of starting a big drive in the spring of 1872.[13] A start toward the foreign-language campaign had been made by the preparation of a little manual for German emigrants.[14] The Northern Pacific's own material was supplemented by an order of 1,000 pamphlets on Minnesota, published by the State Board of Immigration of Minnesota. It has been impossible to ascertain any facts about the distribution of this material, but we know that it was sent from John Schroeder, clerk of the state board, to Loomis. Seven hundred copies were in English and 300 in German.[15]

Late in 1871, Nettleton was preparing two kinds of publicity matter of a little different type. Whether they were ready in time for distribution before the spring of 1872, we do not know. One was a leaflet that Nettleton indicated he intended to publish every sixty days. He explained that he had, in his files, a great number of letters from prominent individuals commenting favorably on the Northern Pacific road. He had intended to compile these letters into a pamphlet, but decided that there was too much similarity between the individual manuscripts to make interesting reading so he hit upon the idea of using the more striking passages in his leaflet. The leaflet had the additional advantages of being cheap, varied, and readable; and copies could be printed and circulated at less expense than could a pamphlet.[16]

The second device was a Northern Pacific map with wide margins left open for reading matter that could include paragraphs on the land grant, climate, and other matters. Copies of this map were to be mounted on canvas rollers and furnished to 2,000 bank agents to be hung on the walls of their banks.[17] The value of such a scheme is readily apparent when it is remembered that the most likely land buyers, as well as bond buyers, are those who frequent banks.

Through 1871 it is difficult to distinguish between material designed primarily for bond sales and that which officials also hoped would stimulate the sale of land. It is quite a safe assumption, though, that the value the Land Committee in most of the publications mentioned above was indirect and that Nettleton's interests were primarily directed at selling bonds.

In the next year, it is quite obvious that the Land Department was beginning to prepare its own material for the purpose

THE NORTHERN PACIFIC PROGRAM GETS UNDERWAY 13

of stimulating land sales. Pamphlets on Montana and on Washington and Oregon were prepared, a photographer was sent out to the territory adjacent to the road to get views suitable for use in publicity material, and officials were beginning to think about preparing material on the climate west of the Rockies.

A good indication of the volume and nature of the material being used for Land Department advertising purposes is given in a letter from James G. Dudley, chief clerk of the Northern Pacific Railroad Company, to Nettleton in which Dudley asked to be supplied with 5,000 Northern Pacific pamphlets, 5,000 Northern Pacific newspapers for January (probably the leaflet previously mentioned), 3,000 of Garfield's *Climates* (a pamphlet extolling the climate of the Northern Pacific country east of the Rockies), and 3,000 of Kelley's speech. Dudley also explained that he intended to send out 5,000 to 10,000 sets of maps and documents the following week independently of the 10,000 sets sent to prospective members of the Soldier's colony.[18]

During the spring and summer of 1872 the Land Department prepared its first advertising booklets on its western territory. A Montana pamphlet was completed in May, but the Land Committee decided that it should be issued only on request, as it was not known when the road would be built into the state.[19] In fact, publication could have been delayed much longer inasmuch as the entry of the rails into Montana was not made until 1882. The first Washington and Oregon booklet went to press in July, 1872.[20] By November, 30,000 copies of the pamphlet were in Dudley's hands.[21]

A significant step toward the preparation of more attractive material was taken in November, 1872, when a photographer was sent to the line of the road to get views of scenery and farms. The instructions given him are a good indication of Northern Pacific promotional policy. Nettleton wrote to Dudley:

> This time (16 days) should be put in wholly west of Detroit. We want good farm scenes, prairie views, lake views (many of these), railroad views, reception houses, bridges, and above all the photographer must go to the end of the line and take the process of track laying. We want a good

view of each principal valley... We want good views of Ottertail Lake from its most interesting point of vision. Don't let him spend his time on hum-drum subjects. Get in a few homesteads surrounded by stacks and cattle.[22]

Nettleton's insistence on scenes showing prosperity and beauty are a good indication that he intended to feature those two characteristics in future advertising. It must also be noted that he desired to show, by means of the pictures of track laying, that the Northern Pacific was no fly-by-night venture.

The work was completed by the middle of November when Hibbard sent fifty-six photographs to Nettleton. The photographer evidently failed to carry out instructions, for Hibbard explains that the number taken west of Brainerd was limited.[23]

That evidently concludes the activities of the company in preparing documents in this period as no mention is made in Land Department files of 1872 pamphlets. It is certain that the 1872 publications were used to a great extent until the Cooke banking house collapsed. After the collapse advertising activities were sharply curtailed.

Getting Publicity into the Press

It is difficult to coordinate the threads of information gleaned from correspondence so that a complete picture of the newspaper publicity activities of the railroad may be constructed. However, it is possible by the use of samples to give a good indication of the nature of the work, if not the full extent of it.

Two methods were used for getting stories into the press: Northern Pacific employes prepared some of the releases and sent them to the newspapers as press handouts, and friendships were made with prominent and key newspapermen who wrote articles independently for their own papers.

The most important figure in the Northern Pacific employ seems to be John W. Sears, who was doing publicity work in Nettleton's office.[24] James Whitman, agent of the railroad in

THE NORTHERN PACIFIC PROGRAM GETS UNDERWAY   15

St. John, New Brunswick, was contacting newspapers and inspiring, if not actually writing, stories for the press of New Brunswick and Nova Scotia, apparently with considerable success.[25] Similar work was done in Duluth by Luke Marvin, the Land and Emigration Agent there. Marvin reported that he was employed almost full time in answering inquiries of persons who intended to go out onto the road, but he did have time to prepare material on Duluth to send to the New York office. He wrote that one of his stories was accepted by the Philadelphia *Bulletin*.[26] William Wales was doing the same sort of work covering Duluth for Nettleton and the Cooke organization as Marvin was doing for the Land and Emigration Department. He explains his work as being "to deal in readable letters with whatever might help the sale of land, stimulate immigration and advance the growth of Duluth."[27]

Charles Carleton Coffin, the famous Civil War correspondent of the Boston *Journal*, was also preparing articles for publication, but it is impossible to determine just what his connection with the railroad was. There is no indication that Coffin was on the payroll, but he seems to have devoted a good share of his time to Northern Pacific interests, both writing newspaper articles and lecturing.[28]

The man in charge of the railroad land advertising was a certain Mr. Abbott, but beyond the fact that he was in charge of the program during 1872, the writer was unable to discover any information regarding his activities. A letter from Nettleton to Dudley says this of Abbott: "Mr. Abbott who is in charge of our land advertising is very successful in obtaining access to the reading columns of the city papers. Indeed they will do for him anything that he asks which is reasonable."[29]

The excursion plan seemed to be the most satisfactory one for interesting newspapermen in the road. Clark M. Bryan of the Springfield *Republican*, who had been the guest of the Northern Pacific in 1871 along with several other men prominent in the press, was still writing favorable articles in January, 1872.[30] In the summer of 1872, Bertram Snyder of the Philadelphia *North American* visited the line of the road with the dual purpose of taking a vacation and writing descriptive correspondence.[31] In March, 1872, Nettleton furnished railroad passes to F. Montague of the London *Daily Telegraph*, who intended to spend three weeks on the road and then to return to London and write a series of articles. Before Montague's arrival, Sheppard had cabled from London that Montague was "important."[32]

How many more newspapermen availed themselves of the opportunity of making a free trip to the Northwest can not be discovered, but the above evidence is sufficient to indicate that the Northern Pacific officials were well aware of the value of building up friendships with the press, and of getting general information concerning the railroad into the newspapers.[33]

Although it is impossible to estimate how many newspapers may have printed Northern Pacific stories, we may gain some idea as to the success of the program from the limited records which are available. There is definite evidence to prove that stories appeared in the Springfield *Republican*, the New York papers, the Philadelphia *Press*, the Vermont *Watchman*, the Boston *Transcript*, the Duluth *Minnesotian*, the Pittsburgh *Commercial*, and the *Farmers' Union* of Minneapolis.[34] From this we may at least form an impression of the wide geographical area that was reached. In addition to this list the assistant editor of the Philadelphia *Daily Times* offered voluntarily to insert any such items as the Northern Pacific should wish to send him.[35] This offer would seem to indicate that the publicity men had been unusually successful in achieving their goal of friendly press relations.

Public Speakers, Excursions, and Miscellaneous Devices

Some indication was made earlier in this chapter that Charles Carleton Coffin had done some lecturing in the interests of the Northern Pacific. In fact, the Coffin lectures were a part of a definite campaign carried on primarily among Civil War veterans. The campaign was so thorough that Riegel maintains that the Northern Pacific was the first organization of its kind to use public speakers extensively.[36]

Northern Pacific speakers were sent out by the railroad to meetings sponsored by the Emigration division and by the

THE NORTHERN PACIFIC PROGRAM GETS UNDERWAY 17

Boston Lyceum Bureau, a James Redpath enterprise, which booked the speakers through the country. The Soldiers' meetings were addressed by speakers in pairs, a man named Barrows teaming up with Coffin.[37]

Mention has been made previously in this thesis concerning the use of excursions by the Northern Pacific,[38] but an event occurred in 1871 which indicated to perfection the attitude of the railroad toward persons who could possibly be of service to them.

Lord Gordon Gordon, a pseudo Scottish nobleman, appeared in St. Paul in 1870 and spoke casually at times of buying 50,000 acres of land and at other times of 100,000 acres. He had already deposited $20,000 in a St. Paul bank so his story sounded plausible to railroad officials. In 1871 he was taken on a two-months' excursion through western Minnesota by Colonel Loomis, the Northern Pacific Land Commissioner. Tracks had not been laid through this region up to this time so that it was necessary to travel by wagon train. The company made up a caravan of six teams, employed twelve men to pitch tents and do manual labor, a number of negroes with white silk gloves to serve as waiters, and a French cook. The railroad staged a mammoth buffalo hunt at which the historic banner of the Clan Gordon waved beside the United States flag. All in all the party cost the Northern Pacific $15,000. And in January, 1872, the would-be nobleman slipped out of town one jump ahead of the police.[39]

The unfortunate Gordon case did not dampen the ardor of the Land Committee toward excursions, however, as it was late in 1872 that they were pushed the hardest.

An excellent picture of the minor details that the railroad had to consider before sending out parties is given in a letter from Nettleton to Dudley in which the writer suggested postponing, until later in the year, all excursions scheduled for the summer of 1872. He argued that trips during the summer would be harmful to the company's interests because the road through Minnesota was unfinished, station buildings were incomplete, the stopping places were rough and uninviting, nothing had been done to "smooth out nature," and many of the settlers who had gone out the previous year were grumbling and complaining about general accommodations, freight rates, and other matters. Nettleton feared that, in view of these disadvantages, prospective settlers, or land buyers, would not be favorably impressed with the land. He hoped that by the following year the conditions could be righted.[40]

Mindful of the fact that certain small items can be a potent factor in promoting friendly relations or in prejudicing interested persons against a program, the Northern Pacific adopted several procedures of no great importance but which, nevertheless, contributed to its general policy. New settlers who needed immediate cash incomes were given jobs, during off seasons on their farms, clearing timber off railroad land. A system of nurseries for the propagation of forest trees provided an ample supply of trees for distribution to settlers who wanted groves and shelter and an income for those who worked in the nurseries. Reception houses at Duluth, Brainerd, and Glyndon provided shelter for settlers who were preparing to go out onto the land. The largest house at Duluth could accommodate 100 persons.[41]

The attitude of Northern Pacific officials toward a well-balanced public relations program is well summarized in a statement included in a letter from Nettleton to Billings:

> I am well satisfied that our company has got to adopt unusual measures in order to secure the settlement of its land as rapidly as the best interests of the enterprise demand. Newspaper advertising is valuable, to a certain extent, but unless that is supplemented by more tangible things, I fear we shall, in a great degree, shake the tree without getting any fruit.[42]

Advertising in the Newspapers

From an examination of the extent of the work done and of the number of times the program is mentioned in Land Department files, we may safely generalize that newspaper advertising ranked second among the promotional devices used by the Northern Pacific, only the use of printed matter in the form of pamphlets, circulars, and the like exceeding it in scope or bulk. This fact is of considerable significance because the relative

THE NORTHERN PACIFIC PROGRAM GETS UNDERWAY   19

values ascribed to the various promotional media are approximately the same as would be ascribed to them by any promotional organization of the present era. It is also interesting that newspaper advertising should have been considered of such great importance at that early stage in the development of advertising.

The advertising program, or that part of it which was directed specifically at land sales, got under way May 15, 1872, and ran for twelve months.[43] All funds had been appropriated by November 8, so that no new contracts were signed after that date.[44]

The same Mr. Abbott who was in charge of the publicity program was also in charge of advertising, but there are indications in Nettleton's correspondence that much of the actual work of placing the advertisements was done by the S. M. Pettengill firm of newspaper advertising agents, who had offices in New York.[45]

A separate advertising program was handled by the Bureau of Emigration under Hibbard's direction, and a third program was carried on in Canada by James Whitman, the Canadian agent.

The schedule for the main campaign was drawn up by the fiscal agents, Jay Cooke & Co., and involved the use of about 100 leading newspapers of large circulation published in New England, the western states, and Canada. It also included ads in about 1,000 country weeklies in the same sections. Political, religious, commercial, and agriculture journals were all used. The total expenditure amounted to approximately $25,000.[46] Hibbard placed $2.00 and $3.00 advertisements in ten New England papers, mostly in the smaller cities.[47] There is no indication as to how much money was allotted to Whitman, but it is certain that he did have an allowance, and that he did advertise in three or four of the larger city dailies of New Brunswick and Nova Scotia and in several country weeklies.[48]

Nowhere in the documents examined by the writer was there a complete list of the publications in which the railroad advertised, but there were references to individual contracts out of which it is possible to draw a brief sample list. Of the daily newspapers, the Boston *Advertiser* and the New York *Independent* are mentioned. In the Boston paper there was an advertisement praising the climate of the "New Northwest." The New York *Independent* published a wheat-field ad every other week for one year, costing the company $450.

One foreign-language publication, the *Nordisk Folkeblad* of St. Paul, was included among those to which reference was made. There were three agricultural newspapers: the *Farmers' Union* of Minneapolis; and the *American Agriculturist* and the *Horticulturist,* both of New York. There was evidently enough Northern Pacific material in the *Farmers' Union* to make it valuable for publicity purposes as several copies were sent to Sheppard for distribution in England. Hibbard was especially pleased with the publication, because he felt that it could be used by the railroad without appearing to be a Northern Pacific-inspired document.[49] Hibbard bought 1,500 copies at their actual cost which turned out to be $120. The ad in the *American Agriculturist* was published in both the American and German editions.[50]

Advertisements were contracted for in the Minnesota State Fair premium-list publication and in the Minnesota State Fair pamphlet, both for the 1872 fair; in the *Pacific Coast Business Directory,* published in San Francisco; and in *Silversmith's Guide for Tourists, Emigrants and Business Men. The New Northwest,* published in Deer Lodge, Montana, had received a two-year contract starting October 7, 1870, from Samuel Wilkeson, secretary of the company, and Dudley contracted for an additional year on June 8, 1872.[51]

An analysis of the general contents of these advertisements, along with analyses of advertisements placed during other periods of Northern Pacific promotional activity, may be found in Chapter VII of this thesis. An attempt is made there to discover the appeals used by the advertising agents to induce prospective buyers to migrate to Northern Pacific lands.

Arousing Interest Through Exhibits

Before July, 1872, Dudley had formulated a plan for exhibiting products of Minnesota at state fairs throughout the country during the fair season of the year. Coffin recommended

THE NORTHERN PACIFIC PROGRAM GETS UNDERWAY 21

to him that to make the plan a success it would be necessary to place the work in the hands of men who knew how to prepare exhibits, how to reach the public, and how to get notices of exhibits in the newspapers. He suggested that Dudley get a list of all the fairs at once, this being July, and arrange to stage his show at the best of them.[52]

Evidently Dudley went to work on the proposal immediately since we have evidence that exhibits were set up at the Minnesota, New York, and Maryland fairs in that year. There may have been others of which we have no record. Ten thousand copies of a Northern Pacific pamphlet were sent to Dudley by Nettleton for distribution at the New York fair, with the suggestion that they be given out only to substantial and respectable people, and that no boys should receive them.[53]

The Minnesota exhibit seems to have been quite a success. Nettleton reported that he had received a communication from Chief Clerk James B. Power of the St. Paul office, containing what Nettleton termed "most gratifying notices" of the exhibitions of grains and vegetables. Nettleton further said that he expected to have these press notices collated and published in a circular.[54]

Just as great a success was scored at the Maryland fair. An extract from the official report of the examining committee appointed by the State Agriculture Society of the exposition made the statement, "Notice the display of cereals, grasses, roots, building stones, fruits, etc., exhibited by the Land Department of the Northern Pacific . . . We should judge the farming lands on which they were grown to be unsurpassed by any in the country. The samples of rye were particularly fine, the soil is said to be inexhaustible . . . We should advise all seeking western homes to investigate thoroughly the lands and inducements."[55]

Results at the Chicago Exposition of 1873 were less favorable. Unfortunately for the Northern Pacific, its exhibit was put on display shortly after the collapse of the Cooke banking house. The railroad was in general disfavor throughout the country because it was the consensus that it had forced the Cooke firm into bankruptcy and thus precipitated the national financial panic of 1873. The Chicago newspapers were particularly bitter toward the railroad, and the exhibit gave them a chance to give vent to their ire.

C. F. Kindred, who was in charge of the exhibit, reported:

> The papers haven't made the slightest mention of our display and haven't been slow in condemning the road. The *Tribune* and *Times* have so fully committed themselves recently that I doubt the expediency of making any overtures to them at present. The fact that they are pitching into us so strong makes visitors more anxious to see the products from that barren country . . . Still it isn't pleasant.[56]

After the fair season had come to an end, the Land Committee continued its policy of showing exhibits by placing samples of its products in the hands of its traveling agents. There is very little evidence available of this sort of promotion, but from a letter Nettleton sent to Wackerhagen we may construct a general idea of the nature of the plan. Nettleton wrote, "Please put up an assortment of sample grains in small glass jars and send them, securely packed, to J. H. Jenkins, Briggs Hotel, Utica, New York."[57] That mineral exhibits were also used is indicated in a letter from Sears to Hibbard.[58]

Employing Agents and Forming Colonies

Two Northern Pacific promotional activities, the work of land agents and the formation of colonies to take up residence on railroad lands, are so closely allied that the two are lumped together under one topic. It is evident from the information available that one of the main functions, if not the chief function, of agents was to promote colonies and to see to it that those colonies got to the Northwest.[59]

It is rather difficult to determine when the Northern Pacific first employed agents. Communications, dated 1871, indicate that agents were at work in that year showing lands to representatives of colonizing groups or to individual prospects for purchases.[60] However, on January 6, 1872, Loomis wrote to a Rev. F. N. Haskell of Belleville, Illinois: "At present no agents are

THE NORTHERN PACIFIC PROGRAM GETS UNDERWAY 23

employed in the Emigration Bureau except Major George B. Hibbard, commissioner. The work of organizing colonies will be done mostly by those directly interested in the colony."[61] On February 24, Loomis wrote to Charles Seeger of Quincy, Illinois, that the board in charge would meet on March 5 to take up the subject of appointing emigration agents.[62]

It may be that the two latter communications related only to agents to be appointed by the Emigration division, and that the Land Department already had men employed for the tasks, or it may have been that there were two types of agents between which we are unable to find any distinction.

The relationship between the agents and the colonies is well defined in a communication from Loomis on February 22, 1871, when he wrote:

> Our local agents along the line of the road are charged with the duty of showing lands all through their respective districts and receive applications from individual colonists. In the case a whole colony makes selection at once the committee appointed to make selection can designate to the department direct and buy the land in bulk. If you could organize a colony, ... we would compensate you for your influence ... by payment of a commission on the amount of purchases made by the colony.[63]

It is apparent that the railroad had employed some men in Minnesota who showed land to prospective colonists, but that most of the work of building up enthusiasm for colonies was done by individuals who hoped to move West and who used the colonizing venture as a means to that end.

The method to be used by an individual, not connected with the road, in organizing a colony is outlined in a communication from Loomis to C. A. Stewart of Wakeman, Ohio.[64] Loomis wrote:

> Should you conclude to form among the people of your section a colony for movement to the line of the Northern Pacific Railroad I would suggest you first call a meeting for the discussion of such a project, and if you are convinced

you can make a success of the undertaking, organize a society, elect your officers, and open a set of books of membership, requiring each member to pay into a common treasury the sum of $5.00 or $10.00 for the creation of a general fund for contingent expenses. Then from among your number choose two or three good men to act as a prospecting or locating committee and start them to the line of the road. If you can practically organize a colony which will take from 10,000 to 20,000 acres of land we will pay the cost which may have been incurred for transportation of the committee on this journey out and return and when the colonists move we will secure transportation of themselves and goods at reduced rates and local agents near the land selected will render valuable assistance to colonists in getting started.[65]

The Land Department evidently assumed that in a case of this sort the general railroad promotion and the tour of the line of the road would be sufficient to convince the prospective colonists to buy. It will also be noted that there is no offer to pay any commissions on the sale of the land.

Although he could hardly be classified as an agent of the company, the employment of Governor B. F. Potts of the Territory of Montana as a "semi-representative" for the land interests provides an interesting example of the lengths to which the company would go in the use of prestige to obtain favorable attention. Governor Potts' duties in the position, which he accepted in 1872, were to give advice to settlers and to answer questions.[66] Getting the prestige of the governor of Montana behind the land-sales movement was undoubtedly a master stroke on the part of Nettleton and Billings, who seemed to have engineered the deal.

Forerunners of the Public Relations Counsels

In summary, it must be concluded that the period of Northern Pacific promotion described in this chapter is one of organization. It is true that the Land Committee had the extensive

THE NORTHERN PACIFIC PROGRAM GETS UNDERWAY 25

Cooke promotional organization to pattern its activities after. It is also true that General Nettleton, an experienced public relations man, devoted much of his time to the Northern Pacific's interests.

Even with these advantages working in its favor, however, the Land Committee was faced with the task of selling an idea that was entirely new. The Westward movement was common. The Far West had been sold to the public. The wheat lands of Kansas and Nebraska were filling up. But to the average citizen the "New Northwest" of the Northern Pacific was an uninhabited wasteland.

One of the principles of advertising is constant repetition. Before much migration to the Northwest could be expected, it would be necessary to state the case for that territory, and then repeat it, and repeat it over and over again. The brief span of time between 1871 and early 1874 did not permit much repetition. Consequently, this was the period in which the public was first made aware of the new field for settlement. This campaign's greatest value was to be that it provided a foundation upon which subsequent campaigns could be constructed.

It must be said, however, that that foundation was expertly built. To students of promotional activities, it must be amazing that fifty years before the term "public relations counsel" began to receive widespread attention, the Northern Pacific railroad set up a program which embodied many of the techniques which are now considered recent developments of that highly specialized craft.

Advertising, newspaper publicity stories, lectures, excursions, publication of pamphlets, and employment of agents are not new nor striking in themselves, but when organized under the direction of one group of men they attain considerable importance. Then, when these devices are combined with the use of the propaganda techniques of "concealed source," "prestige," and "counter propaganda," they assume great significance.

The use of prestige was evident in the favors extended to Coffin, Bryan, Bowles, Dana, and Taylor. These men responded by writing favorable articles in their publications, and excerpts from their letters to the Land Department were used in railroad circulars.

One of the aims of the Land Committee in respect to newspaper publicity was to induce newspapermen to write stories independently of all Northern Pacific ties. The source of the information was to be concealed and the reader was to believe, as probably actually was the case, that persons not connected with the railroad were thoroughly convinced of the soundness of the project.

Counter propaganda was used to refute the widespread belief that the Northwest was too cold for comfort. It has been recorded that Nettleton wrote to Billings concerning the necessity of adopting unusual measures to get the land settled rapidly and that climate was a great obstacle which had to be overcome. It will be noted that one of the pamphlets distributed widely was Garfield's *Climates*.

The organizers of the Northern Pacific's promotional program were men who understood what students of propaganda and promotional activities now term "symbolic environment," and who were cognizant of the techniques of what would now be termed "symbol manipulation."

As this case study of Northern Pacific promotion progresses to later eras, it will become increasingly evident that in skillful manipulation of public attitudes the Northern Pacific had set up a program that was more than a forerunner of twentieth-century commercial propaganda and public relations; it was the equivalent, but operating without the advantage of the communications facilities available in the later period.

Chapter III
The Period of the Big Boom

Promotional activities of the Northern Pacific Railroad were at a distinct ebb tide from the crash of Jay Cooke & Co. in 1873 until about 1879 when the railroad had recovered from the shock. Because of the fact that some colonies, organized in 1873, moved into Minnesota in 1874, there are some slight signs of life on the part of the railroad in that year, but we hear nothing of the promotional activities of 1875 in the road's correspondence.

Two factors made advertising unadvisable and unnecessary through the years of the deepest depression. The financial condition of the company did not permit any expenditure on land promotion, and so many of the company's bonds were being turned in on land purchases that officials felt it unnecessary to advertise widely to stimulate purchases. Bonds, exchangeable for land at par, were low in price, and land prices maintained their former level so that the exchange was a sound economic move for the bondholder.[1]

The advertising program was not wholly dead in 1876, however. In January, 1877, J. B. Power, Land Agent at St. Paul, reported that a great number of letters were coming in to his office inquiring about lands. He assumed that these letters were in response to the advertising done at "a trifling cost" the previous year. Evidently the company had distributed some circular maps and had somehow inspired some newspaper articles. Power indicated that he expected good sales and a heavy immigration later in the season.[2]

By June, 1877, Power reported that immigration was heavier than at any time since 1872. An agency had been established at Chicago, and plans were going forward for setting up a land and emigration office at St. Paul with other offices of the road which were going to move there. Most of the Northwest land being sold, Power reported, was sold by the government, but Power felt that these sales were directly traceable to efforts of the Land Department to induce settlement.[3]

No more information on promotional activities is available until 1880, the year when the big boom of the eighties actually got underway. In that year Power established local agencies in New York, Boston, and Philadelphia, in addition to the Chicago agency already in operation. Sheppard was sent back to England to reestablish the European bureau which had been discontinued in 1874. Distribution of maps, pamphlets, and circulars was resumed on a large scale, and immigrants were once more arriving in the United States in great numbers.[4]

An unofficial tie-up had been effected with the Villard West Coast companies in 1879 when the Oregon Steamship Company began to use the Northern Pacific land office at Colfax, Washington, as one of its four land and emigration headquarters.[5]

The land office had not yet been moved to St. Paul, but plans had been quite definitely formulated to move it there in the spring of 1881. In the meantime an office was to be maintained at Brainerd.[6]

In an effort to discourage purchases by speculators, a practice frowned upon but not rigidly enforced before this time, the land terms were amended. The rate for sale of land east of the Missouri River was fixed at $4.00 an acre with a rebate of 25 per cent for acreage cultivated within two years of the date of the purchase. One condition was imposed: for each 320 acres purchased, at least 20 per cent had to be in cultivation within the two-year limit. West of the Missouri a flat rate of $2.60 an acre was maintained.[7]

Finally, in 1881, the land office was transferred to St. Paul, and an immigration bureau was established in Portland. Henry Villard had taken over the road by means of his famous "blind pool," and activities of the three Villard companies and the Northern Pacific were coordinated.[8]

Colonel R. M. Newport succeeded Power as General Land Agent in 1881.[9] Shortly after taking over his duties, Newport reported to A. H. Barney, chairman of the Land Committee, "We labor under great difficulties in selling our lands this summer by reason of the limited area of attractive land which we have to offer." At this time the best lands belonging to the company in Dakota were still unsurveyed and thus could not be sold, and the best lands that had been surveyed had fallen into the hands of speculators. These were being held for a rise in value or were being sold at rates less than the railroad was willing to charge. The speculators could afford to make cheap sales because they had obtained the land in exchange for below-par bonds. Newport, however, thought it advisable to sell lands west of the Missouri in present-day North Dakota to any interested persons because in that area there was little danger of speculators making purchases.[10] At this time all Northern Pacific land in the Red River Valley had been disposed of,[11] and most of the land between the James and the Cheyenne was in the hands of the speculators.[12]

L. R. Kidder, clerk of the Land Committee, made a report on the status of lands belonging to the company in June, 1882. The report showed that about 600,000 acres remained in Minnesota, most of it either swamp or timber. There were about 6,000,000 acres in North Dakota, about three-fourths of it west of the Missouri and most of the remainder in the Coteau of the Missouri. In Idaho there were about 625,000 acres, most of it heavily timbered, and in Washington 7,700,000 acres, 2,000,000 of which were timbered. Of the remainder about 1,000,000 acres apparently needed irrigation, but more than 4,000,000 acres appeared to be good farming land.[13]

There were not as many first-class sections available as there were when the railroad was built into Fargo in 1872, but there was still ample land to provide for the needs of many migrants, and the promotional campaign continued unabated. It must be remembered, too, as the railroad built westward and constructed feeder lines, additional acres of the grant were claimed.

In 1882 Villard, who was now president of the Northern Pacific, set up a Bureau of Information to edit and prepare for publication all printed matter of the Land Department and to work with Colonel Newport on any matters with which he needed help. H. J. Winser, an experienced newspaperman, was selected for the position as chief of the bureau.[14]

The year 1883 is important in Northern Pacific history. In that year the dream of the railroad's founders was attained. The trackage, from Lake Superior to the Pacific Ocean, was completed, but the effort expended in finishing the line was too great. The company's financial structure was so badly strained that curtailment of the promotional program became necessary at the end of the year. However, during the early part of the year, the immigration movement into Montana had been strong, and settlements in North Dakota had spread over a much wider area because of the construction of feeder lines. Lisbon, Carrington, and LaMoure all came into existence during 1883, and the new towns of New Salem, Glen Ullin, Richardton, Gladstone, Dickinson, and Belfield grew tremendously.[15]

At the end of the year prospects for the future were dark. A communication from Thomas F. Oakes, Vice President, to Lamborne on October 18 indicates the status of the Land Department then. Oakes wrote:

> It is the desire of this committee [land committee] that your force be reduced by the end of this month [October] so far as may be practicable... It will be proper for you to consider whether it is longer necessary to keep up the organization of the Montana and Pacific coast sub-division; and in the interests of economy generally, you will be expected to make the reductions in your forces, both in respect to the numbers and the salaries of your employes, in the most radical manner, regardless of who may be affected officially or unofficially. The demand for extreme economy is imperative and our committee will not be satisfied with any action on your part unless it is in full accord with this view of the situation.[16]

It is impossible to determine the exact number of Land Department officials who lost their jobs in the economy drive, but Winser was among the group. He left the company at the end of 1883.[17]

Regulations against speculators were relaxed enough late in the year to sell to a syndicate 56,000 acres of land north of Carrington at $5.00 per acre, payment to be made in preferred

THE PERIOD OF THE BIG BOOM   31

stock of the company. The same syndicate contemplated buying additional tracts of 45,000 and 40,000 acres south of LaMoure and north of Bismarck.[18] Efforts were also made to sell large tracts of grazing lands as fast as possible. Only one condition pertained here: the lands were to be sold with regard to streams because grazing land without water is worthless.

The bad financial condition of the company was not enough to stop all land activities. The movement that had been started by the strong promotional campaign of the 1880-to-1883 period continued to have its effects in 1884. A steady and regular movement of settlers continued into the country throughout the year, and the volume of local business increased steadily. Sales were chiefly to actual settlers. Government lands were also going rapidly.[19]

The rapid movement was not continued for long, however, as general business stagnation set in throughout the country and the population movement, although it did not cease entirely, tapered off to a great degree.[20] The promotion movement must have been almost dead during this year, as we find no reference to its operations in 1884 and very little more in 1885.

With this brief study of general organization of the Land Department during the second period of Northern Pacific promotion completed, we may proceed to an analysis of the propaganda techniques which were used to bring the unprecedented influx of settlers to the Northwest.

The Flow of Printed Publicity Resumed

From the evidence that is available we may conclude with a reasonable degree of safety that a greater volume of printed publicity was issued from the Land Department offices during the 1877-to-1884 period than during any other time in the story of the road. And at the same time the variety of titles is greater than during any other period examined. Included in this mass of promotional material is one newspaper, the Fargo *Times,* published in two languages; three magazines, the *New Northwest,* the *Golden Northwest,* and the *Northwest;* a book, E. V. Smalley's *History of the Northern Pacific Railroad;* and a great variety of pamphlets, maps, folders, land and settlers' guides, fly sheets, and pictures.

The earliest promotional publication, after 1880, of which we have evidence is the Fargo *Times* and its Scandinavian edition, the *Budstikken*. No direct statements to the effect that this newspaper was published by the railroad could be found, but it is proved with a reasonable degree of certainty that the railroad had some interest in it by a letter from Power to Stark in which Power wrote:

> The only Scandinavian publication we have published is the *Budstikken*, a Norwegian copy of the Fargo *Times*, of which I send you a package of 25. We had an edition of 10,000 printed about February 1 (1878), and the demand has been active.... In our distribution but few have gone to the old country.[21]

The statement, "We had an edition of 10,000 printed" certainly indicates that the Northern Pacific had some sort of an agreement with the publisher if not a financial interest in it. It will be noted that only a few copies went abroad, the main drive seemingly having been centered in the United States.

That more editions were published at later dates is indicated by a letter from Kidder to Power, dated September 25, 1879, in which Kidder wrote that a special edition of the *Times* was being distributed.[22]

In the same year the company distributed to its stockholders 10,000 copies of the *New Northwest*, a monthly published in Philadelphia by Joseph Creamer.[23] The next year the Land Department was subscribing regularly to 1,000 copies of the magazine. Three hundred went to Power, 100 each to the Chicago and Philadelphia offices, 400 to New York, and 50 to Boston.[24] In May, 1881, the usual edition was doubled.[25]

In 1880 the Land Department started publishing a magazine of its own, the *Golden Northwest*, eight pages of information concerning the road, its lands, the territory served by the Northern Pacific, and its land-sales policies. It was to have been published at irregular intervals, but no evidence was discovered that would indicate that publication was continued after the

THE PERIOD OF THE BIG BOOM   33

first edition. An editorial in the first issue, dated April 1, 1880, describes its purposes:

> This paper is issued by the Land Department of Northern Pacific for the purpose of giving to such as desire it, full and reliable information in regard to the section of the country through which the railroad passes.
> Those who seek homes in new lands look for practical information and such is given without exaggeration. The contents of the new paper consists of reports carefully prepared, and as nothing not known to be absolutely correct is admitted to its columns, the information it gives is vouched for as being perfectly reliable.[26]

Henry J. Winser, whose appointment to the position as Chief of the Bureau of Information was described in the preceding section, was busy during 1882, preparing a variety of material for a great number of publications. He wrote articles for the *Golden Northwest,* assisted in the publication of hand bills, ordered the printing of more than 15,000 copies of a publication entitled the *Pacific Northwest* which he distributed to newspapers and private individuals, edited a travel booklet, and submitted an article on mining in Montana to the Cincinnati *Commercial.* While on the job he toured the line of the road and wrote long letters for the New York *Evening Post,* Villard's newspaper.[27]

An idea of the scope and the bulk of the material flowing from the offices may be gained from the fact that at one time during 1882, 46,000 flat maps were en route from Chicago to St. Paul and 89,000 more were being printed.[28] The record for the whole year showed that the Bureau of Immigration had sent out 2,500,000 copies of descriptive pamphlets, circulars, and folders in English, Swedish, Danish, Norwegian, German, Dutch, and Finnish.[29]

Late in 1883, Lamborne submitted a recommendation for advertising that he wished to have placed prior to April 1, 1884. In his letter to the Land Committee he reported that he had already contracted for publication of 20,000 copies each of *The Great Northern Pacific, The Pacific Northwest,* and *Montana* and 50,000 copies of *Vast Areas Along the Line of The Northern Pacific Railroad Company.* In addition to these four booklets he had ordered printed 30,000 map folders, including 20,000 in English and 5,000 each in Swedish and Norwegian. The total cost of this material was to be $18,760. The expenditure had previously been authorized by the Land Committee. But Lamborne wanted to spend another $10,000 for additional copies of *Montana* and the *Pacific Northwest* and for sectional map folders of North Dakota, a general revised pamphlet on North Dakota, general map folders, a new sectional map of lands in Washington Territory, and various other dodges and folders in English, Swedish, Norwegian, and Danish.[30]

Whether Lamborne's request was granted or not we do not know, but at about the same time that the recommendation was submitted the Northern Pacific began to tighten its belt because of the strained financial condition of the Villard management.[31] Publicity continued to flow in 1884, but the scope was considerably curtailed.

Some mention has been made of the distribution of Montana, Washington, and Oregon pamphlets. In view of the fact that the road was not completed until 1883, it is a curious fact that the Land Department advertised lands that it was not yet in a position to claim. A Washington and Oregon booklet had been published in 1873 in the hope that the road would be completed shortly after that date, but by 1877 it was out of date. At that time the company was planning a revised edition.[32] In 1878 the Land Committee recommended that authority be given to publish maps and information in regard to Eastern Washington.[33] Two days later the board of directors approved the recommendations and promised that a Settler's Guide would be out within a month.[34] A Montana pamphlet was printed during the summer of 1878 in answer to a strong demand for information.[35] In 1880 the company issued a new *Settler's Guide to Washington* which was prepared by General Superintendent J. W. Sprague. At the same time the Oregon Steam Navigation Company, a Villard enterprise that was starting an intensive Oregon drive at this time, issued a general information booklet of which the Northern Pacific ordered 100 copies.[36]

The mass of printed material issued by the Land Department naturally created a great demand for pictures of items along the road that would be likely to appeal to prospective land buyers. It is interesting to study the methods used to get these pictures.[37] In the fall of 1878 Power saw a set of farming pictures in *Leslie's Illustrated Weekly.* Most of the pictures were of the Cass-Cheney farm in North Dakota, an enterprise that had been sponsored by George W. Cass, who was president of the Northern Pacific Railroad Company from 1872 to 1874. Considering the photographs the best he had seen of the Cass-Cheney operations, Power expressed interest in getting duplicates.[38] Within three weeks Power had the pictures, and plans were being made to run them in a special edition of the Fargo *Times.* A month later Power sent Stark fifty prints from the same set. Stark was requested to have display cards made from the set for placement in depots of roads leading westward. He specifically recommended using them in New England and Pennsylvania and suggested that he would have an emigration agent post a lot through northern Iowa, Wisconsin, and Michigan.[39]

F. Jay Haynes, a Fargo commercial photographer who later achieved some attention as the authorized photographer for Yellowstone National Park, supplied the company with views of the North Dakota Bad Lands and of many other points along the main line.[40]

When Winser left St. Paul in 1882 for a trip to the coast, he was accompanied by Baron von Schilling, a German artist who was commissioned to make sketches of interesting points en route. Schilling had previously done some work for the company drawing sketches for earlier publications.[41]

One of the most significant publicity efforts of this era because its connection with the Northern Pacific was concealed was the publication of the *Northwest* magazine. The *Northwest* is doubly significant because its publication was continuous throughout the entire period covered by this thesis.[42]

The *Northwest* was published monthly. It contained articles on the success of farmers in the Northwest states, on the scenery along the Northern Pacific route, on the growth of cities and of geographical areas, on the history of the territory, and on the vast lore which had grown up around the country, As such, its value as an interest stimulator is apparent, not only to the Northern Pacific but to all persons interested in the country.

E. V. Smalley, the *Northwest's* editor, explained that the publication was not only an adjunct of the Land Department but a means of communication with the stockholders and a valuable incentive to immigration. Because it was sent to many leading daily newspapers and because articles were copied by many more dailies, it was able to take the place of many advertising pamphlets.[43]

Originally the *Northwest* had been published in Philadelphia by the Northern Pacific. During the early months of 1883, Smalley, who was both editor of the *Northwest* and an assistant to Winser in the Bureau of Information, started negotiations to purchase the periodical. On July 1, 1883, he entered into a rather complicated agreement with the company which was to give him complete ownership with the aid of a subsidy from the company.

The terms of the agreement were flexible. They specified that Smalley immediately pay $200 toward the purchase of the magazine. The Land Department officials evidently hoped that the purchaser would ultimately give them the entire $2,000 that the publication had cost the company, but no provisions were made for the payment of the additional $1,800. Smalley was to repay one-third of the salary he had earned as Winser's assistant, one-half the rent of *Northwest's* editorial office, and the entire cost of the issues which had been on the exchange and subscription lists. The company assumed the costs of the issues which had been used for advertising and publicity purposes.

Although no terms for a subsidy were included in the agreement, it was evidently assumed by both parties that some form of aid should be extended to the new publisher. At the time that the foregoing agreement was made, Smalley proposed that the company, for a period of three years, promise to purchase 10,000 copies monthly at a rate that would insure him the cost of publication plus a fair commercial profit. If these terms were agreed to, Smalley's salary as an employe of the company should

THE PERIOD OF THE BIG BOOM 37

cease January 1, 1884, and the editorial offices should be removed to St. Paul on the same date.[44]

It is obvious that Smalley intended to continue the periodical as a Northern Pacific promotional medium. We may assume that from his request for a subsidy. But it is obvious, too, that he believed that the appeal to the prospective land buyer should be indirect, should feature prosperity, success, beauty of scenery, rapid growth of population, and recreational advantages.

Lamborne favored neither Smalley's proposal for a subsidy nor his promotional policies. He wrote to Oakes:

> I do not regard a newspaper attached to the Land Department as essential or necessary for the success of any work. I believe that better results can be obtained with an equal amount of money expended on circulars, pamphlets, and special descriptive matter, than by a regular publication once each month...
>
> The amount of newspaper advertising that this company will do during the next year is probably limited... I think all that is necessary for a newspaper advertisement is to call attention to the fact that pamphlets, maps and publications can be obtained by application to this office or elsewhere.[45]

It is interesting to note this conflict between theories of advertising. To this point the writer has praised the Northern Pacific for its skill in promoting land sales through a combination of direct-appeal advertising and indirect-appeal promotion.

Lamborne's more limited concept of promotional methods was vetoed, however, when Oakes proposed to the Land Committee that the Northern Pacific drop the *Northwest* as far as any pecuniary responsibility should be concerned but that the company take a few thousand copies from time to time for foreign use and for certain agencies in the United States. The number of copies should not exceed 5,000 each month and the cost to the company should be slightly above the actual cost to the publisher in order to allow a small profit. Smalley was to continue its publication as his own enterprise. Oakes further recommended that should the company require the preparation of pamphlets, Smalley should be employed for such services.[46]

The final decision of the Land Committee was that the company should take 3,000 copies each month at $50 a thousand and that in return for that financial assistance should be permitted free advertising space. Villard reported that his three West Coast companies would take an additional 5,000 copies under the same terms.[47]

Because the company had originally paid $2,000 for the publication, it was necessary that terms be made with Smalley for the payment of the remaining $1,800 or that the amount be written off the books. It was decided that the unpaid sum should be charged to the Land Department as advertising. Under these terms Smalley got the *Northwest* for $200.[48]

Two of the Oregon companies failed to carry out the terms of their agreement with Smalley, so the editor wrote to the Land Department early in 1884, asking that the Northern Pacific guarantee be raised to 5,000 copies a month.[49] This request was complied with, and it was agreed the rates should be the same as those that had originally been set.[50]

That the company acted wisely in subsidizing Smalley is indicated by the fact, shown in subsequent chapters, that the Land Department's orders often exceeded 100,000 copies a year and that thousands of reprints of *Northwest* articles were obtained for promotional purposes.

One additional promotional enterprise must be included in a discussion of printed publicity in the 1877-1884 period. In connection with the grand celebration staged at the completion of the road in Montana on September 3, 1883, Villard commissioned Smalley, still a publicity employe of the company, to write a history of the Northern Pacific. The book, including a detailed account of company affairs up to that time and a guide book descriptive of the territory through which the road passed, was written primarily for the benefit of Villard's guests on an excursion from St. Paul to the point in Montana where the last spike was driven.[51]

THE PERIOD OF THE BIG BOOM 39

Advertising in the Newspapers

As prospects for the completion of the transcontinental route improved, the Land Department's newspaper advertising increased in volume and in cost until more than $5,000 was spent on land advertising alone in the twelve months ending November 1, 1881.[52]

The cost was stepped up considerably for 1882, more than $7,000 being allotted for running one advertisement of one column width and ten inches depth in seventy-three papers for a period of six months starting November 1, 1881. The list of papers used was compiled by N. W. Ayer and Son advertising agency of Philadelphia in conjunction with Colonel R. M. Newport, who was General Land Agent for the Northern Pacific at the time. The list covered the weekly editions of the best papers in Boston, Portland, Rochester, Buffalo, New York, Philadelphia, Cleveland, Cincinnati, Columbus, Indianapolis, and Detroit, and the "best agricultural newspapers of the northwest."[53]

In 1883, advertisements were inserted in 167 newspapers in the United States, twenty-five in Canada, and forty divided among publications in Germany, Sweden, Norway, and Denmark.[54] At the end of the year, the only outstanding contract was for a two-inch ad in the family magazine the *Youths Companion*, which Lamborne considered the best advertising medium in the country.[55]

Plans for 1884 were even more extensive, however. Lamborne proposed in December, 1883, to spend about $5,000 in the first three months of the coming year. He intended to insert brief notices in 200 or 300 papers in the first three months of 1884. He recommended that approximately $2,000 of the $5,000 total be expended on newspapers published in Scandinavian-and-German-language and about $3,000 in English-language journals.[56] His plans were carried out almost to the letter as the total advertising for the year included the use of 200 English-language newspapers, sixty-eight German, and thirty-two Scandinavian, all published in the United States.[57]

In making plans for this advertising, Lamborne emphasized the fact that more than nine-tenths of the settlers on Northern

Pacific lands came from the states and territories west of the Alleghenies. He also directed his program so that it would reach the farmers during December, January, and February, the months in which they were most likely to make plans for moving.[58]

Although compensation for most of this advertising was made in cash, there is one instance of publication, the *Advance* of Chicago, taking payment in land.[59]

Keeping Up An Agitation in the Press

With a Bureau of Information, manned by two men, devoting a good share of its attention to getting items into the daily press, it is quite natural that the Northern Pacific should receive favorable space in many of the leading newspapers during the Winser regime.

Villard, too, was vitally interested in squeezing as many items as possible into newspapers. Winser wrote to Newport, concerning Villard's attitude on publicity, "Mr. Villard has urged him (Smalley) as well as he has urged me, to keep up an agitation in the press on these subjects by sending news paragraphs etc., to the journals with which the company advertises."[60] The technique of sending reading notices along with advertising was developed to a much higher degree in the 1897-to-1902 period, but Winser was using the practice to the greatest extent that he could at this time.[61]

Henry W. Raymond, literary editor of the Chicago *Tribune,* seems to have been one of the best friends of the Northern Pacific. Raymond helped Winser get into print an interview with a prominent Dakota farmer, a story on mining in Montana, and some information on Washington Territory. Winser also made arrangements with the Chicago *Tribune* man to print a series of letters concerning Winser's trip west during the summer of 1882.[62]

Another good friend was Murat Halsted, editor of the Cincinnati *Commercial,* who saw to it that stories concerning mining in Montana and Winser's travel experiences found their way into the *Commercial's* columns.[63]

It may be more than coincidental that Villard had, at various times, been on the editorial staffs of both these newspapers. His intimate acquaintance with newspapermen, gained through his many years of experience as a reporter and correspondent and through the fact that he was, at this time, publisher of the New York *Post* and *The Nation,* must certainly have worked to the advantage of Winser and his aides in the Bureau of Information.

The list of papers using Northern Pacific publicity stories was undoubtedly lengthy. Winser wrote to Smalley in 1882 in regard to an interview with the Dakota farmer mentioned above, "It has occurred to me that you might make use of some of the more important facts . . . among the many *[sic]* newspapers to which you have the entree."[64]

Use of Miscellaneous Publicity Techniques

Northern Pacific officials were satisfied with neither straight advertising nor press agentry nor a combination of the two to achieve their goals. They also gained attention and thus promoted land sales by such divergent devices as exhibiting products at fairs, sending out exhibit cars on tours of the country, giving away free lots to churches and newspapers, promoting excursions both for land seekers and newspapermen, staging a mammoth celebration marking the completion of the road, and employing district land agents to keep up the Northern Pacific fever in local communities.

The exhibit car, an ordinary railroad passenger coach carrying samples of products from the Northwest country, was sent out for a three-months' tour in 1882. During those three months, it stopped at sixty-five important towns in ten states and was visited by more than 50,000 persons. Ordinary exhibits were set up at annual fairs at Chicago, St. Louis, and Minneapolis.[65]

One of the most interesting of the smaller public relations practices of the Land Department was the gift of a lot in Livingston, Montana, to George Wright and Joseph Hendry as an aid in starting the Livingston *Enterprise.* Hendry and Wright paid $1 for the deed to the lot, which was to be in their permanent possession after they had published their paper for one year.[66] The donation of lots was nothing new, however, as it had been the practice of the road to give lots varying from a 100-foot to a one-half block front to schools and churches in towns laid out by the company.[67] There is no need of commenting on the importance of this device in gaining good will.

From a national publicity standpoint, one of the most important of all Northern Pacific moves was an excursion to Yellowstone Park organized by the railroad for prominent daily newspaper editors. Again the influence of the newspaper-wise Villard is evident. The trip was taken in August, 1882, and Winser served as guide to the party.[68]

The grand celebration marking the completion of the Northern Pacific's road bed from Lake Superior to the coast was the zenith of all staged publicity projects. Villard desired to attract European attention, so he decided to make an international event out of the driving of the last spike, which took place on September 3, 1883. Villard, himself, describes the event in the following terms:

> The company extended invitations to the members of the United States government and the governments of the seven states traversed by the road, to leading members of the United States Senate and House of Representatives, to over a hundred representative men from all parts of the country, and the leading newspapers, to be present at the driving of the last spike. The whole diplomatic corps was also invited, as well as several score of prominent Englishmen and Germans. As nearly all those invited accepted, it was necessary to arrange four special trains from the East and one from the Pacific Coast.[69]

The huge excursion left the East on August 28 when two trains started westward from the Atlantic coast. One train was added at Chicago and another at Minneapolis and St. Paul. Included in the party were former President U. S. Grant, several of President Arthur's cabinet, seven governors, more than a score of journalists, and a host of other dignitaries, foreign and American, important and unimportant.

THE PERIOD OF THE BIG BOOM 43

The trip west was a constant procession of parades, receptions, salutes, entertainments, and celebrations, with vast numbers of people lining the tracks to watch the special trains roll by. Speeches were made, cornerstones were laid, and, in Montana, Crow Indians danced a war dance for the party.

Naturally the press could not fail to take notice of such an imposing event, and it became a leading topic in both American and foreign journals.[70]

With one stroke Villard had interested prominent officials who would write and talk about his road and lend prestige to it, had manufactured a constant barrage of front-page news for the press, had built up enthusiasm among thousands of people who witnessed the celebrations along the line, and had focused the attentions of both Europe and America on the new transcontinental line, which, it is important to note, still had land to sell.

There was much less drama in the employment of traveling land agents and district land agents, but this practice, too, was an integral part of the Northern Pacific promotional program.

Traveling land agents had been employed throughout the period. Their duties were to promote excursions, assist in the formation of colonies, and aid the Bureau of Information in the distribution of publicity.[71] Their specific function for the Bureau of Information was to disseminate information out of which newspapermen could construct their own news stories. Articles that had their inception in interviews with these agents would obviously have none of the "canned" aspects of the articles which were prepared in Winser's office, and it was much more likely that they would get into print.

Use of district agents was recommended to Oakes by Colonel Newport in 1881. Newport suggested paying commissions of 5 to 7½ per cent on sales and thereby secure active talkers for the railroad throughout the country.[72] Evidently nothing was done because R. J. Wemyss, who became General Land Agent in 1883, made a similar proposal in November of that year. He suggested employment of agents in localities where the road might expect to find land buyers. The agent was to be paid a commission consisting of 1 per cent on sales to persons coming from his district of whom he had not advised the company, 2 per cent sales to persons of whom he had advised the company, and 4 per cent on sales to those persons he personally escorted to the Northern Pacific land.[73]

On December 27, 1883, the Land Committee finally authorized the appointment of the district agents, but the commission scale was considerably different than the one proposed by Wemyss.[74] Instead of the sliding scale from one to four per cent, the Land Committee decided that there should be a flat commission of two per cent on all sales of land east of the Missouri River and two-and-one-half per cent on sales of land in Dakota west of the Missouri. There should be no commissions paid on sales of company land west of Dakota. An additional one-half per cent should be added to the compensation when the agent personally brought the purchaser to the land. The agents were expected to distribute advertising matter and canvass their districts thoroughly.[75]

How well this melange of publicity and public relations methods succeeded may be seen by an examination of the census reports for 1880 and 1885, included in Chapter VIII of this study. It is sufficient here to say that 1880 to 1885 was the period of most rapid growth in the history of northern Minnesota and eastern North Dakota. It was on sale of lands in these two areas that the Northern Pacific was concentrating its promotional efforts at this time.

Chapter IV
The Period of Drought, Crop Failures, and Large-Scale Land Sales

The Northern Pacific's land-sales campaigns from 1885 to 1892 are marked by a constant series of adversities. The period began while the company was still shaken by the failure of the Villard management (Villard had resigned the presidency in 1884). Recovery should have begun by 1886, but then the country was faced by a general business depression partly occasioned by the financial crisis of 1884. The depression was magnified in the Northwest by the drouth and crop shortage of 1886. Crops were better by 1888 but received another setback in 1889. Conditions were little better in 1890 but recovery had set in during 1891. When prospects were finally bright again, the company crashed in 1892 and went into the hands of receivers.

Undoubtedly the Northern Pacific was doing a substantial amount of advertising during this period in spite of the forbidding business prospects, but beyond a general summary the records are inadequate to construct a complete picture. This may be partly due to the fact that much of the publicity concerned lands in the Western District, and thus was handled by the Western office, whose records were not available to the writer.

Notwithstanding the above difficulties, it is possible to piece together the threads of the story by a study of business conditions and land sales, by a breakdown of Land Department advertising expenditures, and by an account of minor promotional activities.

The *Annual Report* for 1885 pointed out that two factors, general business conditions throughout the country and the low prices received by farmers for their crops, checked immigration somewhat. In the face of these facts, however, there was a steady, if not large, movement into the Northwest, particularly to the lands west of the Missouri. Land sales were made in small tracts almost exclusively to actual settlers. Crops during 1884 had been large but prices were very low.[1]

In 1886 the Dakota wheat crop suffered an almost complete failure, causing general suffering in that territory and checking immigration to the area. Dakota's loss was the Pacific Slope's gain, however, as land sales boomed in eastern Washington as well as in Montana. There was also a considerable movement into western Dakota in the spring of 1887.[2] Railroad officials were still hopeful of staging a strong western Dakota campaign, because, as they pointed out:

> It cannot be long before a new and continuous movement of population will flow into this immense territory. Nowhere else can there now be found such large areas of unoccupied land, ready for cultivation without the expense of clearing, and with no need of irrigation.[3]

Land sales were limited in Dakota for the fiscal year of 1888. In Montana operations of the Land Department were hindered by the limited area covered by government surveys. Minnesota sales showed a fair increase, but it was in Washington that most of the activity took place. There land sales showed an increase of 68 per cent, and the population was up 30,000 from the previous year, according to the company's estimate.[4]

Dakota was still in a slump in 1889, partly because of the fact that the West Coast was getting the largest share of the attention of prospective buyers and partly because of memories of the crop failures. In an effort to overcome the fear of wheat-crop failures, the Land Department started to direct attention to the fact that Dakota lands were well adapted to diversified farming.[5] Prospects were good in the spring but drouth hit again in the summer with great severity.[6]

Business in North Dakota, which had become a state in 1889, continued quiet in 1890 with crops below average and little demand for land. However, 1891 promised one of the

THE PERIOD OF DROUGHT, CROP FAILURES... 47

highest grain yields in history and prices were high.[7] Excessive rainfall affected the quality of the wheat and cut down somewhat on the total yield, but at the end of the year general conditions were good.[8] The demand for Montana land was down in 1892 but came back well in 1893.[9]

As the country was on the threshold of the panic of 1893 and the Northern Pacific was getting dangerously closer to its bankruptcy of the same year, prospects in 1892 seemed good. Migration to the lands was no higher than in the previous year, but the bountiful wheat crop of 1891 had revived interest in Minnesota and North Dakota and talk of irrigation was stimulating demand for Montana and eastern Washington grazing lands.[10] But then came the crash and with it, evidently, the curtailment of almost all of the promotional program.

Two large-scale sales of land were negotiated during this period. On July 22, 1885, the company entered into a contract with "certain parties" for the sale of all unsold land in Dakota east of the Missouri River. A total of 2,430,000 acres was to be included in the contract, which called for $2.00 an acre payable in preferred stock of the company. Before the publication of the *Annual Report* of 1886 the company had selected more than 1,700,000 acres of the total, 670,000 acres remaining unsurveyed.[11]

That the transfer of this huge quantity of land took some time is evidenced in the *Annual Report* of 1888, which says of the contract:

> A contract for the sale of 1,600,000 acres of place lands in Dakota, east of the Missouri River, had been authorized and executed, and as the tracts embraced there-in are designated by the purchasers, and are paid for, they will be conveyed and the sales will be regularly taken up in future reports.[12]

During 1890 and 1891 a total of 143,268 acres of timber lands in Minnesota were sold to Frederick Weyerhauser and associates. By July 1, 1891, conveyance of the entire purchase had been made.[13]

Advertising During the Adverse Years

During the 1885-1893 period the Land Department's message was carried to the public by means of four separate types of promotion. A constant barrage of newspaper advertising was placed in a great number of papers; sectional land maps and short circulars were sent out by the thousands, and the *Northwest* magazine was distributed widely.

During the fiscal year ending July 1, 1888, the company advertised in 3,385 newspapers at a cost of more than $2,700. The advertisements were of a one-column by one-inch size. During the same year 500,000 sectional land maps and 650,000 short circulars were sent out as were 90,000 copies of the *Northwest*.[14] In 1889 the number of newspapers had been increased to 4,156 but the total cost was down to about $2,300. A total of 508,412 land maps, 848,000 circulars, 87,000 *Northwests*, and 145,000 reprints of articles in the *Northwest* were also used.[15]

The year 1890 was a peak year for newspaper advertising, the total number of papers reaching 6,829 at a cost of $3,170. The number of sectional land maps had dropped to 250,249, short circulars to 584,000, and *Northwests* to 84,000 plus 11,000 reprints.[16]

Advertising fell to 3,166 newspapers in 1891 but land maps had increased to 423,155 and circulars to 665,000. *Northwests* remained constant at 84,000 with no reprints.[17] In the last year of solvency, 1892, the Land Department used 2,820 newspapers at a cost of $1,901, set out 300,450 maps and 84,000 *Northwests*. The use of circulars hit a peak in this year, the total reaching 1,491,650, almost double the highest previous year.[18]

TABLE I
Advertising Expenditures by Years, 1888 to 1893

	Cost Newspaper Adv.	Number Newspapers	Sectional Land Maps	Short Circulars	*Northwests*	Reprints
1888	$2,759.32	3,385	500,000	650,000	90,000	
1889	$2,297.08	4,156	508,412	848,000	87,000	145,000
1890	$3,170.08	6,829	250,349	584,000	84,000	11,000
1891	$2,348.19	3,166	423,155	423,155	84,000	
1892	$1,901.20	2,820	300,450	1,491,650	84,000	

In addition to the above material, which was used as direct advertising for the Land Department, the Northern Pacific was distributing pamphlets which emphasized, for the most part, the scenery along the road. Persons taking land-seeking excursions were given several booklets which described the country through which the railroad passed. Available for distribution were a pamphlet on North Dakota, one on Montana, one on Idaho and eastern Washington, and one on western Washington. There was also a map of the entire Northern Pacific country and one of Yellowstone National Park.[19]

A display of agricultural, mineral, forest, and grazing specimens was exhibited at the council chambers of the Court House in St. Paul for some time.[20]

That the practice of cultivating influential newspapermen was carried on during this period is indicated by the fact that L. E. Quigg, a correspondent of the New York *Tribune,* wrote a series of letters while on tour of the Northern Pacific country. The letters were compiled in pamphlet form by the railroad and used for advertising purposes.[21]

At the very end of the period a marked change in the land-sales policy was forced upon the company by a decision handed down by Judge Joseph J. Jenkins of the Circuit Court of the United States for the Seventh Judicial District, Eastern District of Wisconsin. Judge Jenkins ruled that the receivers of the Northern Pacific should be in the future restrained from accepting preferred stock in payment for land purchases, a policy that had been in use since the first land sales were made.[22]

Undoubtedly the story of the promotional activities of this period would have been far more extensive had the work of the Western District Office been included. It is true that the placement of advertisements and the distribution of pamphlets, circulars, and *Northwest* magazines measured up well with preceding periods of promotion, but the slump was most noticeable in the variety of indirect methods of attracting attention to the Northwest that had been used previously. As a consequence, the Eastern office of the Land Department between 1885 and 1893 maintained only an advertising agency, not the highly skilled promotional machine that had functioned so ably prior to 1883.

It is probable that this curtailment in the promotional program was based, for the most part, on the fact that very little good, surveyed land was available for sale. The boom years of the early eighties had taken up thousands of acres and the bulk sale of 1886 took more than 2,000,000 acres more. Then, the Eastern district office was handicapped by adverse crop conditions that eliminated the desire for purchasing lands in this region. When the latent desire to purchase land is absent, it is self-evident that the promotional expert has no bases around which to design his pressures, and an extensive campaign would have been wasted effort.

When prosperity returned to Minnesota and North Dakota and large areas of desirable land were once more available, as will be noted in the following chapter, Northern Pacific promotion was fully as varied and fully as skilled as it had been in the earlier periods of land sales.

Chapter V
Newspapers Become the Dominant Medium, 1897 to 1902

A marked shift in advertising policy dominated the period of Northern Pacific Land Department promotion that began in 1897 and ran through 1902. Almost all efforts were directed to reaching prospective land buyers through the country press. F. W. Wilsey, the official in charge of land advertising, who started as Eastern Land Agent and was advanced to Assistant Land Commissioner, expressed this new policy when he wrote to George W. Spinney, president of the road, "This department has millions of acres that it is daily making an effort to sell. My experience teaches me that the best known method of communicating the fact to the proper public is through the country press."[1]

With that theory in mind Wilsey set out to advertise widely, to offer transportation to newspaper publishers and editors in exchange for advertising in an effort to interest them in the Northern Pacific territory, to inspire favorable letters to newspapers, and to fill the newspapers with press handouts.

True enough, the railroads ran land-seekers' excursions, employed solicitors and agents to sell the lands, sent out exhibit cars, and used other, sometimes devious, methods of attracting attention; but when each of these devices was used, Wilsey was careful to see that the press got notices.

Another fundamental shift of policy saw most of the advertising going into publications in the Middle West, not in the East and in the East North Central states as formerly. Most of the ads were placed in Iowa and southern Minnesota, but some were also contracted for in Nebraska and some in South Dakota.

Wilsey took over his new job January 1, 1897. Some advertising had been done in 1896. There had been advertisements in nineteen papers in Minnesota and sixteen in Iowa.

Paying for Advertising in Transportation

Because so many of the features of the 1897-1902 land sales publicity depended upon the system then in vogue of paying for advertising in transportation, it is necessary to start a discussion of this period by analyzing the system used and the multitude of results which were brought about by this method.

Advantages of using transportation were many. Wilsey pointed out that exchange of advertising for tickets on the railroad would cut down on the cash outlay necessary to carry out the advertising program, thus making it possible to use more papers, and it would permit publishers to travel to points of interest, including Yellowstone Park. The final point, however, is of great importance: "Every publisher favored with transportation would undoubtedly record in the columns of his paper the experience of his trip thereby benefitting the passenger as well as the land department."[2]

The system started slowly for two reasons: many of the publishers, especially those in Iowa, were at so great a distance from St. Paul that they hesitated about paying their fares to the Minnesota terminus of the road, and the Interstate Commerce law had placed a prohibition against issuing transportation through any office of the railroad excepting the Passenger Department. It was not, then, possible without an agreement with the Passenger Department to issue any transportation at all, and the General Passenger Agent had issued all the passes possible for the 1897 season, with about thirty or forty exceptions, in payment for passenger advertising.[3]

On Wilsey's recommendation, however, President Mellen heartily approved the transportation-payment plan in December of 1897 so from then on it was possible to issue transportation through the Passenger Department in any amounts that Wilsey saw fit.[4]

In issuing the transportation the Northern Pacific officials in charge had to be careful not to violate any Interstate Commerce law provisions. Tickets could be issued only to the proprietor of the advertising medium personally or to his assistants.[5]

As the plan was finally worked out, the Northern Pacific Land Department offered, in exchange for its two-columns by six-inch advertisements, round-trip transportation, first class, to the most remote point on the line that would be covered by the cost of the amount of advertising done.

Tickets were to be issued only to the publisher, the publisher and his wife, and editor, the editor and his wife, "a representative of the newspaper certified to be such by the publisher, and bearing credentials issued by the publisher stating that the bearer is a regular employe of the newspaper, that he is engaged in no other business, and that he proposes using the transportation for no other business than the newspaper business or for recreation," or to that employe and his wife. The transportation was to be issued at St. Paul and was limited to use on the company's own line.[6]

Publishers were told in the spring of 1898 that most of the advertising to be done by the company from that time on would be paid for in transportation.[7]

Advertising in the West

The most interesting features of the newspaper advertising campaign carried on from 1897 to 1902 were the facts that almost all of the papers used were situated in Iowa, Minnesota, Nebraska, and South Dakota; that the advertisements were much larger than they had been in previous periods; and that brief announcements called reading notices were invariably sent along with ads. Provisions for these reading notices were usually included in the advertising contracts.

It has already been mentioned that the advertising program for 1896 included advertisements in nineteen newspapers in Minnesota and sixteen in Iowa.[8] When Wilsey took over the land office at St. Paul on January 1, 1897, he immediately signed contracts for the first six months of the year with 171 newspapers distributed as follows: eighty-four in Iowa, forty-seven in Minnesota, sixteen in South Dakota, twenty in Nebraska, three in Wisconsin, and one in Illinois. There were also two special contracts, one a general ad in the *German Evangelical Report* and the other, a write up of Aitkin County, Minnesota, in the Des Moines *Homestead*.[9]

Total advertising contracts for 1897 were 262, with 153 in Iowa, sixty-three in Minnesota, twenty-two in Nebraska, sixteen in South Dakota, four in Wisconsin, two in Illinois, and two in New York. The total for 1898 was down to seventy, sixty-three in Iowa, six in Minnesota, and one in Wisconsin but rose again in 1899 to 133, sixty-six of which were in Iowa, thirty-seven in Minnesota, eight in Illinois, one in South Dakota, and one in Wisconsin.[10]

TABLE II
Advertising Contracts for the Years 1897, 1898, and 1899

State	1897	1898	1899
Iowa	153	63	66
Minnesota	63	6	37
Nebraska	22	0	0
South Dakota	16	0	1
Wisconsin	4	1	1
Illinois	2	0	8
New York	2	0	0
Total	262	70	113

The average price paid for each of the advertisements, over the three-year period, varied from $12 to $15, depending on the circulation of the paper, for a three-months' run.[11] Rates were generally computed on the basis of $10 for each 1,000 of circulation.[12]

The amount of transportation given in payment for advertising contracts signed up to April 30, 1897, may be learned from the following table:

TABLE III
Advertising Contracts Made up to and Including April 30, 1897

State	Total Cost	Cash	Transportation
Iowa	$1,212.53	$975.13	$237.40
Minnesota	614.11	507.63	106.48
South Dakota	206.00	143.00	63.00
Nebraska	288.50	187.00	101.50[13]
Wisconsin	58.80	58.80	
Illinois	39.70	39.70	

Most of the advertisements were placed by Wilsey and Drummond, but there is also evidence of the use of advertising agencies. The H. P. Hall Advertising Agency of Minneapolis placed ads in more than thirty Minnesota papers in 1897,[14] and David R. McGinnis of St. Paul signed a contract December 1, 1898, to do $10,000 worth of advertising with ten selected publications during 1899.[15]

The McGinnis contract was to cover only large agricultural journals. In the list were the *Dakota Farmer* at Aberdeen, *The Farmer* of St. Paul, the *Iowa Homestead* of Des Moines, *The Nebraska Farmer* of Omaha, *The Wisconsin Farmer* of Madison, *The Livestock Indicator* of Kansas City, the *Farmer's Voice* of Chicago, the *Indiana Farmer* of Indianapolis, and the *National Stockman and Farmer* of Pittsburgh. Each publication was to receive $250 for each three months or $1,000 for the year.[16]

McGinnis was to prepare the copy for the advertisements but was to submit it to the Land Department before forwarding it to the publications. He was to use the $10,000 as a maximum sum to be spent but was to try to get as much advertising as possible above the figure at no additional expense. Lands to be advertised were those in Kidder, Burleigh, and McLean counties in North Dakota.[17]

The compensation to be paid to McGinnis was a commission of 25 cents an acre on land sold to actual settlers not already in the counties mentioned in the foregoing, the commission not to be paid in full until at least 75 cents had been paid on each acre of land purchased. In the promotion of the land sales McGinnis was to be permitted to organize land excursions for publishers. On these excursions the Northern Pacific offered to furnish transportation but no more.[18]

The fact that most of the Northern Pacific advertising in this period was in the states immediately adjacent to Minnesota and North Dakota has been pointed out. That Wilsey had definite objectives in mind and a well-formulated policy for the placement of advertisements is apparent from a study of some of his correspondence with publishers.

The Iowa advertising was carefully placed. Early in his regime Wilsey wrote that it was to be confined to the central and western parts of the state and that none would be placed in the river towns.[19] In 1898 he explained that he was especially desirous of working the Boone, Iowa, vicinity thoroughly that year.[20]

Another rule followed by Wilsey was that no advertising was to be placed in newspapers in the vicinities of the lands advertised. He believed that everybody in those localities knew that the land was for sale and that there was no point in spending money to inform them of the fact.[21] On the basis of this regulation, all the Minnesota advertising was placed in the southern section of the state.

There were a multitude of other regulations to which Wilsey adhered. There was to be no advertising in the city papers and none in dailies.[22] Up until March, 1898, he reported that he had placed none with monthly publications and might not in the future.[23] Very little advertising was done in summer months because Wilsey thought that it would be difficult to get the attention of the farmers during that season.[24]

Wilsey was also careful to insist that all advertising should go on local pages because he felt that those pages would be read by subscribers. "I would not give a dollar for certain positions in some papers," he wrote, "and unless I can have reasonably good position I do not care for the advertisement." He had a particular aversion to having his ads thrown on pages devoted to supervisor's meetings or next to boiler plate.[25]

When some local land solicitors wrote that they thought some publishers would be willing to take land in exchange for advertising, Wilsey wrote to Spinney that he considered such a policy of great value to the company. He felt that it would be desirable because if the publisher owned land in the sections advertised, he would be inclined to favor the Northern Pacific's program.[26]

In explaining his choices for his advertising list to Spinney, Wilsey wrote that he made up the list on the basis of three considerations: recommendations of local land solicitors, knowledge of the papers that had in the past rendered good service and in which the advertising was beneficial, and through a careful study of the map of Iowa. By studying the map Wilsey was able to distribute his contracts throughout the state in such a way as to strike those towns where prospects for sales were the best and to cover the entire field without any duplications.[27] A regular form was sent to solicitors asking them which papers in their territories they thought would do them the most good; which type of advertising, a standing display ad or frequent reading notices, would bring the greatest returns; and whether it would be possible for them to secure much gratuitous advertising.[28]

After his lists were made up, Wilsey sent contracts to the chosen papers. In the standard contract was a provision that the reading notice which was submitted with a two-column by six-inch advertisement would be inserted next to reading matter on a local page. One display ad was generally left standing and run each week for a total of thirteen weeks.[29] Only the "readers" were changed from week to week.

The reading notices were generally very brief, not more than ten lines, and were used primarily to call attention to the facts mentioned in the display advertisement. They were sometimes, too, used to announce homeseekers' excursions to North Dakota.[30]

Inspiring Favorable Letters in the Press

Through 1897 and 1898 the weekly papers, primarily in Iowa, kept up a running series of long interviews praising Northern Pacific lands in Minnesota and North Dakota. Most of these interviews came from residents of the towns in which the stories were printed and described excursions to some point on the Northern Pacific line.[31] A person studying these articles casually would assume that they were bona fide communications from the persons named, but a closer perusal shows that there is amazing similarity between some of the accounts. In some cases, in fact, whole paragraphs are exactly alike.

The similarities between accounts are sufficient reason to assume that Wilsey, or some other Land Department employe, wrote the stories and handed them to the excursionists for the purpose of getting them printed in the home paper. There was very little danger of being exposed because in most cases the towns in which similar articles were printed were sufficiently far apart that it was quite improbable that anyone would read both papers.

Even if we assume that some of the interviews were actually in the words of the persons to whom they are ascribed, they are a testimonial to the public-relations policies established by Wilsey. They all speak of the excellent treatment accorded to them by the Northern Pacific on their excursions and of the prosperous farms that they saw.

One of the most flagrant examples of duplication of facts in interviews is found in clippings from the Perry (Iowa) *Advertiser*, the Perry *Chief Reporter*, and the Adel (Iowa) *News*. The *Advertiser* clipping is dated January 7, 1898, the *Chief Reporter*, November 25, 1897, and the Adel *News*, February 16, 1898.

In the Perry *Chief Reporter*, Harvey Willis, a resident of Perry, is reported to have said:

> Carrington is a town of about 700 inhabitants, the county seat of Foster county, and has four churches, two banks, a 75 barrel roller mill, a $10,000 school building and a fine new court house. The town is located on the Devil's Lake branch of the Northern Pacific Railway and is the terminus

of the Sykeston branch which will probably extend westward in the spring, thus opening up a large new territory of fine farming land. The Soo Railway line connects with the Canada Pacific north, and other lines at St. Paul give the town splendid railroad facilities and easy access to markets.

The same paragraph, identical in all respects, was printed in an interview with William Nash, another Perry resident, in the Perry *Advertiser* almost six weeks later, and again in an interview with J. T. Gudgel in the Adel *News* almost three months after the Willis story. It is hard to believe that Willis, Nash, and Gudgel all thought of the same paragraph to utter when confronted by the press.

There is the possibility that the interviews were written by George Heaton, the Land Department's representative in Perry, as both Willis and Nash commented on the fine choice made by the Northern Pacific when the road employed George Heaton to represent it. Both, too, recommended that prospective land buyers see Heaton for information.

The type of information in all three interviews is exactly of the type that one would expect to come out of Wilsey's office. Nash commented that the region around Carrington was rich farming country, that there was no snow or extreme cold, and that only one-half a day's work was lost in the months of October, November, and December on account of the weather.

Willis was enthusiastic about the splendid market facilities; the fact that one could work outside all day in the cold, dry weather; that the water was as good as any he had tasted; that the soil was richer and deeper and good for any small grain or for pasturage; and "this section promises by far the largest and surest returns on a smaller investment than any farming section in the middle western states."

A job that could not have been done by the Northern Pacific office was well taken care of by Gudgel when that Adel citizen pointed out the advantages of Carrington on the Northern Pacific line over Cardo on the Great Northern. Gudgel said that all the good land at Cardo was taken up, that the Great Northern terms were not as good as the Northern Pacific's, and that there were no good homesteads within twenty miles of the railroad at Cardo. If the story, as we may assume, was sponsored by Heaton or Wilsey, it is evident that the Northern Pacific was, in a respectable fashion, taking a slap at the Great Northern.

Another story in the Adel *News* would indicate that the Land Department was setting up a counter propaganda to combat the stories of the short crops in the 1890 period. In a certified statement, A. D. Parker of Carrington wrote to the paper that there had not been a failure in the Carrington vicinity in thirteen years, that the average yield of wheat was more than seventeen bushels an acre, that there was no sandy land, and that the poorer lands made excellent pasturage. He also reported that he had invested $800 in sheep in 1890 and by 1895 had realized $2,998 on his investment. On January 1, 1896, he still had sheep on hand worth $600. Again we have no proof that the Northern Pacific was in any way involved in the publishing of the article, but in view of the duplications of the Carrington paragraph and of the obvious value to the road, we certainly have some basis for assuming that Wilsey's hand was involved somewhere.

In addition to showing the nature of the interviews being given to the press on returning from such excursions, an interview with W. E. Stephens in the Churdan (Iowa) *Reporter* September 24, 1897, indicates the nature of the excursions themselves. Stephens reported:

> I must say that it is the pleasantest outing that I have ever taken. We had a tourist car, slept and ate on the car all the time we were gone. When we arrived at Carrington Mr. Vanbergen (the Northern Pacific's land representative at Carrington) had arranged to have four double seated buggies to drive us into the country at the expense of the railroad company. We drove from 25 to 50 miles a day and looked at the most beautiful prairie country I ever laid my eyes on. The soil is black loam with yellowish clay sub-soil, which makes it the garden spot of the world for wheat, oats, rye, flax, barley, and vegetables ... They have plenty of good water, as good as any I ever drank, and they get it at from 18 to 30 feet.

A great many people who had moved from Iowa, Kansas, Indiana, Illinois and other states ... told me that they would rather winter in North Dakota that in any of these states.

The *Reporter*, in addition to the Stephens interview, published a brief notice similar to the reading notices used by Wilsey, calling attention to the fact that the Stephens interview would be found elsewhere in the paper.

One of the most interesting cases discovered was a letter from Steele, North Dakota, to the Winona (Minnesota) *Herald* printed in the *Herald* October 15, 1898. It is interesting for two reasons: it was written by a David R. McGinnis and it includes a paragraph on climate which has a strangely familiar ring.

On December 1, 1898, the Northern Pacific signed a contract with a David R. McGinnis of St. Paul to place $10,000 worth of advertising in ten selected publications during 1899.[32] There could hardly have been two David R. McGinnis's with so great an interest in Northern Pacific lands.

In the paragraph on climate, McGinnis wrote:

The climate here along the Missouri is remarkably mild for its latitude. The only explanation is that western North Dakota partakes in those strangely mild winds which wafted from the Pacific ocean in winter carry their mildness to this Northern slope.

In 1871 the Hon. S. Garfield, delegate in Congress from the Washington Territory, wrote a pamphlet entitled *Climates of the Northwest* which was published in Philadelphia by the Northern Pacific.[33] In his pamphlet Garfield included a paragraph which read:

Warm southwesterly winds ... spreading ... over Eastern Montana and Dakota ... together with the lower elevations of the northern districts give them a mildness of climate both incomprehensible and incredible to those who have given the subject no particular attention.[34]

Garfield's theory, which dominated his pamphlet, was that the climate of Dakota and Montana was milder than that of the states to the south because Pacific winds were able to reach them through low passes, and, because they were on the northern slope, their altitudes were lower and thus not subject to the rigorous temperatures of high mountain country.

If Wilsey did not write the letter himself, then someone in close connection with the Northern Pacific had schooled McGinnis thoroughly on Garfield's theory of climate. It certainly seems reasonable to believe that the letter was either Northern Pacific-written or Northern Pacific-inspired.

The foregoing is by no means a complete list of the letters written to the press by apparently disinterested persons during this period, nor is it a complete account of duplications found. It should be sufficient to indicate, however, that Wilsey was doing an exceedingly skillful job of either inspiring news stories written exactly as he wanted them or of getting his own stories placed in newspapers under the by-lines of persons who had no connections with the Northern Pacific. The evidence would seem to indicate that the latter was the case.

Publicity Techniques with Source Unconcealed

In the case of the letters mentioned in the foregoing section, no one, not even the editor of the newspapers to which the letters were sent, could be sure of the source. In the case of news stories sent directly from the Land Department office in St. Paul, at least the editor knew that they came from the Northern Pacific although Wilsey made every effort to make it appear to the reader that they were written by disinterested persons.

The letter technique was used as extensively for direct Land Department-to-publisher publicity as it was for the indirect private individual-to-publisher type. The *Mower County Transcript* of Austin, Minnesota, in 1898 published a lengthy letter to its editor signed "Hometaker."[35] "Hometaker" could have been nobody but Wilsey.

NEWSPAPERS BECOME THE DOMINANT MEDIUM 63

After praising North Dakota extravagantly for its universal fertility of soil, its fabulous yields of grain, its superb grazing land, its healthful and its unexcelled opportunities for making money, the letter concludes that more detailed information may be procured from F. W. Wilsey. It is noteworthy, too, that in listing the best localities in North Dakota for land buying, without a single exception every locality is on the Northern Pacific line.[36]

Additional proof that the article came form Wilsey's office may be found in the fact that the same article was published, word for word, in another newspaper and signed by the same "Hometaker."[37]

An article of the same type signed "Minnesota Dairyman" received even wider publication, if the files of the Land Department may be accepted as an indication. The article, with not a word changed, was printed in at least four newspapers: the Madelia, Minnesota, *Messenger*, the *Christian County Courier* of Taylorville, Illinois, and two others whose names could not be determined.[38]

The story is a description of the Aitkin county exhibit at the 1898 Minnesota State Fair, which is harmless enough in itself, but which takes on a distinct publicity flavor when it suggests that readers write to F. W. Wilsey for information concerning the abundant government and railroad land which is for sale in the county.[39] It could hardly be regarded by the editors of the newspapers as timely since the fair took place in the fall and publication not until January.

Praise was just as effusive as in the "Hometaker" piece. "Minnesota Dairyman" extolled the climate, the abundance of timber and of rainfall, the fertility of the soil, the mildness of the temperature (there was not too much snow, but enough), and the excellence of the exhibits at the fair. He concluded his story with testimonials from two persons who had migrated to Aitkin County.[40]

It is impossible to learn how many stories of this type may have been sent out or to how great a number of papers they may have gone, but the practice certainly must have been widely used. Two more clippings were found of long news stories which were used in their entirety. One was printed in the

Homestead of Des Moines in April, 1898, and the other in the Grand Forks (North Dakota) *Herald* in January, 1898.[41]

The *Homestead* story is a description of Northern Pacific land-sales policy during the three years after William H. Phipps became Land Commissioner in 1895. It mentions low prices, liberal terms and a rapid increase in settlement. The story is concluded, "So writes F. W. Wilsey of St. Paul, Minnesota."[42]

The same material is included in the story in the *Herald* but that article lays more stress on the rapid movement to Northern Pacific lands. It records that "people have come to North Dakota during the past year [1897] from almost every state in the union," but that "Iowa is furnishing the larger portion of the new settlers."[43]

This story differs from the others in that it was datelined "Carrington, N.D." That might mean that it was prepared by the Northern Pacific land solicitor at Carrington, or it might mean that it was written in the St. Paul office and mailed to the Carrington solicitor who sent it on to Grand Forks. It could, of course, have been written independently of all Northern Pacific influence, but that is unlikely in view of the fact that the entire story is devoted to the railroad.

Willis Drummond, Wilsey's assistant, was evidently busy writing news stories of various sorts. In November, 1897, he wrote to the *Evening Telegraph* at Superior, Wisconsin, that he was submitting an article about development of the country near Superior. "I trust you will find it satisfactory and not too much of an ad," he concluded his letter.[44]

In August, 1898, he wrote to the Primghar (Iowa) *Democrat* that he was enclosing an article for the *Democrat's* special Red River Valley edition. "I have tried to make it as brief as possible but fear it will make more than a column," he wrote. But the length did not deter him from sending along a half-tone view of an Aitkin County farm "for which I will thank you to run in the article over the caption 'A Good Start in Timber'."[45]

Each of the articles mentioned above was evidently submitted without accompanying advertising, with the exception of the Des Moines *Homestead* story, for which payment was made. Liberal advertising contracts may have induced editors to print

NEWSPAPERS BECOME THE DOMINANT MEDIUM   65

the stories more readily, but there was no contract regulation specifying that they must be printed.

Such was not the case with the "reading notices" that were sent with all advertisements contracted for by the Land Department.[46] The "readers" were single-paragraph stories of fifty to seventy-five words with centered single-line headlines of four or five words. They could hardly be classed as news stories but were more closely related to advertisements. Most of them were announcements of landseekers' excursions or of terms of payment for land. Unlike the longer stories which were aimed at specific newspapers, only one "reader" was prepared each week, and it was then sent to all newspapers carrying Land Department advertising.

This is by no means a complete record of all the news publicity stories sent out from the Eastern Land Agent's office, nor of all the activity of that office in the placement of this sort of promotion. We may assume, on the basis of the samples presented here, that a constant barrage of newspaper articles left the St. Paul office during this period.

A skillful bit of promotion, which was to produce the maximum of promotional value with the minimum of expenditure, was conceived in the Land Department office early in 1897. The plan, as outlined by Phipps and Wilsey, was to start, on April 1, the publication of a monthly bulletin to be devoted to the "country, lands, and matters of general interest along the company's route." The publication was to be distributed primarily from the company's World Fair products car, which was scheduled to visit every section of the United States south and west of St. Paul during the year. An additional several thousand copies of the publication were to be mailed from St. Paul.[47]

Circulars with the above information were printed and sent to ninety-five manufacturing firms through the country. The manufacturing firms were asked to advertise in the bulletin at the rate of $3.00 a column inch for each insertion.[48]

The exhibit car, which was already on a tour of the country, was an ordinary passenger coach carrying a complete display of products grown along the line of the Northern Pacific and literature descriptive of Northern Pacific lands.[49]

Success for this plan would make it possible for the Northern Pacific to actually make a profit on its promotional venture, or at least to break even. The advertisements would serve to add prestige to the periodical. The cost of distribution would be eliminated because the exhibit car was to be on the road anyway.

The car itself is an interesting promotional device. An article printed in the Iowa City *Iowa State Press* describes it in detail. D. M. Stewart, a traveling emigration agent, and A. W. Parker, traveling land agent, were in charge. Displayed in the car were collections of grasses, grains, minerals, fruits, and game, and on the walls were photographs of scenery along the railroad line. Mr. Stewart told visitors about Central Minnesota, its timber, prairies, lakes, and fish.[50]

The information given to visitors by Stewart and Parker indicates the general content of the promotional material of the time. Minnesota and North Dakota, they reported, were attracting the attentions of Iowa people. "Over 1,200 Iowa people," they said, "bought lands along the line of the road last season and it is expected that fully 1,500 more will visit that country this coming season." One of the chief arguments used for buying land in Minnesota was that the state "has today $20,000,000 in its school fund which was obtained from the sale of swamp lands."[51]

They explained that the railroad was running excursions to Minnesota and North Dakota the first and third Tuesdays of every month for one fare plus $2.00.[52]

These excursions have already been mentioned in connection with the reading notices that were sent to newspapers along with paid advertisements. The general practice was the one-fare-plus-$2.00 system, but cheaper fares were occasionally made available.

On April 1 and April 7, 1897, the railroad promoted excursions for Iowans, the fare for which was only $2.50 from St. Paul to Carrington, North Dakota. Sleeping cars were to be left on the tracks at Carrington until the excursionists should be able to find "temporary or permanent accommodations." If twenty or more persons would join in one party, the fare from their homes to St. Paul should be computed at two cents per mile.[53]

Free passage was not handed out indiscriminately, however, to all persons who maintained that they were interested in buying land or had prospects for the sale of land. Wilsey wrote in 1901, "It is not the practice on the part of this company to issue transportation to any and all parties who claim that if some were granted they could go to South Dakota or into other states and be instrumental in bringing to North Dakota a large immigration."[54]

Wilsey did concede that if the person should be willing to make the trip at his own expense and as a consequence bring about the sale of sufficient land to make a refund of transportation worthwhile, the railroad would make the refund.[55]

Reactions to the excursions were evidently quite favorable. Editor Adrian Cross of the Churdan (Iowa) *Reporter* went to Carrington on an excursion in October, 1897. He wrote back to his paper praising George Heaton, the Churdan solicitor for the Northern Pacific, who had made arrangements for the trip, and his treatment all along the line. He first went to St. Paul where he got a letter of introduction from Wilsey to Vanbergen, the Carrington solicitor. Of his experiences in Carrington he wrote:

> Our letter of introduction to Mr. Vanbergen brought us before one of the most genial, pleasant and entertaining men we have ever met. He has the sale lands belonging to the Northern Pacific Railway Company in that section of North Dakota. He takes care of all land seekers and is always pleased to show them any portion of the country they may desire to see. He is assisted in this work by H. A. Hogue, one of the pioneers of North Dakota and a former newspaper man.[56]

The value to the Northern Pacific of getting so favorable an endorsement from one with an editor's prestige is obvious. That the Land Department was doing its best to make the excursions a success goes without saying.

The Job of the Land Solicitor

Reference has already been made to the fact that land solicitors were placed in all the districts in North Dakota where the railway hoped to sell land and in all the areas where it hoped to find buyers. These land solicitors were a key factor in the promotional program of this period. Much of the newspaper publicity was handled through them. Facts for news stories were uncovered by them. They organized parties of excursionists and showed the excursionists the lands which were for sale. And, finally, they sold land.

Two types of contract were drawn up. One contract specified duties and commissions for those employed in the districts from which the land buyers came. The other did the same for those who were in the districts where the land was to be sold.

The duties of the men employed under the first type of contract are indicated in an agreement dated May 1, 1897, between H. C. Dodge of Morris, Minnesota, and the receivers for the Northern Pacific Railroad. Dodge was assigned to sixteen counties in Iowa. He was to travel through the territory assigned and to appoint sub-solicitors. These sub-solicitors were to be visited continually and their names were to be reported to the Land Department office.[57]

In return for his services Dodge was to get a 5 per cent commission on small sales and 25 cents an acre, including the 5 per cent, on all sales of more than 5,000 acres. The Northern Pacific was to furnish his transportation "where it can get it." In case of prior colonization attempts in these sixteen counties, the solicitors were to refrain from attempting to sell the land and were to get no commissions on sales that were made. The Land Department promised to give Dodge and his solicitors the benefit of all advertising done in the territory and to mention specific names in advertisements.[58]

An agreement with John F. Robinson of Steele, North Dakota, is typical of the second type of contract. Robinson was to receive 5 per cent commission on all sales originated by him and 2 1/2 per cent on sales he made to parties sent out by the Land Department.[59]

It would appear, then, that on a sale to an Iowa buyer the Northern Pacific would pay 7 1/2 per cent in commissions, 5 per cent to the Iowa solicitor who originated the deal, and 2 1/2 per cent to the North Dakota solicitor who consummated it.

A little different type of agreement was drawn up with J. M. Rhodes, who was to work in the Miles City, Montana, territory. Rhodes was to receive 2 1/2 per cent on all sales of less than $5,000, and on the first $5,000 of sales greater than that figure. On the amount between $5,000 and $10,000 he was to receive 1 1/2 per cent and on the amount above $10,000, 1 per cent. It was specified that Rhodes was at no time to represent himself as an agent of the company. He was invariably to be known by the term "Sales Solicitor."[60]

A third method of payment, straight salary, was found in two cases and may have been used widely, particularly in those cases where the solicitor spent much of his time doing general promotion work for the company. Karl Simmon, who was General Sales Solicitor for Montana with headquarters in Billings and Helena, was paid a salary of $208.33 a month.[61] J. Vander Las, the solicitor in Dickinson, received $90 a month and his expenses.[62]

The use of sales solicitors reached its peak late in 1898 when a total of 140 were at work. The project started as a widespread practice in 1896, when eighty-five were employed, continued strong through 1900, and tapered off in 1901. By 1902 the program was almost dead. The greatest number of men was employed in Iowa, the state toward which the greatest promotional effort was directed during this period. Minnesota and North Dakota held second place at various times, North Dakota at the beginning of the period, Minnesota at the end.

TABLE IV
Number of Solicitors at Work 1896 to 1900

State	1898	1898 (Sept. 24)	1899	1900
Iowa	52	55	89	76
Minnesota	35	16	29	11
North Dakota	36	36	4	1
Montana	3	3	1	1
Nebraska	1	1	1	1
South Dakota	1	1	2	3
Illinois	0	9	3	1
Wisconsin	0	19	0	0
Totals	128	140	129	94[63]

As has been pointed out previously, most of the promotion was concentrated on Iowa during this period. It is also interesting that solicitors were employed in South Dakota and Nebraska, states to the west of Minnesota and to the south of North Dakota. The migration movement had shifted from an east-to-west direction to a south-to-north and even, to a slight degree, west-to-east.

One of the techniques used to keep up enthusiasm among the solicitors was an excursion to the West Coast given, free of charge, to fifteen representatives from Iowa, southern Minnesota, southern Wisconsin, and northern Illinois. The party left St. Paul August 20, 1898; stopped for a day at Brainerd, a day at Wadena, one at Wahpeton and Breckenridge, another at Fargo and Moorhead, one at Jamestown and Carrington, one at Bismarck, one at Dickinson, and then went through to the coast.[64]

Elaborate entertainments and cordial receptions were arranged for the party at all stops. Before leaving St. Paul the guests of the company were taken for a ride in a tally-ho coach, which cost the company $10, and were entertained at a luncheon at the Commercial Club Cycle club for which the bill was

$8.00. Pullman berths for the entire trip were paid, costing the company $280.[65]

The large-scale use of the land solicitor probably came to an end in 1902. Early in that year the Northern Pacific disposed of all its western North Dakota land holdings and consequently had no further use for its elaborate organization which was built up largely for the purpose of selling that land. Vander Las was dropped from the company's payrolls in July of that year as there was no further reason to have a representative in Dickinson and its neighboring towns.[66]

There is no indication of either the employment or the dropping of other solicitors, but we may logically assume that the organization was for the most part disbanded. It will be remembered that the trend in the number of solicitors employed sloped off from the peak year of 1898. With no more land remaining in North Dakota and very little in Minnesota, there would be little need for any large-scale promotional campaign. And, further, there is no record available of such a campaign. Land sales held up through 1902 but plummeted rapidly after that year until the Redwater, Montana, drive of 1926 and 1927.

1897 to 1902 in Review

The Northern Pacific land-sales campaign of 1897 to 1902 was easily the most interesting of those studied. There was a greater variety of techniques used, and those techniques were more skillfully employed. Advertising and news publicity were far better organized than they had been in previous periods.

This improvement was to be expected. Wilsey and his associates had the experiences of past Northern Pacific Land Department officials to draw from. They had the advantage of a superior press to deal with. And they had the experiences of other firms doing the same sort of promotion to profit by.

Even taking all these factors into consideration, however, Wilsey and Drummond must be credited with having done a skillful job. They formulated a definite policy for the placement of advertising. They conceived that advertising campaign to cost the company the least possible amount, yet to produce the greatest possible yield.

The policy of paying for advertising by means of free transportation cost the company little yet resulted in much free newspaper publicity. Its scheme of furnishing letters extolling the Northern Pacific lands to excursionists for submitting to home town publishers gave them access to news columns but, more than that, gave the stories the added prestige of having come from home town residents. Inclusion in the advertising contracts of the reading-notice clause insured space in favorable locations for free publicity.

The practice of employing solicitors insured the Northern Pacific of having articulate boosters in all sections where there were possibilities of land sales. Further, those solicitors were of great aid in securing further newspaper space.

In short, Wilsey and Drummond did the work that a major business firm would today divide among three departments: public relations, publicity, and advertising. They handled all three tasks and, if land sales are to be accepted as a criterion of judgment, handled them admirably.

Chapter VI
The Campaign in Europe

Perhaps the most glamorous of the Northern Pacific's promotional campaigns was its extensive drive in northern Europe. How the railroad was able to induce farmers, fishermen, artisans, and laborers to leave their established homes in their native countries, cross the Atlantic, and then travel across 1,500 or more miles of the United States is a fascinating story.

The story becomes doubly fascinating when one considers the fact that a large share of today's population of Minnesota and North Dakota, the two states toward which almost all the activity was directed, is only one or two generations removed from migrating Germans, Norwegians, Swedes, Danes, or Finns. It seems evident from superficial observation, that the Northern Pacific's campaign was attended by great success.[1]

It must be remembered, however, that no matter how efficient the Northern Pacific's promotional machinery may have been, it could not have succeeded unless there existed in Europe a latent desire to migrate. That such a desire did exist is the contention of students of immigration.[2] It has been pointed out elsewhere in this thesis that most migration to the American West was motivated by a desire for cheap land, that the greatest single factor inducing persons to migrate to the West was the quest for economic betterment. It was the task of the railroad to root out these causes of unrest and design its promotion around them. With these factors present, it is certain that the Northern Pacific could succeed if its promotion were skillful enough.

Machinery for the European migration was set up concurrently with the plans for the first intra-national movement, an account of which is found in Chapter II. In 1871 George B. Hibbard was appointed Superintendent of the Bureau of Emigration, a subsidiary of the Land Committee, and George Sheppard was named General European Agent with headquarters in London.³ As soon as Sheppard had set up his office in 1872 the drive was underway.

The purposes of the European campaign were two-fold: first, to sell bonds, and second, to encourage emigration and the sale of lands. Consequently, Sheppard's problem was to circulate information that would reach those with surplus funds that they desired to invest, in addition to appealing to those persons who were interested in emigrating.⁴

The story divides itself into two parts. Part one begins with Sheppard's arrival in London in 1872 and continues until the Cooke financial debacle of 1873 put a temporary end to all activity. Part two opens with Sheppard's return to London in 1880 and ends when financial collapse again appeared imminent, this time late in 1883. The large European staff was permanently disbanded in that year and efforts in succeeding years were haphazard, most of the promotional material in the later periods being directed at residents of the United States in the section west of the Alleghenies.⁵

It is evident from Sheppard's early communications that both he and his superiors in the Bureau of Immigration and the Land Department had a well-defined plan of action. The selection of Sheppard himself is an indication of the thoroughness of the Cooke firm's preparations. In a letter to Billings, Jay Cooke wrote, "I regard Sheppard as a great prize. His power over the press in England and on the continent is very great and the work he does in this line could not be done at five times the cost through any other party."⁶

Access to editorial offices and the columns of leading newspapers seems to have been of paramount importance in the selection of almost all of the European representatives.

A certain Colonel von Corvin was employed during 1872 solely for the purpose of maintaining a press service in Germany. Corvin was a German by birth but was a naturalized citizen of the United States. He had been a Central European correspondent for the London *Times* and the New York *Times* and during the Franco-Prussian war was a correspondent for "a leading Frankfort journal."⁷

THE CAMPAIGN IN EUROPE 75

His chief qualification for employment by the Northern Pacific was apparently the fact that he was on intimate terms with the leading newspapers of Germany and Austria.

A second major requirement for employment specified that the agent must be familiar with the territory in which he was to work. Sheppard was selected because he was familiar with England and with the European press. He in turn chose men to work in smaller areas who were widely known in those areas. He wrote to Billings that it would be possible for the railroad to obtain the utmost confidence of the public by employing men known to the residents of the districts in which they were to labor. He sent a Welshman to Wales, a Scot to Scotland, a native of the Midland counties of England to that section, a native of the Northern counties to the North, and a native of the Southern counties to the South and Southwest. These men were to cooperate with the local agents who had already been engaged to represent the bureau in their home cities and villages.[8]

Two Americans, widely known for previous work in the interest of railroad and state emigration activities, were sent to Europe in 1872 and 1873. The first was Dr. J. P. Tustin, a Scandinavian minister who had previously worked for land-grant roads in Michigan, and the second was Colonel Hans Mattson, a Scandinavian who had once served as secretary of the Minnesota State Board of Immigration and was, at this time, a representative of the Lake Superior and Mississippi railroad.[9]

These men were of great value to the railroad because, as Scandinavian-born Americans, they were able to obtain the cooperation of influential Norwegians, Swedes, and Danes. Tustin was especially successful in obtaining the support of clergymen. In Sweden he induced two Church of Sweden ministers and one Baptist clergyman to organize colonies for him. In Denmark he won the aid of a leading Danish bishop. In both Denmark and Norway he succeeded in winning over several ministers who aided him in preaching the gospel of the "Great Northwest."[10]

Colonel Mattson confined his promotional efforts to Norway and Sweden. Because of his experience and prestige, the

Northern Pacific had been, since the organization of the Bureau of Immigration, especially desirous of obtaining his services. The Lake Superior and Mississippi, however, refused to grant his release until late in 1872. Mattson started for Scandinavia as a Northern Pacific agent early in 1873.[11]

He, too, paid careful attention to the prestige factor in the choice of his assistants and in the choice of the men through whom he worked. As assistants he selected men who had visited Minnesota or who had actually spent a period of residence there and who were acquainted with both sides of the Atlantic. Men influential in local affairs provided a means by which he gained the attention of prospective migrants.[12]

Although the activities of the agents varied considerably according to the locality in which they worked, the duties Sheppard outlined for Armand Goegg in Germany, Switzerland, and Alsace-Lorraine indicate the general nature of the central European campaign.

Goegg, who worked in conjunction with Colonel von Corvin, the press publicity expert previously mentioned, did some of the individual contact work that characterized the efforts in the Scandinavian countries, but his principal task was to popularize the Northwest through lectures and printed promotional matter. The terms of his contact with Sheppard indicate the scope of his duties. During the twelve months starting in July, 1872, he was to spend 200 days lecturing in Germany and Switzerland for which he was to receive two pounds a day. In addition to his lectures, he was to publish in Switzerland a monthly emigration bulletin "which, without being avowedly in the interests of the Northern Pacific, should really encourage emigration to its route." He was to publish 2,000 copies each month of this bulletin for which the railroad agreed to pay the expenses, four pounds a month for postage and four pounds a month for printing. In addition to his lecturing and publishing duties he was to serve as an agent for the company in Switzerland and Germany for which he was to receive twenty pounds a month.[13] Goegg's total income for the twelve months would, under these terms, approximate $3,000, with an additional $450 for expenses incurred on his monthly bulletin.

THE CAMPAIGN IN EUROPE 77

Personal contacts, lectures, and the distribution of publications were not enough to bring emigrants to the Northwest, however. These media served to induce migrants to start for the United States but did not insure that those migrants would ever reach Northern Pacific land. Competition between a number of land companies was severe during this early period of Northern Pacific activity.[14] Those companies that had previously established emigration agencies in Europe had also entered into agreements with steamship lines to route emigrants to their lands. They had also stationed agents at Castle Garden, the point at which immigrants entered New York City. At Castle Garden the agents re-routed bewildered land-seekers to the districts they represented. Thus, unless the Northern Pacific could make advance arrangements with the steamship lines and could have adequate representation at Castle Garden, all the efforts of the European agents could go awry.

Consequently, the Land Department was forced to enter into agreements with the Cunard, Inman, National, and Allen lines, the principal trans-Atlantic carriers, to insure that persons interested in Northern Pacific lands would get to the Northern Pacific territory. As a by-product of this agreement the railroad was able to get promotional material distributed in Europe by steamship line agents.[15]

The method used was simple. Agents of the steamship lines were given books of tickets making it possible to sell passage directly to Duluth or St. Paul. Such routing freed the immigrants from the necessity of buying additional tickets in New York and insured the railroad that they would arrive in Minnesota. Some resident agents of the steamship companies also served as agents for the Land Department. To make certain the continuation of this system the Northern Pacific exercised particular care to maintain friendly relations with steamship lines.[16]

The Castle Garden problem was a far more serious obstacle, it appears, from the worried attitude that permeates correspondence regarding it. In January, 1873, Nettleton wrote to Hibbard that he expected a good many people from Great Britain in the spring. He advised Hibbard: "While they will come to America predisposed or fully intending to settle on the line of our road in Minnesota, nothing will be easier than to divert them to other localities unless they are taken care of from the moment they reach Castle Garden until they are on the line of the road. You are fully aware of the many influences at work adversely to our own enterprise and to the country through which the road runs."[17] Nettleton concurred with several recommendations made previously by Sheppard that an emigration office be set up near Castle Garden.[18]

It was recommended that John W. Sears, who had been handling publicity in Nettleton's office, should be put in charge of the new office. Every effort was made to contact all individuals who had started out from Europe with the intention of settling along the Northern Pacific line and to assist them to get transportation to points along the road.[19]

The Jay Cooke financial crash of 1873 forced the liquidation of the European staff and brought about the recall of Sheppard. There is no evidence of any activity between that year and 1880, when Sheppard was sent back to England and an even more elaborate organization established.[20]

The general pattern of the second European drive was essentially the same as the first with the exception that it was on a much larger scale. Sheppard set out for England in February, 1880, and remained in charge until 1882 when A. Roedelheimer took over his position.[21] The end of the campaign took place in the same fashion as that of the first; it was withdrawn when financial retrenchment became necessary late in 1883. Immigrants continued to come to the Northwest after 1883, but their coming was evidently not due to any concerted effort on the part of the railroad as from that time on the road's policy was to concentrate on residents of the United States only.

As in the case of the earlier campaign, the actual contact work with prospective migrants was carried on by local agents. Arrangements were again made with steamship lines for two purposes: to distribute pamphlets and circulars and to sell through tickets to Minnesota points. Printed promotional material flowed into Europe in quantities far exceeding those of 1872 and 1873, and newspaper advertising was again an important feature of the drive. Agents, armed with samples of grain and other products from the Northern Pacific territory, set up exhibits at fairs, agricultural shows, and grain markets.

THE CAMPAIGN IN EUROPE 79

The campaign started on a relatively small scale but grew rapidly until its liquidation in 1883. During 1881 Sheppard had local agents working in eighty-three towns in England, Scotland, and Wales. During that year he visited Sweden, Norway, Denmark, Switzerland, and northern Germany, making arrangements with local agents in those countries to forward emigrants to points on the Northern Pacific line. "Judicious" advertising had been done in a number of newspapers in Great Britain at a "very moderate expense." Arrangements had been made with the only steamship line operating directly from Denmark to the United States to bring the advantages of the Northern Pacific land to a large number of Danes.[22]

An exceedingly clever promotional policy pursued during this period was the employment of a large number of Scandinavian and German laborers in the construction work on the Yellowstone division of the line. It was expected that these laborers would purchase land from the company as soon as the line should be finished.[23] This device is important because one of the chief obstacles to land sales was the fact that income during the early years of land cultivation was so small that it made payments difficult. In fact, in some cases, it was necessary for the railroad to provide "made work," such as timber cutting and plowing, to get the new settlers through the first hard years. With quantities of cash already in the hands of the land buyers as a consequence of their construction work, land sales were made easier and no paternalism on the part of the road was necessary.

Careful training of the European land agents seems to have been a Land Department policy. When a special agent for Germany was appointed in the spring of 1881, he was taken on a tour of the land tributary to the railroad before he was sent abroad to begin his work.[24]

During the last half of 1882 and the first half of 1883 the European campaign reached its peak. A total of 748 new agencies were established in the British Isles during those twelve months so that, in July of 1883, there were 831 active local agents in the United Kingdom. Of the total, 20 were in London, 689 in the large towns and villages of England and Wales, and 122 in Scotland and Ireland. On the continent there were

124 general agents in Norway, Sweden, Denmark, Holland, Switzerland, and Germany.[25]

The agents in the British Isles were supplied with printed material from the Liverpool office and with samples of grain and other products that they displayed at various sorts of exhibits. Continental agents did essentially the same type of work, distributing pamphlets and circulars through sub-agencies in smaller towns and villages.[26] It is noteworthy that most of the publications went to the villages, where contacting rural migrants would be a much simpler task than it would have been had the agents concentrated on the cities.

The extensive scope of the work may be gained from the evidence that 632,590 pieces of promotional material were distributed during the fiscal year of 1882 and 1883. This literature included pamphlets, maps, cards, and posters printed in English, German, Swedish, Dutch, Danish, and Norwegian, and regular monthly editions of the *Northwest* magazine.[27] In an editorial paragraph the *Northwest* indicates that during the entire campaign 2,500,000 pieces of promotional material in all the above languages plus Finnish were mailed out in answer to 60,000 letters of inquiry.[28]

Relationships with steamship companies were maintained on the same basis as during 1872 and 1873, but agreements were entered into with a greater number of lines. From Liverpool alone there were seven lines that booked 1,172 passengers for points on the Northern Pacific during 1882.[29] Reference has already been made to a line operating from Denmark to the United States which aided the Northern Pacific enterprise, and it has already been noted that other steamship companies were aiding in the distribution of publications. From these facts we may gather that the total number of cooperating lines was well above the four with which the railroad had agreements in 1872 and 1873.

The 1883 *Annual Report* points out, however, that the policy of booking passengers directly to the Northwest was not meeting with overwhelming success. The Land Department had made arrangements with seven lines operating from Liverpool to the United States, but there were forty-one additional lines with which no contracts had been made, and the report points out that "English passengers have a prejudice against through booking, and mainly prefer to buy their railroad tickets on this side."[30]

The cost of maintaining the foreign agencies, after the amalgamation of the Northern Pacific with the two Villard West Coast companies, was borne 60 per cent by the Northern Pacific, 24 per cent by Oregon Railway and Navigation Company, and 16 per cent by the Oregon and California Railroad. This does not include the costs of the various pamphlets, maps, and circulars that were shipped from the United States. Most of those pamphlets were paid for by the Northern Pacific alone with the exception of those dealing with the Pacific Northwest, in which case the cost was divided.[31]

Although we have no means of interpreting costs of the European agencies in terms of the current value of the American dollar, we can gain a general impression of expenditures of those offices from a letter submitted by L. R. Kidder, clerk of the Land Committee, to the committee. During the year the expenditures of the general agency at Liverpool were $9,995, of the Berlin agency, $3,450, and of the Frankfort agency, $1,958. The Liverpool expenses were divided into: $4,000 salary for A. Roedelheimer, the general agent; $1,500 salary for the assistant agent; $50 salary for the office boy; $1,810 for traveling expenses; $1,800 for freight, postage, printing, and stationery; $585 for office rent; and $350 for advertising.[32]

R. Goerdeler, the Berlin agent, was paid $2,000 and C. Jaeger at Frankfort $1,500. Berlin did the heaviest advertising, $575 of the total expenditures there being classified under that heading. Frankfort listed $28 for posters but none for advertising.[33]

For a more complete picture of the activities of the European agents and agencies it is necessary to break the work down into its separate functions and analyze each type of promotional endeavor, item by item. Individual contact work, which was analyzed in some detail by previous writers on this subject and which has been touched on here, probably is the most important single type of work done. Distribution of printed publicity literature evidently takes second rank, followed by newspaper advertising, exhibits at fairs, and a variety of minor promotional features in approximately that order.

Before a detailed analysis of these methods, excluding the individual contact work which has been adequately described both in this thesis and in previously written articles, it is interesting to note the policy of the Northern Pacific in regard to the desirability of immigrants from various sections of Europe.

The Land Department Chooses Its Prospects

It might be assumed that the organizers of high-geared promotional machinery such as the Northern Pacific was using would not erect barriers to impede the free motion of that machinery. It would appear most likely that the Land Department would welcome any prospect who had been attracted by its promotional activity. But such was not the case. The Northern Pacific was quite careful to choose only those persons who it thought would make successful settlers on its land. It could obviously not cull out specific individuals, but it could keep its promotional material from flowing into areas whose inhabitants were considered unacceptable by the company's officials.

That is the policy the Northern Pacific followed. It is a most logical policy. The company could not afford to have disgruntled settlers on its land because of the effect of such disaffection on other prospects. It could not afford to run the risk of foreclosures both because of the effect on further promotion and because of the cost involved.

Whether the company's policy was sound or not is for the reader to determine, but its importance here is that it indicates the thoroughness of the railroad's promotional campaign. Merely getting the buyer's signature on the sales slip and transporting him to the line of the road was not enough. Land Department officials were far-sighted enough to see that the future of their promotional campaign depended to at least some degree on a successful record in the past.

All through a study of the company's foreign campaign one is compelled to ask, Why was all the promotional pressure exerted on Northern Europe? The answer is that officials believed

THE CAMPAIGN IN EUROPE   83

that only natives of Northern Europe could successfully adapt themselves to the climate of Minnesota and the Northwest.

French were discouraged from migrating to Northern Pacific lands. "Common sense dictates the expediency of taking climatic influences into account when judging the probable destination of various people," Sheppard wrote to Billings. Sheppard's reasoning was that the French, being Southern Europeans, naturally seek the South when they migrate to the United States. "We must seek our emigrants among the Northern peoples of Europe," he wrote.[34]

An added reason caused the Northern Pacific to hesitate before encouraging French to migrate. Very few French farmers felt disposed to leave their homes. Most of the French discontent was among artisans in the larger cities, and artisans were of no use in the development of the Northwest.[35] The railroad was interested in farmers who would buy land and raise products to keep freight moving on the new railroad.

Alsace and Lorraine offered a slightly different problem. Because of the fact that they had been ceded to Germany following the Franco-Prussian war, there was much discontent in the two provinces in 1872 and 1873. The Paris agent estimated that approximately 500,000 persons would leave Alsace and Lorraine during the summer of 1872.[36] Consequently there was a fertile field for Northern Pacific promotion, but the company was honest enough to emphasize the advantages of the Pacific coast where the climate was considerably milder than in Minnesota and Dakota.[37]

Although it has already been noted that the company's European headquarters were in England and that there were more agents working in England than in any other European country, still company officials were not unqualifiedly favorable toward English emigrants. "English emigrants are in many respects peculiar and troublesome," Sheppard wrote to Billings.[38]

Chief criticism of the English was that they were uncooperative.[39] Considerable difficulty with English colonies which had been transported to Western Minnesota had made officials wary.[40] However, before the 1880 campaign the colonization policy had been largely discontinued and there is less evidence to indicate that English, when sent to the Northwest as individuals, were not satisfactory migrants. It is also true that much of the pressure in the United Kingdom was exerted on Irish and Scotch, about whom there were no complaints.

Of equal importance with the geographical location of the prospective emigrants in Europe were their occupational characteristics. It has already been noted that the railroad discouraged the French since many of the French who desired to migrate were artisans and were considered by the railroad as unsuitable. The greatest pressure was exerted on the class whom officials termed "practical farmers."[41]

James B. Power, who became General Agent for the Land Department in 1873, expressed the policy when he wrote to Hibbard that it was "advisable to use every effort to deter men who are depending upon daily labor for support..." He added, "Our greatest difficulty has been with that class; they have been led to expect immediate work at good wages and many of the first two parties reached here almost destitute and without any of the independence and individuality of the American people."[42]

The great fear of the Land Department was that these disgruntled settlers would leave the Northern Pacific territory in search of employment and carry with them unfavorable impressions.[43] Those unfavorable impressions, officials believed, could cause more damage than could be righted with reams of counter propaganda.

They recognized the need for mechanics, merchants, laborers, and the like but felt that those persons would naturally follow the general migration when the demand for their services asserted itself. Until such time, however, the crying need was for farmers to clear the timber, break the sod, and raise crops to keep the freight trains busy.[44]

Another clue to Northern Pacific policy in regard to prospective migrants may be found in an analysis of the factors which caused Europeans to be receptive to Land Department promotion. As has been emphasized previously, the company's promotional material had to be designed to be effective with the discontented elements.

It has already been pointed out that economic unrest was the greatest factor impelling Europeans to migrate to the United

THE CAMPAIGN IN EUROPE 85

States. In localized areas, however, there were other factors on which the Northern Pacific had to play if its campaign were to be successful.

A Mennonite group wanted to leave Southern Russia to avoid compulsory military service.[45] In Schleswig-Holstein there was a desire to escape enforced naval service; in Mecklenburg and other sections of Prussia, parents wanted to remove their children from the liability to military service.[46] A conflict between Catholics and Protestants drove large numbers of Protestants out of Posen, and migrants left Pomerania because it was practically impossible to acquire land there.[47] Land ownership was also the dominant reason for emigration from Holland.[48]

These factors are mentioned here because they indicate the need for designing a different style of promotion for each area in which the Northern Pacific's agents worked. The overall policy of the railroad was undoubtedly to choose those areas from which it thought it could get the most desirable immigrants and then aim its promotion to appeal to the peculiarities of that district. The soundness of such a policy is self-evident.

Printed Promotional Material Flows to Europe

That the Northern Pacific's European agents were well armed with promotional material for distribution to prospects has already been indicated. The next task is to analyze the composition of the more than 600,000 copies of pamphlets, circulars, maps, and leaflets that were sent across the Atlantic.

The publications used bear the same titles as those that were distributed in the United States during the corresponding periods.[49] They were translated into the languages of the countries in which they were to be used and then sent to Sheppard in England for redistribution to sub-agents.

The contents of a box sent to Sheppard in 1880 indicate the general nature of the material used. The box contained 30,000 leaflets, 10,000 each in Norwegian, Swedish, and German; 1,000 *Golden Northwests*, all printed in German; 500 map circulars in English; twelve posters; twenty-four farm scenes (photographs); twelve copies of the Fargo *Times*; and miscellaneous matter. Also included were 300 copies of the *New Northwest* and a like number of copies of the Helena *Herald*.[50]

Additional evidence on the nature of the material is provided by a requisition sent by T. F. Oakes, vice president of the road, to the Land Committee in 1883. In that requisition Oakes ordered a total of 241,000 map folders printed in six different languages. One hundred thousand were to be in English, 66,000 in Norwegian, 35,000 in Swedish, 20,000 in German, and 10,000 each in Danish and Dutch. He also requested 11,500 copies of Sly's pamphlet in five languages and 18,500 copies of the *Pacific Northwest* in five languages.[51]

Because these media were published by the Northern Pacific and distributed by the Northern Pacific's agents, they are not as interesting to the student of promotion methods as the more indirect devices used. Officials of the Land Department were well aware that the best publicity was that which did not ostensibly come from the railroad itself.

There were many opportunities for placing valuable pamphlets and booklets throughout Europe that would not disclose Northern Pacific authorship. In 1872 a young Swedish lawyer, Alex Nilsson, was preparing a booklet on Swedish emigration to the Northwest. Nilsson intended to publish about 30,000 copies to sell for 25 cents each. He told Colonel Mattson, who was representing the Northern Pacific in Sweden at the time, that he would emphasize the Northern Pacific and its land as the best place for Swedes to go if the railroad would pay one half the cost of publishing the volume, a sum approximating $500. Colonel Mattson recommended to Nettleton that the offer be accepted because, as he put it, "It will not be considered partial to America because it will be written by a Swede."[52]

Nettleton wrote to Dudley only two months later, "Today I have paid Colonel Mattson's draft for $500."[53]

At about the same time Edward Young, chief of the Bureau of Statistics at Washington, decided to republish his manual of information for immigrants with the aim of distributing it in Great Britain. Young offered, at a price of $50 a page, to include immediately following the last page of his manual the fourteen-page Northern Pacific publication, *Guide to the*

THE CAMPAIGN IN EUROPE   87

Northern Pacific Lands. Nettleton, without consulting Billings, immediately paid Young $500 of the $700 total, explaining:

> This official document, as thus republished, will be sold at all the news stands throughout the British Empire, mailed to leading statesmen, politicians, trade-union men, steamboat agents, emigration agents, etc. Our Mr. Sheppard will use a good number for distribution among his own agents. The fact that our guide appears substantially as a part of the text of the book, under official seal, will give it great currency, value and influence.[54]

The last sentence of the quotation is striking proof that Northern Pacific promotional experts were aware of the advantages of publicity with a concealed source. In both the Nilsson and Young publications the chief value to the Northern Pacific depended upon the fact that the booklets were written by apparently disinterested persons, thus lending credence to the railroad's claims. If the Northern Pacific stamp had appeared on the booklets, the reader would have had an opportunity to allow for promoter's license.

Roedelheimer used essentially the same method to insure wide circulation of steamship and railroad fares to points on the Northern Pacific line. It was his objective to get publications in circulation that would include information from which total fares to points in the Northwest could be computed. To attain this goal, he published a four-page folder which told the exact cost in English money of transportation from all American and Canadian ports to all possible destinations on the Northern Pacific.[55] He ordered only 3,000 copies of the folder, but by circulating these folders to all the steamship companies involved he was able to get his information reprinted in 15,000 publications distributed by the steamship lines.[56] Here, too, with the exception of the 3,000 copies published by the Northern Pacific, the identity of the Northern Pacific was not revealed, and, for the cost of only 3,000 copies, the information was printed in 18,000.

Distribution of the independently published booklets was, of course, handled largely by the authors or publishers themselves, but with its own publicity the Northern Pacific had a major problem. Where it had agents, the agents armed themselves with the material and handed it to prospects. But where there were no agents it was necessary for the Land Department officials to discover some device through which they could learn the names of prospective land buyers in Europe.

Nettleton hit upon a clever scheme. He recommended to Dudley that arrangements be made with the postmasters of various leading towns and cities in the United States, "whereby you can obtain a list of the addresses of all letters mailed at such addresses within a given time to people in those European countries which we wish to reach."[57]

These addresses were to be used as a mailing list for the railroad's land guides. Nettleton's theory was that the recipients of the guides would assume that they came from their friends in America.[58] By this device Nettleton was aiming to reach the persons who would be most interested in the United States, because of the fact that they had close friends in this country, and at the same time he was increasing the prestige of the publication by making it appear that it came directly from the friends and not from the railroad which had land to sell.

It must not be assumed that the Northern Pacific was concealing the identity of all its publicity nor that it was resorting only to clever tricks. It has already been indicated that a huge mass of promotional material, published by the Land Department, was distributed by agents obviously in the employ of the road. The significance is that the Land Department was using techniques that are still considered sound by public relations firms who have all the advantages that experience and improved communications facilities have provided.

Placing Advertising in European Newspapers

It has already been pointed out that there were substantial allotments in the budgets of the London and Berlin agencies for newspaper advertising.[59] Many scattered and brief references are made in Land Department correspondence to advertising done in the journals of various European countries. But nowhere

THE CAMPAIGN IN EUROPE 89

was the writer able to discover any complete record of this form of promotion.

We are justified in concluding, however, that newspaper advertisements were a very important part of the entire promotional campaign. Sheppard, early in 1872, estimated that it would be necessary to spend about 100 pounds a month for advertising.[60] His total expenditures for June of that year were 178 pounds, of which 110 pounds was for advertising.[61] In several letters he emphasized the fact that considerable newspaper advertising would be necessary to bring the Land Department's cause before the people of Europe. Agents of the road thought, too, that advertising was of great importance. Leopold Lindau, one of the German agents, wrote to Sheppard in 1872, "Believe me ... this is the best way to come in direct communication with emigrants and any reasonable sum spent upon this, you will have no cause to regret."[62]

If it were possible to gain access to the news columns without paying for advertising space, Sheppard preferred that less costly method, however. He wrote to Billings that he didn't believe it necessary to set apart any large sums for advertising in Germany in the fiscal year starting in July, 1872. He explained that advertisements in the columns of the large Berlin and Frankfort journals would not reach the class of emigrants the Land Department wanted and that Colonel von Corvin was attempting to place publicity stories in the rural papers, which were certain to reach the desired classes. He recommended slight expenditures in the small provincial papers, but he hoped that the work Colonel Corvin was doing would "demonstrate the feasibility of using them [the provinical papers] for the dissemination of information without direct payment."[63]

One who is conversant with the vigorous campaign now being carried on by the National Editorial Association against the printing of free publicity under the guise of news stories will recognize that the Northern Pacific's policy is still being practiced today by a substantial number of the nation's leading advertising and merchandising firms.

Considerable advertising was done in Germany notwithstanding the desire for free space. Lindau placed advertisements in forty provincial weeklies and semi-weeklies and two Berlin papers prior to December 1, 1872. He indicated to Sheppard that he was very well satisfied with the results. "The first ad appeared last Saturday," he wrote, "and on my return to Berlin I found 32 letters, all direct from persons wishing to emigrate; my opinion about advertising has been justified by the results."[64]

The writer was unable to discover proof that advertising was placed through agencies, but there is evidence that the Land Department asked the Charles Meyer and Company advertising agency of New York for prices on advertisements in thirty of the best German papers (weekly editions) and in 100 good German weeklies.[65] That it is probable that a contract was entered into we may assume from the fact that this method of placing advertising was often used by the Land Department in its domestic campaigns.

It is also difficult to determine how much advertising was placed in Scandinavia and where it was placed, but the writer did have access to a letter from O. J. Johnson, General Scandinavian Agent with headquarters at Christiania, to James B. Williams, assistant to the President of the Northern Pacific, in which Johnson wrote, "Our Northern Pacific country is well advertised in Scandinavia." He continued, "I have used considerable printer's ink to make known the country and what was awaiting immigrants on their arrival in the Golden Northwest."[66]

The total picture of newspaper advertising is sketchy, but it is evident that the Northern Pacific was spending substantial sums of money on European newspaper advertising, that it was distributing that advertising through the rural areas by using weekly newspapers, and that it was supplementing the advertisements by the use of what we would now term "press handouts."

Exhibiting Products of the Northwest

The Northern Pacific apparently never failed to set up an exhibit at an exposition which promised to attract the attention of a large number of people. The International Exposition at Vienna in 1873 gave the Land Department its first opportunity

THE CAMPAIGN IN EUROPE

to display products of the "New Northwest" on a large scale. The extent of preparations for this exposition indicates the seriousness with which officials regarded it.

Preparations for the Exposition were started during the fall of 1872. The Engineering department was asked to make "collections of specimens" in Dakota and Montana. Dudley wrote to D. C. Linsley, assistant engineer-in-chief, that he already had a large exposition of cereals on hand but he still needed typical grasses of the country west of the Red River, specimens of the soil at various points with statements as to the depth and character of both surface and subsoil, specimens of lignites and coals, of the various types of timber growing along the line, and anything else that would be of value in illustrating the potentialities of the Northwest country. Evidently Dudley also desired to cater to the widespread interest in Indians. He wrote, "I deem it of importance that the manners and customs of the Aborigines should not be overlooked, and whatever tends to illustrate this question will be of value."[67]

There were evidently no restrictions on quantity as Dudley expected to fill "at least half a dozen cabinets."[68] In those half dozen cabinets were to go building materials, woods, stone, minerals, cereals, fruits, vegetables, manufactured articles, maps, plats, charts, and other publications. Probably not into the cabinets but at least along with them was to go a locomotive of the type the railroad used on its line.[69]

But that was not enough. Hibbard was not going to overlook anything in the Northwest that grew, walked, or crawled. Two days after the locomotive was requested he asked for "the stuffed skin of an elk with the antlers thereon, the skin of a bear, of an antelope, of a badger, and of other animals, and anything else ornamental to our stand that will make it attractive to the eye of the sportsman as this feature will go a good way with our European friends."[70] In short, an entire museum was to be transported across the Atlantic.

Behind this magnificent exhibit was to be a map of the entire Northern Pacific route, forty-two feet long and ten feet high.[71]

Hibbard was in an excellent position to maintain direction of the Northern Pacific exhibit as he had been appointed

Assistant United States Commissioner to the International Exposition at Vienna.[72] He was thus in Vienna representing the United States government and not the Northern Pacific railroad.

It is apparent that the exhibit was undertaken purely as a good will measure and not to produce any immediate results. Sheppard at one time wrote to Nettleton that the expenses would be large and the "immediate results nil" but that statement caused no slackening of the program.[73]

Sheppard was unable to contract for space at the Smithfield show in England in 1872 because his application was submitted too late, but he went ahead to set up a cereal display in the Land Department offices. Attention was attracted to the display by newspaper advertising and news stories. The news stories turned out to be just about as costly as the advertisements as it was necessary to pay fees to publishers and writers to insure publication.[74]

In 1887 the Land Department set up an exhibit of farm, forest, and mine products at the American Exhibition in London. The 1887 *Annual Report* indicates that the exhibit was visited by "many thousands of people and was favorably mentioned by the London Press." "Its influence in attracting settlement to Northern Pacific territory is already felt," the report continued.[75]

It is apparent from the foregoing examples that the Land Department officials were well aware of all the benefits that were to accrue from making full use of opportunities to exhibit products of the Northwest. Those exhibits, it will be remembered, were not limited to the most important crops grown in the territory. They included as well a display of recreational opportunities. In short, the Land Department made an attempt to portray the Northwest as a land with every opportunity for a well-rounded existence. It is noteworthy, too, that the Northern Pacific saw the secondary advantages that were to result from the exhibits. They saw that the displays would have an effect not only upon those persons who saw them but also upon those who read of them in newspaper accounts.

The Promotional Devices Summarized

To the student of propaganda, the promotional devices used by the Northern Pacific railroad between 1870 and 1884 must appear strikingly similar to those used by any strong public relations firm today. True, Land Department officials lacked the communications facilities which make the task of the promotional expert easier today, but they lacked none of the ingenuity of today's public relations counsels and advertising and publicity men.

The railroad used its own agents for person-to-person contact. It placed newspaper advertising from its central office, through its agents, and through advertising agencies. It employed trained newspapermen with ample press contacts to get space in the news columns of the newspapers. It kept a constant stream of promotional material (which now would be known as direct-mail advertising) flowing into the hands of its prospects. It exhibited its products at all possible fairs, shows, and exhibitions, and employed widely-known men to lecture for it.

And to direct attention to its advertising and its publicity, to make the task of selling land easier for its agents, the Northern Pacific's Land Department officials used a multitude of miscellaneous techniques which would do credit to a promotional program of today.

Already mentioned have been subsidies to authors, agreements with steamship lines, contacts with postmasters, excursions for publishers and lecturers, cooperation with church officials, and construction of reception homes.

A couple of additional devices are worthy of mention here. An attempt was made in 1878 to interest consular agents of the United States stationed in Sweden and Norway in spreading information about Northern Pacific land. Samples of Northern Pacific literature were sent to them and letters written asking them if they could cooperate.[76] Whether they did or not has not been disclosed, but the incident is significant because it indicates the resourcefulness of the Land Department officials.

Skillful use of counter propaganda became necessary when heavy snows caused discontent in Minnesota in the winter of 1873. English settlers had written letters home which began to get into the English press. The Northern Pacific countered this blow by getting letters from satisfied settlers and finding means to get them into the newspapers.[77]

One other technique is of great interest. When John Miller of Goodhue county, Minnesota, a former Minnesota legislator, returned to Sweden for a visit, he took with him a bundle of the Northern Pacific's Swedish pamphlets for distribution there.[78] This is another excellent example of the Northern Pacific's interest in utilizing prestige. Miller was valuable to the railroad because he was a successful Swedish immigrant.

The foregoing list of promotional activities is by no means complete. But it is adequate to indicate the skill of the Northern Pacific's mid-nineteenth century promotional experts. By all present-day standards of advertising and publicity, the Northern Pacific should have succeeded. That it did succeed is proved in Chapter VIII of this thesis which analyzes the results of the promotional campaigns.

Chapter VII
An Analysis of the Pressures Exerted

Pouring an unending flood of advertising and publicity material into the Eastern United States and Europe would obviously not attract enough settlers to fill up a single Northwestern county, unless that publicity and advertising material, first, captured the attention of its readers and, second, appealed to the latent desires to emigrate which have been proved to exist.

We have already noted the abundance of promotional material that left the Philadelphia, New York, Boston, Chicago, St. Paul, and Portland offices. Now we must set up some yardstick for the measurement of the influence that material wielded in inducing persons to leave their established homes and to move hundreds of miles to the unsettled West.

It will be remembered from foregoing chapters that economic unrest was the greatest motive causing persons to migrate.[1] The urge to own land probably ranked ahead of all other factors, but land ownership alone was not enough. It was necessary that the land should be inexpensive and soil good, that there should be educational opportunities for the children and religious opportunities for the whole family. Fear of compulsory military and naval service was a major source of irritation to some scattered groups in Europe.[2] Political and religious conflicts forced many Europeans to seek new homes. But transcending all was the economic motive with all its implications.

In order to make any sort of an evaluation of the worth of the Northern Pacific's promotional campaign, we must formulate some set of standards to determine whether the railroad exerted its pressures on the causes of unrest, which were outlined in the preceding paragraph, and whether it utilized every seed of discontent as the basis for an appeal to the persons whom it sought to migrate to its land. Finally, we must know whether the Northern Pacific gave each of these causes of unrest its proper value in its promotional scheme. A quantitative analysis of the appeals on which the Northern Pacific centerd its promotional program will provide us with some basis on which we can evaluate the campaign as a whole.

Such a study would necessarily have to be limited to advertisements, because no other division of promotional material would provide sufficient uniformity. Pamphlets are difficult of analysis because of their length. While this writer found a number of circulars, there were too few to justify an analysis that would equal the appraisal of advertisements. News stories were often directed at specific reading publics, thus causing them to lack a universal appeal. They are also of doubtful value to this study because it is not certain that they were all written by paid Northern Pacific employes. The pamphlets, circulars, and news stories are of sufficient importance, however, to make imperative an analysis of their contents in subsequent pages of this chapter.

Advertisements overcome all the objections ascribed to other forms of promotional material. It is possible to employ them for a study of the frequency of mention of reader appeals for several reasons. A sufficient number were uncovered by the writer to indicate the general nature of the entire campaign, particularly of 1897 to 1902. Space requirements kept them brief and it was certain that they were prepared by Northern Pacific officials. It is probably true, too, that paid advertisements reflected more adequately than any other form of promotion the exact bases on which the company was appealing to its prospects.

In order to make a study of appeals, it was necessary for this writer to eliminate all advertisements with only a specialized selling point – advertisements of grazing lands in stock growers' publications, of land seekers' excursions in the weekly press, of wheat lands in agricultural periodicals, and the like. These were not considered because each ad had only one feature to exploit and each attempted "to sell" that feature to a reading public with only one major interest. A grazing advertisement in a stockgrowers' periodical would limit itself to grazing lands alone, but a grazing ad in a weekly newspaper, aimed at the

AN ANALYSIS OF THE PRESSURES EXERTED 97

general reading public, would feature the grazing element and include many other inducements to buy Northern Pacific land.

With those factors in mind, a quantitative study of the reader appeals in twelve advertisements, designed for general distribution, was made. The number was set at twelve, only because twelve ads of that type were found in the archives. Most of the ads used were of the two-column by six-inch type employed in the 1897 to 1902 campaign for distribution to all newspapers with whom contracts had been made. There are obvious weaknesses in the analysis. The number is too limited. It was difficult to draw clear-cut lines of demarcation between appeals, and no attempt was made to weigh in the amount of emphasis given to various items through size or blackness of type.

No air-tight conclusions may be drawn from such an analysis, but it is possible to derive a general indication of the importance that the Land Department attached to various arguments designed to bring settlers to Minnesota and Dakota. The writer believes that the results clearly indicate the nature of the stimuli used by the Northern Pacific to attract land buyers.

Low land prices and the possibility of buying on liberal credit terms were each mentioned in eight of the twelve advertisements.[3] These factors ranked first on the list. Seven mentions each were given to "good soil," "nearness to markets," "nearness to railroads," and "nearness to schools." Five of these first six items, it will be noted, are direct appeals to the money-making motive.

"Nearness to churches" was mentioned six times. This fact, combined with the high rating given to "nearness to schools," indicates that educational and spiritual welfare ranked second only to the money-making urge in frequency of mention. It is quite evident, however, that taking the promotional program as a whole—including news stories, pamphlets, and circulars—climate and health both received greater emphasis than these factors.

"Availability of ample supplies of good water" ranked next with five mentions. In a tie at four each were "good crops and a large yield," "plenty of timber and fuel," "climate," "health," and "opportunity for diversified farming." "Beauty of surroundings" was mentioned three times; "possibility for fruit raising," "prosperous homes," "comfortable homes," and "good grazing and feeding" twice each. Mentioned once each were the possibility of buying "low priced land for the children," "ample rainfall," "no rent to pay," and "a good environment for the children."

TABLE V
An Analysis of the Frequency of Mention of Various Appeals to Readers in Northern Pacific Advertisements

Low Prices	8	Healthful climate	4
Liberal terms	8	Diversified farming	4
Good soil	7	Beauty of surroundings	3
Nearness to markets	7	Fruit raising	2
Nearness to railroads	7	Prosperity	2
Nearness to schools	7	Comfortable homes	2
Nearness to churches	6	Good grazing and feeding	2
Much good water	5	Low priced land for children	1
Good crops, big yield	4	Ample rainfall	1
Much timber and fuel	4	No rent to pay	1
Pleasant climate	4	Good place for the children	1

Fourteen of the above items, mentioned a total of forty-seven times, could be lumped under one general heading, economic welfare. Four of the items, mentioned sixteen times, deal with the general topic of pleasantness of environment; three, mentioned nine times, advertise the Northwest as an ideal situation for the children. Nearness to churches, with six mentions, remains as the fourth general topic, if such a classification is to be used.

A further indication of the values given to these appeals by Northern Pacific officials may be gained by noting the items that received the greatest display in each of the twelve advertisements.

The economic factor again leads all others by a wide margin. Low prices were emphasized in four ads, prosperous self-owned homes in three, and big crops in one. The healthfulness of the environment was given the most important position in one, possibilities for raising fruit in one, and a general exhortation

AN ANALYSIS OF THE PRESSURES EXERTED

to live on the farm in one. The twelfth featured no one argument above any other. That the Northern Pacific was playing upon those motives which students of immigration believe to have been the most important in bringing about migration is obvious. The desire on the part of migrants to own prosperous farms which could be purchased inexpensively on liberal terms gave the Land Department the motive around which it could design the largest share of its advertising. That it did just that is proof of its skill in adjusting its promotional media to the pre-existing attitudes of its prospective customers.

The Contents of the Advertising Arguments Analyzed

Frequency of mention of various appeals to readers of advertising is not enough to prove success or failure of the Northern Pacific's promotional efforts. The effectiveness of the material used can be judged further by an analysis of the contents. We cannot be satisfied with an analysis of advertising content only, as advertisements constituted only a small part of the total promotional campaign. Before drawing any final conclusions as to the worth of the program, it is also necessary to evaluate the contents of the booklets, pamphlets, circulars, and leaflets that were distributed by the thousands.

Such an analysis must necessarily be isolated from the remainder of the thesis. It was not possible to discuss the general promotional program in previous chapters without making reference to the contents of the various materials used. In this section it is proposed to dissect that material much more thoroughly and subject it to closer scrutiny. It would be easy to do a job of "muckraking" by using only those examples which have since proved to be greatly exaggerated. Such a job would be unfair to the Northern Pacific. True, there are many cases where promoter's license has been used. The Land Department officials became too enthusiastic at times, but when the promotional campaign is taken as a whole, the Northern Pacific was probably no more dishonest in its claims than any other large business firm at the time and, probably, considerably more honest than many. Most of the strongest claims, it will be noted, are quoted from persons who were considered to be authorities.

In the process of making this qualitative study of the appeals that the Northern Pacific communicated to its prospective migrants, paragraphs were taken from news stories, pamphlets, booklets, articles, and circulars. These paragraphs were then organized under seven general topics: "crops," "profit," "fast growth of the country," "climate," "health," "churches and schools," and "pleasant environment."

It has already been noted that these are in general the same topics that were emphasized in the newspaper advertisements analyzed in the first section of this chapter. The frequency of mention and amount of space given to the various items in the general promotional material followed the same pattern as did the advertising. Ownership of land and prospects for making a good profit dominated the whole program. The Northern Pacific was aiming primarily at the economic urge. Next to the economic factor came climate, health, churches and schools, and the beauty of the country in approximately that order.

Probably the most constantly used claim of the Northern Pacific was that its land grant provided the best available land in the United States for growing bountiful crops. One of the railroad's first bulletins, published by Jay Cooke & Co. in 1871, included the paragraph, "Pages of incontestible evidence can be introduced here to prove that nowhere in the world can larger crops of wheat, barley, rye, oats, potatoes and other roots be raised than on the land grant of the Northern Pacific Railroad."[4]

The statement is far too sweeping in its claims. If it had been narrowed to the United States and made to include only large unsold portions of land, it would probably have been true. But it does indicate the general tenor of Land Department policy to attract persons by the prospects of raising large crops.

In the much-quoted *Climates of the Northwest* (1871), Garfield wrote, "The belt of country from the Mississippi to the Pacific Ocean, having the best climate and consequent greatest fertility, lies between the forty-fourth and fifty-fourth parallels."[5] This belt of land includes the northern half of Minnesota and all of North Dakota, Montana, and Washington. Garfield's thesis

AN ANALYSIS OF THE PRESSURES EXERTED   101

was often used by the Northern Pacific as a basis for its claims. A delegate to Congress from the Territory of Washington, Garfield carried much prestige.

By 1874, the Northern Pacific was ready to maintain that "The bountifulness of crops in the Red River Valley is already proverbial."[6] It was a little early to term the bountifulness "proverbial," but the few settlers who had drifted in during 1872 and 1873 were evidently having a good deal of success, and even after seventy years of cultivation, the Red River Valley is still considered good farming country.

There is no doubt about the exaggeration in a paragraph of a news story sent to the Primghar (Iowa) *Democrat* in 1898: "Whenever seed is sown (in northern Minnesota counties), crops of outstanding proportions are the result.[7]

The railroad used scientific authority to support its claims in an 1897 news story in which one paragraph read, "Prof. W.M. Hays of the Minnesota State Experimental Farm discloses that this mixture of the extremes, sand and clay (found in the region between Aitkin and Lake Superior), constitutes the golden mean in soils. These soils are warm early in the season, easy to work, quick in giving up their fertility to crops and adapted to a wide range of crops."[8] Aitkin county had been praised as early as 1880 when an article in the Golden Northwest included the sentence, "The crops ... have been prolific."[9]

The prestige of science was brought to bear more thoroughly in another article, in the *Golden Northwest*, published in 1880. For that article Prof. Samuel P. Sadtler of the University of Minnesota did a complete analysis of the soil in the Red River Valley, which probably meant little to the prospective migrant, but which must have looked quite impressive.[10]

If it had limited itself to the United States, the Northern Pacific would not have been overstating itself when it reported that Dakota Territory "has been proved to be superior to any other portion of the world yet developed for the production of spring wheat."[11] At any rate, it was a powerful argument to use on prospective land buyers.

Quotations from successful farmers constituted a large part of the land-sales argument. One of the strongest of these reported, "One of the largest land owners in the Northwest, who had possessions in all the Northwestern states, says he will give two acres in southeastern Dakota for one acre in Becker county (Minnesota)."[12]

The Land Department probably taxed its advertising license a little too heavily when it wrote, "As an instance of the enduring fecundity of the soil in this valley, it may be stated that the Postmaster at Georgetown, North Dakota, is now working a farm on the bank of the river which has for twenty-two years been continuously cropped and he asserts that it is still too rich."[13] It is somewhat difficult to think of soil as being too rich, but certainly such an endorsement would not deter a land buyer.

Scores of other examples could be quoted to indicate the methods the railroad used to convince its prospects that Minnesota and Dakota lands were capable of producing superior crops. Those quoted above, however, will suffice to show the general arguments used. It must be remembered that they are the most striking paragraphs and thus are exaggerated more than the average appeals.

In its general appeal to the desire to make profits, the Northern Pacific used specific examples replete with figures. One of the most striking examples of this method was a circular distributed at Webster City, Iowa, by J. H. Richard, a sales solicitor for the railroad.[14]

The circular compared the cost of renting a farm in Iowa with the cost of buying one in North Dakota. Ten years' rent on a 160-acre Iowa farm, the circular explained, would cost $400 a year or $4,000 for ten years. During the same ten-year period 160 acres of land could be bought in North Dakota for $1,036. Included in the $1,036 total is the original cost of $800 at the rate of $5.00 an acre and $236 interest. This leaves the buyer with a saving of $2,964 in cash, but that is not the only advantage. At the end of ten years, with improvements on his land, his North Dakota farm would be worth $25 an acre or a total of $4,000. The profit on his investment is now the $2,964 saving on his original purchase plus the present worth of his land, or $4,000, which makes a grand total of $6,964.[15]

This argument must have sounded impressive. Under the financing plan then in force, the land purchase would take very

AN ANALYSIS OF THE PRESSURES EXERTED 103

little capital. Eighty dollars down payment would earn title to 160 acres. The remainder of the payments could be taken out of year-to-year profits. Of course, this highly imaginative speculation does not take into account the fact that profits are made, not on comparisons with land costs in other sections, but on sale of produce at the end of each growing year.

Another choice bit of speculation in a newspaper story assumes that a farmer has a $1,500 mortgage on 160 acres of Iowa land. He sells his 160 acres at $50 an acre for a total of $8,000, from which the $1,500 mortgage is subtracted. This leaves him $6,500 in cash. He then buys 640 acres in North Dakota at $3 an acre, a total of $1,920. This transaction leaves him with $4,580, of which he spends $1,000 for a house and some of the reminder for a barn, livestock, and other necessary items. He now has a fully equipped, debt-free farm of 640 acres and cash to spare in contrast with his former 160 acres with the $1,500 mortgage.[16]

Both the above examples compare Iowa with North Dakota to the disadvantage of Iowa. A third statistical argument shows just how inexpensively one could purchase government land near the Northern Pacific in North Dakota and start farming on that land. The article explains that a man with $500 could make a good start. He would first pay a land-office fee of $14. The material for a simple home of single boards would cost him $35; stove, furniture, and crockery another $50; oxen, plow, and wagon, $225. His total expenditures to this point would be $324, leaving him $176 for living expenses until he could market some of his produce. This $176, the article explained, could be increased by $150 by working for neighbors.[17]

The three examples quoted above take into consideration the three types of individuals who might buy Northern Pacific land: the established landowner in an older state who desired to expand his operations, the renter who preferred to own his own land, and the person with limited capital who saw the possibility of improving his financial status by buying cheap land in the West. In each case the financial advantages of North Dakota are exploited to the ultimate.

Allied to the crops and price arguments is the plea to "buy immediately because the country is growing rapidly and prices will go up." This theme is that the Northwest is destined to greatness. This gospel is found in an editorial in the *Golden Northwest*:

> The man who is so fortunate as to be located on the Northern Pacific railroad when it is completed will find himself on the main artery of traffic, on the great highway across the continent. He will be like the tradesman, who by fortunately locating on main street of a town, which afterward grows to be a great city, becomes a merchant prince and enjoys much greater commercial benefits than those who come after and are found to occupy more retired localities away from the great traveled thoroughfare.
>
> The Northern Pacific Railroad will become to the American continent what Broadway is to New York and the Strand to London. Other lines may occupy important positions but all must be subordinate to the grand route by which the production of the world will pass, as it will be the most direct and most feasible and hence the cheapest and fastest.[18]

Nothing could be more typical of the spirit of the American frontier. It is "Go West, young man, and grow up with the country," in different phrasing. And, of course, the financial inducements are not overlooked.

The Northern Pacific constantly repeated this theme. Its publicity spoke of growing cities, prosperous homes, heavy demands for lands, and counties filling up rapidly. But always not too rapidly. There was always some cheap land remaining.

On the subjects of climate and health the promotion men scorned caution and promised almost everything. Almost everything is accurate, as will be noted in the following quotation. "Hundreds of people," one article read, "may be found in all parts of the country whose lives have been spared through the climate (of northern Minnesota) . . . Their lungs being terribly diseased are now entirely healed . . . It must not be expected that even this atmosphere possesses the miraculous power of creating new lungs."[19]

AN ANALYSIS OF THE PRESSURES EXERTED

Aside from creating "new" lungs, however, the advertising and publicity men claimed just about every medical property for the healthful air.

On a map circular was the statement, "The state [Minnesota] is one of the most popular resorts for invalids, no fever and ague and the dry tonic atmosphere is a specific for incipient consumption."[20]

The same claim is made in one of the early pamphlets published by the company: "There are many people in the state [Minnesota] who formerly were threatened with consumption, but who in their new homes are enjoying perfect health; . . . fever and ague and kindred malarial diseases are unknown. It may be classed as one of the most healthful climates in the world."[21]

A new medical property of the pine tree is introduced in one article which includes the sentence, "Brainerd is quite celebrated as a resort for invalids, the pine forests having a remarkable curative effect, especially on people suffering from pulmonary complaints."[22]

A chart comparing the death rate in Minnesota with other states in the United States was used as final proof of the healthfulness of Minnesota's climate. Minnesota's death rate was purported to be 1 to 155. Its closest rival was Nebraska with 1 to 75 followed by Kansas with 1 to 74, Missouri with 1 to 67, Texas 1 to 64 and Massachusetts 1 to 57. The United States average was said to be 1 to 74 and the English average 1 to 46.[23] Even if these figures were accurate, as they may well have been, they prove very little. Minnesota's residents, in 1880, were very young. Almost all the population in the northern part of the state had come in since 1871, and it is the young who migrated, not the old. The table only proved that Minnesota's population was younger than the populations of the older states.

Closely allied to health in the Northern Pacific promotional program is the matter of climate. Claims for the climate of the Northwest included a wide scope of beneficial factors. There was ample rainfall, not too much snow (but enough), timeliness of snowfall, timeliness of rainfall, salubrity of climate, mildness of temperature, no fear of rigorous winters, no fear of extreme heat, and in general, the climate was the best in the world for humans, livestock, and crops.

Garfield's reasoning in his pamphlet, *Climates of the Northwest,* forms the basis of much of what the Northern Pacific's Land Department men wrote about the climate of the section. The theory, as has been explained previously in this thesis, is that lower altitudes have milder climates and that passes in the Rocky Mountains permit warm Pacific winds to penetrate the inland areas. Garfield explained that from Colorado and Wyoming, which form an east to west ridge through the western United States, the country slopes to the north. Consequently, Montana's climate was as mild as states far to the south. The northern tier of states was also benefitted, according to Garfield, by the fact that passes in the Rockies are lower west of Montana than they are west of Colorado and Wyoming. That permitted warm, moisture-laden breezes to penetrate far into Montana and North Dakota. The pamphlet was written in scientific terms and undoubtedly carried much weight.[24]

It is quite evident that many persons whom the Northern Pacific considered likely prospects to buy land feared the rigors of the climate in states as far north as those through which the railroad ran. General Nettleton was cognizant of this fact in 1873. In February of that year he wrote to Billings:

> Blink at it as we may, the question of climate is a sockdalager, and this obstacle, it seems to me, can only be overcome by convincing people that, in spite of the long and cold winters, they can live comfortably and make money on the line of the Northern Pacific road.... [25]

Because of this obstacle it was necessary for the road to maintain a constant counter propaganda campaign to convince prospective buyers that the climate was not severe and that they could live comfortably.

A paragraph from Garfield's pamphlet indicates the general tenor of this campaign. Garfield wrote, "In delightfulness and salubrity of climate much of it [the New Northwest] far exceeds any portions of the country lying east of the Father of Waters; the general temperature and the sublime scenery produce an exuberance of spirits, a luxury of existence, an intense enjoyment of animal life nowhere else experienced on this continent.[26]

Notwithstanding the delightfulness and salubrity of climate, it was necessary for the Land Department to marshal its promotional forces on several occasions to combat unfavorable stories of severe blizzards which came from settlers on the line.

One would never suppose that there could be blizzards in the Northwest if he had read Garfield's paragraph concerning the warm, southwesterly winds which spread over eastern Montana and Dakota. These, Garfield wrote, "together with the lower elevations of the more northerly districts, give them a mildness of climate both incomprehensible and incredible to those who have given the subject no particular attention."[27] Nor would he have any fears of cold weather if he had believed a news publicity story sent to an Iowa paper, in 1898, in which was the paragraph, "The climate is the finest on earth. The residents of Northern Minnesota have no fears of the rigors of Minnesota, for they know from experience that they are far preferable to the same season back East or farther South. In summer, cool nights follow the warmest days."[28]

Even the natural factors which control rainfall cooperated with the Northern Pacific to make the New Northwest the finest farm land in the country. A paragraph in a railroad pamphlet explained that "The timeliness of rainfall over this district will command attention. It mostly occurs when it is wanted. Its function is to make crops and not snow."[29]

In case any doubters feared that cool springs might retard crops, *Golden Northwest* explained that "Springs are cool but coolness gives strength to the plant and the rapid passage to hot weather is what gives a superiority to the productions of this district." For those who might believe that the country had insufficient rainfall, the article continued, "In the Northern agricultural belt, the dryness and purity of the atmosphere is one of the potential causes of perfect development in vegetation and the remarkable healthfulness of the people and products." The article adds a line, "Extreme cold is exceptional."[30]

There is not much doubt that the claims concerning health and climate are greatly exaggerated. It is true that only the most flagrant examples are quoted here, but those examples are sufficient to show that the bonds that held the Northern Pacific to truth were pretty badly strained. The reason for the excesses in describing the salable land is not hard to discover. It wasn't hard to prove that the soil in the Northwest was exceptional, it wasn't hard to convince prospective land buyers that land could be bought at a bargain in the Northwest, but it was hard to lure people to a region as far north as that country through which the Northern Pacific runs. The main objective seems to have been to prove that the climate of the New Northwest was no more severe than that of New York and the New England states.[31]

The fact that the Northern Pacific made constant references to the numbers of churches and schools in its territory has been mentioned often in the foregoing chapters. There were no articles found that devoted themselves entirely to pointing up this factor, but reference to religious and educational facilities was made in many of the advertising circulars, advertisements, and newspaper stories that were distributed. The railroad's policy is well indicated in a letter from Nettleton to Billings, in 1872, in which Nettleton wrote, "It occurs to me that it would considerably strengthen Mr. Rogers at home [England] if he could say, on his return, that his people would find several hundred American Congregationalists already on colony lands to welcome them."[32]

It has also been pointed out that it was part of Northern Pacific policy to donate land to communities for building churches and schools.[33] In one of the earlier circulars which the railroad distributed, it was emphasized that Minnesota already had normal schools at Winona, Mankato, and St. Cloud, a state university at Minneapolis, and Carleton College at Northfield.[34]

Usually references to churches and schools were included in sentences that praised the Northwest in general as in an advertisement sent to the Dodge county, Minnesota, *Fair Book* in which there was the sentence, "They [these lands] have fine soil, splendid water, and are close to railroad stations, churches and schools, and the best markets of the West."[35]

The recreational advantages to be found in the Northern Pacific territory were never made the subject of entire advertisements nor of entire articles, but very little promotional material concerning Minnesota was published that did not mention this feature.

Brainerd was advertised as a paradise for hunters and anglers.[36] The Park Region in the vicinity of Detroit Lakes, then Detroit, was described as "One of the most beautiful regions under the sun."[37] A news story sent from the Land Department office reported that "One of the chief beauties of this part of Minnesota [northern part] is the numerous lakes and streams. The lakes number several hundred and range in size from one-half an acre. They all contain the purest cold water and are plentifully stocked with fish of all kinds."[38]

It was noticeable, however, that in almost all cases the beauty of the country was subordinated to its profit-producing potentialities. Forests were important because they provided shelter and fuel and were not hard to clear. Lakes were important because they insured an ample supply of cold, clear water.[39]

Taken as a whole, it is evident that the Land Department was designing its promotional material to appeal to those urges in people that would be most likely to cause them to move to a new country. First, and most important, in Northern Pacific publications was the argument that in the Northwest it was possible to buy cheap land. Allied with cheap land was the prospect of making big profits. Following these arguments were the inducements to come to a territory where it would be possible to provide a good education for the children, to go to church, to grow with the country, to maintain good health, and to enjoy life. All evidence points to the fact that, during the frontier period of American history, those were the factors that motivated men to push westward.

An Analysis of Individual Articles

To complete a study of the Northern Pacific's promotional material it is necessary to study some of the railroad's articles and publications in their entirety. Previous sections of this chapter have extracted items and paragraphs from this material and organized them under topic headings. To fully judge the impact of any one of these articles or bulletins, however, the publication must be analyzed as a whole.

The promotional materials used varied from one-page circulars to multi-page bulletins and newspaper and magazine articles. With very few exceptions these materials presented a great variety of inducements to buy Northern Pacific land.

One of the first of these media used was a 32-page bulletin, "Guide to the Lands of the Northern Pacific Railroad in Minnesota," published by the Land Department in 1872.[40] It was divided into chapters under such headings as "Fruit," "Timber and Fuel," "Markets," "Increase in Value of Property," and "Climate." There were no illustrations.

A great variety of topics was discussed. In addition to those mentioned above were wood resources, grasses, scenery, soil, treeless land, health, education, and railroad facilities. In succeeding pages the bulletin described methods used in the formation of colonies, including colonies for soldiers. The concluding sections were devoted to more technical subjects, including information on the outfit that the prospective settler should have before he started out, how he should arrange for free transportation, and where he should stay while he was land hunting.

One interesting argument for buying Northern Pacific land, that has not been described previously, was employed in this bulletin. The pamphlet praised the "convenience" of the land. Northern Minnesota had many wooded fields. The new settler could clear the fields to get fuel and fence posts, and when that job was done, he would have good soil on which to raise crops. He was getting a three-in-one package.

The April, 1880, issue of *Golden Northwest* has been quoted extensively in this chapter. *Golden Northwest* was an eight-page magazine published at irregular intervals by the Land Department of the Northern Pacific. In the April, 1880, issue, which could be procured free by writing to James B. Power, Land Commissioner, according to a statement in the magazine, were one-and-one-third pages of advertising and six-and-two-thirds pages of copy divided into four articles, several paragraphs of miscellaneous information, and an editorial.[41]

The first article was entitled, "The Northern Pacific Railroad, Its Route, Its Connections, Its Lands." This article, starting

AN ANALYSIS OF THE PRESSURES EXERTED 111

with St. Louis county on Lake Superior in Minnesota, described every county on the Northern Pacific route between Lake Superior and the Missouri River.

There was general comment on each county. In the Aitkin county, Minnesota, paragraph the article reported, "The crops, although not in what may be called strictly an agricultural district, have been prolific. Clearings in the hardwood forest make extremely fine farms."

Concerning Crow Wing county was the comment, "Corn matures perfectly in this locality," and, "Settlers are going in fast." There was also a plug for the resort city of Brainerd: "Brainerd is quite celebrated as a resort of invalids, the pine forest having a remarkable curative effect, especially on people suffering from pulmonary complaints."

Of Wadena county the article said, "For diversified farming, no better location can be found." It also reported of this county that wheat had been raised there for eight successive years without a failure.

Comments on other Minnesota counties were essentially the same as the foregoing. Populations were also included and these populations were invariably set higher than the census figures. For instance, Becker county was credited with 5,000 persons, but the 1880 federal census report listed it at 4,459.[42]

Before launching into a county-by-county description of Dakota Territory, there was a paragraph on the northern part of the territory, later to become North Dakota, as a whole. Dakota was described as "That wonderful prairie country whose fame has reached to all the civilized portions of the world."

Cass county, Dakota Territory, was praised because "Wheat, oats, corn, barley, and all vegetables grow to wonderful perfection." An added paragraph on Fargo, in Cass county, said that this city "is probably the most prosperous and enterprising frontier city in the country." It added, "Its citizens occupy as fine residences as are found in the oldest and wealthiest towns of Minnesota."

The paragraph on Barnes county was similar to those already quoted, but on Stutsman county there was more. Stutsman lies along the James River about midway between the Red and Missouri. "This district," the article read, "in point of fertility and general adaptability for agricultural operations differs none from that we have passed through since leaving the Red River Valley. The same natural causes have conspired to create a soil especially adapted to the production of wheat in its highest degree of perfection and to the growth of other grain and all vegetables in abundance and of marked flavor and nutritive qualities."

Stock raising was featured as the strong point of Kidder county. "The richest grasses grow here," the paragraph reported. Of Burleigh county, on the Missouri, it was said, "The soil is extremely rich and productive. Wheat grows to perfection." That concluded the article.

The second article in the magazine was a more technical discussion of prices of land along the Northern Pacific route and the third analysis of soil in the Red River Valley by Professor Samuel P. Sadtler of the University of Minnesota, which has been quoted previously.[43] A story on the climate of the Northwest, which was largely a condensed re-hash of Garfield's pamphlet, and an editorial, "The National Highway,"[44] which has been quoted previously, filled the remaining pages.

The pamphlet and the magazine discussed in the foregoing paragraphs are a fair sample of the longer publications distributed by the Northern Pacific. The shorter circulars included the same sort of material, but in a condensed version. Many of them have been described in previous chapters.[45]

Conclusions on the Worth of the Promotional Material

On the basis of all the evidence available, it must be concluded that the Northern Pacific's promotional policies were expertly adapted to the conditions which might cause men to move to Northern Pacific land. Historians and sociologists are agreed that people migrated for economic reasons. Students of the history of the American West insist that the American frontier movement was motivated by a desire for cheap land.

The causes of discontent and the urge to migrate were present in Northern Europe and the older sections of the United States. The Northern Pacific Land Department designed its

AN ANALYSIS OF THE PRESSURES EXERTED

promotional program to prove to these discontented elements that they could own their own land and make profits on that land if they would move to the New Northwest. The additional advantages that they could be comfortable, that they would have ample churches in which to worship, and that they could educate their children were subordinated, but were not omitted.

It would be difficult to substantiate many of the stronger claims made by the Northern Pacific, but that is probably more indicative of the general expansionist nature of the time than of any conscious dishonesty on the part of Land Department officials. Garfield was probably confident that his findings were scientifically sound. Whether the Land Department was as certain that the conclusions were true is more questionable, but it must be remembered that the late nineteenth century was famous for its optimism and its ruthlessness in its business dealings.

Whether the campaign was wholly ethical or not, we must concede that the railroad's propaganda was aimed at the most prominent causes of unrest and that its counter propaganda was designed to overcome fears of a rigorous climate. That being the case, it is evident that the Northern Pacific's promotional methods were skillful and the contents of its promotional material likely to draw settlers to the Northwest. One question remains unanswered. Was the promotion actually successful in bringing the settlers to the country?

Henry Villard (ca. 1888), seventh president of the Northern Pacific Railroad, 1881-1884. Courtesy Minnesota Historical Society.

Jay Cooke (ca. 1887), financier for the Northern Pacific Railroad. Courtesy Minnesota Historical Society.

Northern Pacific Railroad's first general offices in Brainerd, Minnesota (ca. 1871). Courtesy Robert Kolbe.

Laying line on the Northern Pacific Railroad near Valley City, North Dakota (ca. 1881). Courtesy Robert Kolbe.

Northern Pacific transfer being loaded on Missouri River ferry at Bismarck, North Dakota (ca. 1883). Courtesy Robert Kolbe.

PHOTOGRAPHS

Northern Pacific Railroad locomotive No. 829 at Blatchford, Montana, 1896. Courtesy W. R. McGee.

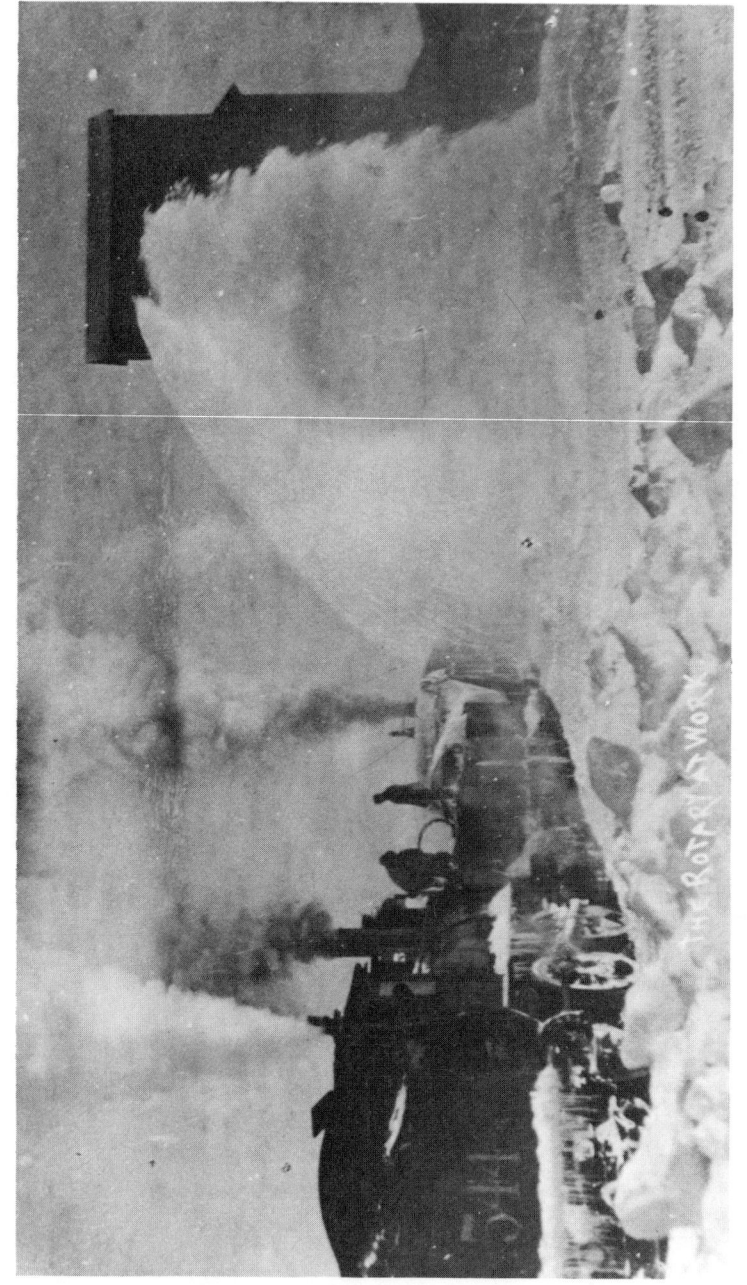

Northern Pacific Railroad locomotive No. 544 clearing snow at Berea, North Dakota, 1897. Courtesy W. R. McGee.

PHOTOGRAPHS

Northern Pacific Railroad locomotive No. 468 in Twin Bridges, Montana, 1898. Courtesy W. R. McGee.

Northern Pacific Railroad observation car on the North Coast Limited at Como, Minnesota, for initial run of April 29, 1900. Courtesy W. R. McGee.

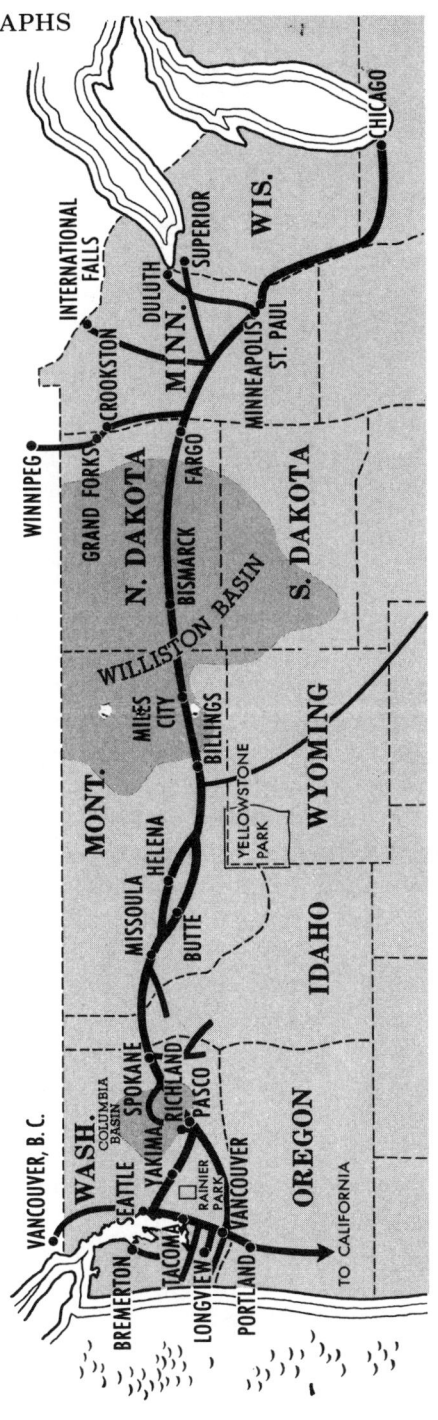

Map of the Northern Pacific Railroad line, showing the 6,900 miles of track in operation in 1958. From *Brief History of the Northern Pacific*. Courtesy Don L. Hofsommer.

Chapter VIII
Results of the Campaigns

The earlier chapters of this study have analyzed the origins of the Northern Pacific's promotional campaigns, the goals sought by such promotion, and the techniques that were employed to gain the attention of prospective settlers and convert them to the desirability of buying the Northern Pacific land. Some sidelights have been thrown on the results accruing from the campaigns, but a careful analysis of the effectiveness of the promotional effort requires extended study in this chapter.

The major objective of the Land Department, as this writer has many times pointed out, was to sell Northern Pacific land to actual settlers. Subordinate to this goal was the desire to attract population to the entire territory adjacent to the railroad.

That the vast prairies of the Northwest were placed under cultivation is indisputable. That population moved in at a spectacular pace is a matter of record. On the surface it seems evident that the Northern Pacific succeeded.

Such reasoning, however, does not take into account the multitude of other factors which were attracting persons to the Northwest. The westward movement was so irresistible a phenomenon that it undoubtedly would have continued even if there had been no Northern Pacific promotion. The purpose of this thesis is to establish the fact that the pressures exerted by the railroad hastened the movement to the West and, further, attracted persons to Northern Pacific lands whom the Land Department desired to have there.

In order to establish this thesis with any degree of certainty, it is necessary to determine whether the periods of greatest land sales and population increases in Northern Pacific territory followed the periods of heaviest railroad promotion and whether the land buyers and immigrants came from sections in which the railroad was exerting pressures.

RESULTS OF THE CAMPAIGNS

There are three general sources of information from which our facts may be drawn. Records of sales of Northern Pacific lands will tell us in general whether the Land Department was succeeding in its fundamental purpose of selling land, but they will not show whether a fairly large acreage was going to speculators who intended to hold it for price advances or to small operators who intended to move to the Northwest. These records, too, are limited to Northern Pacific holdings only and cannot show the influence of the railroad in attracting buyers for government land.

Census reports will help fill in the gaps. They will show whether land sales were followed by migration. They will also record the influx of population to the areas adjacent to the road and not to railroad lands alone.

Land-sales reports and census figures, however, do not indicate which lands were sold nor where the migrants were coming from. We must, so far as it is possible, ascertain the direction of the flow of population to make sure that persons were migrating from those districts in which the promotional campaign was operating. For example, Chapter II records that between 1871 and 1873 pressures were exerted on residents of New England and Europe. If most migrants came from those areas during that period, it is reasonably certain that they were affected to some degree by the promotional pressures exerted upon them by the railroad. Similar reasoning can be applied to subsequent periods.

Even with these problems solved, we have no method of evaluating the influences of state immigration bureaus, land companies, successful residents, or of the general expansionist tendency. But if land sales were high and population increases great in periods when the Northern Pacific's promotional machinery was most active, if migrants came from the regions in which Northern Pacific pressures were exerted, and bought lands in regions that were being advertised, then we may be reasonably certain in concluding that the railroad's promotion was effective.

Sales of Northern Pacific Lands

That the Northern Pacific sold land in great quantities there is no doubt. Land Department records show that up to June 30, 1903, the company had sold at least 26,429,931 acres of its grant.[1]

That the largest sales of lands were made during the periods of greatest intensity of Land Department activity is borne out by a study of sales during each of the periods of Northern Pacific promotion.

TABLE VI
An Analysis of Land Sales by Periods of Promotional Activity

Period	Total Sales		Average Sales Per Annum
1870 to 1874	699,214	(approx.)	139,842
1876 to 1884	3,379,405		422,427
1885 to 1893	3,159,650		394,956
1894 to 1896	889,465		222,366
1897 to 1902	16,079,473		2,641,912
1903 to 1907	4,285,997		480,521[2]

As would be expected, little land was sold during the first flurry of promotional activity. Not much could be done before late in 1871, and, after the financial crash of 1873, the Land Committee was dormant. It must also be remembered that the Northern Pacific set out on an entirely new venture. It is only logical that results should flow slowly from the first promotional campaign.

The second period, 1876 to 1884, was marked by an increased tempo of promotional effort. It will be remembered that it was during those years that the European staff was at its largest and the flow of promotional publications at its greatest.

The fact that annual land sales averaged more than 400,000 acres a year in this second period indicates that the promotion was bringing results. The accuracy of this generalization is

RESULTS OF THE CAMPAIGNS   127

strengthened by the fact that there was a slight decrease in the annual land-sales average during the third period, which extended from 1885 to 1893. During this period there was a noticeable slump in sales effort. The decrease from an average of 422,427 acres a year from 1876 to 1884 to an average of 394,956 acres annually from 1885 to 1893 is slight, but it reverses the general upward trend which reached its peak in the fourth period.

Between 1893 and 1896, when the company was in receivership and there was practically no promotional activity, land sales reached a low average of 222,366 acres a year. But when Wilsey and his associates were carrying out their heavy newspaper campaign in the fourth period, from 1897 to 1902, sales jumped to an average of 2,641,912 acres annually. Promotion was cut off in 1903, and sales for the next four years averaged only 480,521 acres a year.

These figures would seem to justify the conclusion that extensive promotional effort brought about heavy land sales. The first period of activity gave the sales drive its start. The second, which was very intensive, increased those sales approximately 300 per cent. During the third period, when the trend should have been upward because of the promotion that had preceded it, there was a falling off. This was a period of only average activity. When promotion was greatly curtailed after the receivership, sales dropped to the lowest point since 1874. When promotion was revived again in what is probably the strongest campaign of all, sales reached their highest point in Northern Pacific history. Once more activities were curtailed and sales dropped to approximately their 1880 level.

These generalizations fail to take into consideration an important factor, the business cycle. In the early 1880's Land Department efforts were aided by bumper crops and high prices. After 1883 they were deterred by poor crops and low prices. There were minor upward trends but no sustained prosperity until after the depression of 1893. The year 1897 marked the beginning of a new era of prosperity which lasted for about ten years.[3]

The fact that Northern Pacific promotional efforts closely paralleled trends in the business cycle does not detract, however, from the effectiveness of the railroad's promotion. It rather indicates that the Land Department was taking advantage of upward surges of the cycle. During periods of prosperity, when persons were most likely to move,[4] the Land Department exerted its greatest pressures. In 1880, when yields were strong and prices high, there was a demand for land to which the company catered. In 1887, when crops were poor and prices low, there was less demand and promotion was curtailed. Crops improved and prices rose in 1897, and the Northern Pacific followed the trend with its strong campaign, which lasted until 1902. This campaign would probably have been continued through the prosperous years after 1902 if most of the high-quality land had not been sold by that year. It is also true that Northern Pacific fortunes rose and fell with business conditions. Consequently, it was necessary to curtail promotional expenditures in times of business depressions because of the weakened financial condition of the company. These factors make it evident that the business cycle affected Northern Pacific promotion, but they do not refute the contention that the migratory movement was, in a large part, motivated by Northern Pacific promotion.

Land sales by years from 1875 to 1907 will further bear out the contention that the greatest quantities of land were sold during the periods of the most intense promotional activity. The ebb and flow of land sales follows closely the fluctuation of promotional efforts, as the following table will bear out:

TABLE VII
Land Sales by Years from 1875 to 1907

Year	Sales	Year	Sales
Prior to Sept. 1875	699,214	1891	366,152
Nine months ending		1892	553,214
June 30, 1876	149,791	Calendar year 1893	275,175
Year ending		Calendar year 1894	98,178
June 30, 1877	254,827	Calendar year 1895	126,359
1878	702,387	Calendar year 1896	389,753
1879	506,685	Calendar year 1897	453,449
1880	291,752	Fiscal year 1897-98	6,576,652
1881	835,209	Fiscal year 1898-99	1,032,137
1882	467,418	Fiscal year 1899-00	2,873,903
1883	771,236	Fiscal year 1900-01	2,757,443
1884	478,116	Fiscal year 1901-02	2,385,889
1885	344,557	Fiscal year 1902-03	2,363,912
1886	370,925	Fiscal year 1903-04	396,908
1887	310,355	Fiscal year 1904-05	1,135,500
1888	392,256	Fiscal year 1905-06	175,752
1889	573,214	Fiscal year 1906-07	213,923[5]
1890	278,322		

The first marked increase in sales took place in the year ending June 30, 1878. This was at the beginning of the second period of sales promotion. The total sales for this year are probably higher than they normally would have been, however, because company finances were still suffering from the 1873 crash. Bonds, which were exchangeable for land at par, were depreciated in value. Consequently, there was a tendency to trade the low-value bonds for land, which seemed a far sounder investment.[6]

The table shows that sales for 1880 were very low, but it must be remembered that the figures are for the year ending June 30. Results of the heavy promotional campaign would be reflected in 1881 sales, which were considerably above any previous year. There was a decrease in 1882 followed by a strong increase in 1883. As would be expected, there was a tapering off after 1883 into the mediocre years, which lasted until 1897. Records for 1889 show that sales for that year were relatively strong but not nearly as strong as 1881. This is to be expected on the basis of the amount of effort exerted by the Land Department during the two years.

An all-time low was struck in 1894. This can be attributed to the general depression and to the curtailment of promotion by the railroad. There was a slow rise through the first half of 1897 and then the overwhelming 6,576,000 figure of 1898. This coincides with the intensity of the promotional effort. Sales remained in the millions until June 30, 1903, when they dropped below 400,000. Again the coincidence between promotion and sales is marked.

It may be concluded from the foregoing figures that there was a distinct correlation between business conditions, promotional activity, and land sales. It could be assumed that business conditions were alone responsible for causing fluctuations in the disposal of the land, but that is unlikely. It is more logical that Northern Pacific promotion capitalized on prosperous years to direct capital toward its land grant.

There is one further check that we may apply to records of land sales to determine the effectiveness of Northern Pacific efforts. We may note the districts in which the railroad was selling the most land from year to year and compare them with areas which were advertised most strongly in the promotional material that was distributed. We know from the foregoing chapters that after 1880 very little advertising was directed at the sale of Minnesota land until the final period of activity. In that final period northern Minnesota was publicized extensively.

Land Department records show that between 1884 and 1890 the largest acreage sold in Minnesota in any one year was 18,413 acres. This high point was reached in 1888. In 1900 (immediately following the heavy campaign of 1898 and 1899) the total sales had risen to 522,998 acres. By 1904 the total was down to 760 acres.[7]

The record of North Dakota sales is similar. During the late eighties the Western division of the Land Department was more active than the Eastern division, and sales were much greater in Washington than in Minnesota and North Dakota. North Dakota's best record for the period was compiled in 1885 when 178,529 acres were disposed of. There was then a drop to 10,521 acres in 1887 and a rise to 99,597 acres in 1889. This figure was the highest for any one year until 1898 when the astounding total of 4,481,834 acres was sold. And 1898 was the year of newspaper advertising, news publicity stories, Homeseekers' excursions, and land solicitors. It is important, too, to note that in 1889 the Land Department organized a special campaign to prove that North Dakota was well adapted to diversified farming, and in that year sales rose greatly above 1888.[8]

It is also highly significant that 1887 was the first year in which Washington sales exceeded combined Minnesota and North Dakota sales. The West Coast ascendancy held through 1890. It was during these years that more effort was directed to selling West Coast land than to selling in Minnesota and Dakota.[9]

It is true, to a certain degree, that regional business conditions affected these sales. But it is certainly evident from the records that Northern Pacific promotion was able to direct migrants to the areas in which it desired to sell lands. In years when promotional efforts directed attention to Washington, land sales in that state were higher than in the Eastern district. When North Dakota and Minnesota lands were featured, their totals exceeded Washington's. The fact that this record was achieved is sufficient to prove that prospective land purchases were affected by the railroad's pressures.

The Growth of the Northwest's Population

The data presented in the foregoing section adequately proves that the Northern Pacific promotion was effective in selling the railroad's land. A study of census records will show whether buyers actually moved to the land which they purchased. If populations of counties and towns adjacent to the railroad line increased rapidly, we may safely assume that the

Land Department was achieving its major objective of selling its grant in small parcels to actual settlers, as well as its secondary objective of populating the entire area that would be dependent upon Northern Pacific for transportation.

That the population of the entire area grew at an incredible pace is a matter of record. We have three possible means by which we may analyze that growth. We may investigate the populations of the states as a whole, of the counties along the railroad's line, and of the cities along the road. In each of these political divisions the growth is reflected.

TABLE VIII
Populations of the Northwestern States, 1870 to 1920

Year	Minnesota	North Dakota	Montana
1870	439,706	2,405	20,595
1880	780,773	36,909	39,159
1890	1,301,826	182,719	132,159
1900	1,751,394	319,146	243,329
1910	2,075,708	577,056	376,053
1920	2,387,125	648,872	548,889[10]

It would be straining logic to try to draw any major conclusions from the population growths of the states other than that they grew rapidly from the time of the beginning of the Northern Pacific campaign until the end. A year-by-year breakdown might be valuable in proving the effectiveness of individual promotional drives, but the ten-year census records show only that the population did increase. In the case of North Dakota, however, the records show to some degree that North Dakota's growth is coincident with the Land Department's efforts. The same is quite true of Montana.

An analysis of population growth of the counties through which the Northern Pacific passed and of those counties adjacent to the Northern Pacific line is of greater value in proving that almost all of the population came into the country after the Land Department started its land sales campaign. The great increases between 1870 and 1904 are evident in the following table:

TABLE IX
Populations of Counties in Minnesota Along the Northern Pacific Line

County	1870	1875	1880	1885
Ramsey	23,085	36,333	46,168	116,227
Hennepin	31,609	48,725	66,760	148,737
Anoka	3,930	5,709	6,394	10,089
Sherburne	2,051	3,018	3,860	5,647
Stearns	14,210	17,797	22,552	28,712
Benton	1,558	1,974	3,019	4,721
Morrison	1,683	2,722	5,877	9,406
Todd	2,038	3,818	6,126	9,643
Wadena		210	2,086	3,565
Ottertail	1,961	9,174	18,740	31,520
Becker		2,256	4,459	7,433
Clay	264	1,451	5,900	10,362
Washington	1,810	14,751	19,553	29,751
Chisago	4,359	6,946	7,997	9,765
Pine	648	795	1,365	2,186
Carlton	286	495	1,234	15,965
St. Louis	4,519	3,517	4,553	20,453
Aitkin	177	205	370	1,388
Crow Wing	190	1,931	2,307	8,743
Cass		239	250	1,135

TABLE IX (con't)

County	1890	1895	1900	1905
Ramsey	139,796	147,537	170,554	206,330
Hennepin	185,294	217,789	228,340	292,806
Anoka	9,884	11,181	11,313	12,113
Sherburne	5,908	7,137	7,281	7,961
Stearns	34,844	39,925	44,464	47,120
Benton	6,284	7,793	9,912	11,256
Morrison	13,325	19,163	22,891	24,853
Todd	12,930	17,674	22,214	24,638
Wadena	4,053	6,976	7,921	9,317
Ottertail	34,232	39,453	45,475	48,229
Becker	9,401	13,725	14,375	18,490
Clay	11,517	15,154	17,942	19,457
Washington	25,992	27,417	27,808	28,884
Chisago	10,359	13,118	13,248	14,341
Pine	4,052	8,361	11,546	14,869
Carlton	16,532	7,458	10,017	15,287
St. Louis	44,862	78,575	82,932	117,513
Aitkin	2,462	5,224	6,743	9,537
Crow Wing	8,852	11,561	14,250	16,731
Cass	1,245	3,425	7,777	11,012[11]

The population tables of the urban counties of Ramsey, Hennepin, Stearns, and St. Louis are of relatively little value to this study because their population growths depended upon industrial factors as well as agricultural. The predominantly agricultural counties more adequately illustrate the results of Northern Pacific pressures. Becker, Clay, Wadena, Crow Wing, and Aitkin counties are especially significant since it will be remembered from foregoing chapters that more publicity was given to these counties than to any others.

Clay county of this group had the greatest population in 1870, 264; Wadena had no white residents; Becker had none; Crow Wing had 190; and Aitkin 177. The most significant columns in the chart are those that followed the heaviest

RESULTS OF THE CAMPAIGNS

promotional drives. Much of the 1872-1873 promotion advertised lands in Becker, Clay, and Crow Wing counties. The 1875 column strikingly shows the results. It is evident that the migratory trend, set in motion during this period, carried on through 1880.

The next period of intensive promotion took place during the early eighties. A comparison of the 1880 and 1885 columns will show heavy gains in all counties. Most of the railroad's promotion between 1885 and 1889 advertised West Coast lands. There are gains in all counties during the 1885-1890 period but these advances were not nearly as great as those in the preceding five years.

Reasonably strong gains between 1890 and 1895 are harder to explain except for the fact that an effort was being made to direct more attention to the Eastern district lands again after the lull prior to 1889.

Becker and Clay and the northern timbered counties were heavily promoted again starting in 1897. There were moderate gains between 1895 and 1900 and strong gains between 1900 and 1905. If figures for 1898 were available, a comparison between that year and 1905 would probably show even more striking results.

This reasoning does not take into consideration the multitude of other factors that might have influenced population movements, but the remarkable correlation between Northern Pacific promotion and population gains must surely indicate that the Land Department's efforts were an important element in bringing migrants into the counties analyzed.

Similar results are indicated by a study of North Dakota counties through which the railroad passed:

TABLE X
Population of the Dakota Counties Through Which the Northern Pacific Passed

County	1870	1880	1890	1900	1910
Cass		8,998	19,613	28,625	33,935
Barnes		1,585	7,045	13,159	18,066
Stutsman		1,007	5,266	9,143	18,189
Kidder		89	1,211	1,754	5,962
Burleigh		3,246	4,247	6,081	13,087
Morton		200	4,728	8,069	25,289
Stark			2,304	7,621	12,504
Billings		1,323	170	975	10,186
Foster		37	1,210	3,770	5,313[12]

The counties are listed in order from east to west with the exception of Foster, which is on a feeder line north of Stutsman. It is particularly significant that there was not one single white resident in any one of the Northern Pacific counties at the time of the 1870 census and, further, that there were only 1,523 persons in Northern Pacific counties west of the Missouri River in 1880.

Cass was the only North Dakota county to profit greatly from the earlier Northern Pacific promotional campaign. That campaign described the village of Fargo, which had not yet been founded at the time of the taking of the 1870 census, as the prospective metropolis of the Red River Valley. Results of the advertising are reflected in Cass county's 1880 population of 8,998. It was uninhabited in 1870.

Not much publicity was given to North Dakota before the late seventies and the early eighties, and then attention was directed primarily to the counties east of the Missouri River. The results of this publicity are evident in the large gains indicated in the 1890 column.

The West River counties of Morton, Stark, and Billings, and the eastern county of Foster were featured in the campaign

RESULTS OF THE CAMPAIGNS 137

of 1897 to 1902. It will be noted that their most striking gains were recorded between 1900 and 1910.

The statistics indicate, even more strongly than in the case of Minnesota, that the greatest population gains took place when the Northern Pacific was exerting the greatest promotional pressures and in the locations where the Northern Pacific sought to sell its land.

An analysis of Montana county populations is a more difficult task. Mining and grazing attracted many settlers to Montana independently of any Northern Pacific promotion, and we do not have as much evidence of Northern Pacific promotion in that state as in other western commonwealths. However, some conclusions may be drawn from a study of Montana counties east of the Belt Mountain range.

TABLE XI
Population of Montana Counties Through
Which the Northern Pacific Passed

County	1870	1880	1890	1900	1910
Wibaux					
Dawson	177	180	2,056	2,443	12,725
Prairie					
Custer		2,510	5,308	7,891	14,123
Rosebud					7,985
Treasure					
Yellowstone			2,065	6,212	22,944
Stillwater					
Carbon				7,533	13,962
Sweet Grass				3,086	4,029
Park			6,881	7,341	10,731[13]

The only period in which we have evidence of much promotion for Montana lands is from 1897 to 1902 when land solicitors were maintained in the state.[14] There was no Montana promotion before 1880 because the line had not been built into the state before that time. A few pamphlets and circulars that mentioned

Montana were distributed during the 1876-1883 period, but interest in the state was kept subordinate to North Dakota.[15]

That there is a correlation between the growth of population and promotional efforts is borne out by the fact that the greatest increase took place during the years that the Northern Pacific featured Montana lands most strongly. The increases are reflected in the 1900 and 1910 populations. It is also significant that the company did not stage its greatest eastern Montana campaign until 1925 and 1926. This would account for the fact that four of the counties were devoid of population in 1910.

The growth of cities is important as it relates to the Northern Pacific promotion campaign only because it indicates the need for distribution centers. The Northern Pacific made no effort to attract city and town dwellers, believing that that class would naturally follow after the farm lands had filled. City and town growths, however, indicate the general growth of the entire community and for that reason will throw some light on an analysis of the results of Land Department promotion.

TABLE XII
Population of the Minnesota Towns and Cities Along the Northern Pacific Line

City	1870	1875	1880	1885
St. Paul	20,030	32,678	41,738	111,397
Minneapolis	13,073	32,711	46,887	129,200
Duluth	3,093	3,058	838	18,085
Anoka	1,497	2,420	2,706	5,103
Brainerd		930	1,865	7,110
St. Cloud	2,176	2,672	2,462	5,048
Little Falls	417	387	508	2,630
Wadena		138		855
Detroit		388	973	1,323
Glyndon		244	793	543
Aitkin		205		705

TABLE XII (con't)

City	1890	1895	1900	1905
St. Paul	133,156	140,292	163,065	197,023
Minneapolis	164,738	192,833	202,718	261,974
Duluth	33,115	59,396	52,969	64,942
Anoka	4,252	3,812	3,769	4,953
Brainerd	5,703	7,031	7,524	8,133
St. Cloud	7,686	9,178	8,663	9,422
Little Falls	2,354	5,116	5,774	5,856
Wadena	895	1,252	1,520	1,868
Detroit	1,510	1,810		2,419
Glyndon	295	278	250	
Aitkin	737	1,670	1,719	1,896[16]

The most important conclusion to be drawn from the foregoing table is that the populations of Minnesota communities grew steadily during the period of Northern Pacific promotion. It is significant that these cities and towns had very few residents in 1870 and that they grew most rapidly between 1880 and 1885 when Northern Pacific pressure was at its greatest for the entire area.

Glyndon is a particularly interesting case because it was used as a center for the establishment of colonies between 1870 and 1880. When the colonies had been established and other towns grew up around it, the Northern Pacific evidently had no further use for the town and the population dropped off again.

While the validity of the data may be open to question, Northern Pacific publications give a more adequate picture of population growth by recording results at the ends of periods of heaviest promotional activity. Land Department estimates for 1881 and 1882 are a clear reflection of the influx of population that took place following the census of 1880. These figures are particularly valuable to this study because they record the results of an intensive promotional campaign which directed attention to a relatively small area embracing only the western section of Minnesota and the eastern counties of North Dakota.

140   SIG MICKELSON

The *Annual Report* for 1882 recorded that cities along the St. Paul branch of the Minnesota division, including Minneapolis and St. Paul, had increased 69 per cent in population in the one year following the taking of the 1880 census. During the same period the populations of the ten most important towns along the Minnesota division had increased 200 per cent, the ten counties on the Minnesota division 63 per cent, the leading towns along the Dakota division (from Fargo to the Missouri River) 60 per cent, and the five counties traversed by the Dakota division 150 per cent.[17]

In 1882 the Land Department compiled another series of estimates of population growth for the two years following the 1880 federal census. The results show tremendous gains in every political division investigated, as the following table indicates:

TABLE XIII
Estimated Populations of Minnesota Cities
1882 Compared with Census of 1880

City or Town	1880	1882 (Est.)
St. Paul	41,473	70,000
Minneapolis	46,887	80,000
St. Cloud	2,462	3,300
Little Falls	508	1,000
Sauk Rapids	598	1,000
Aitkin	366	500
Audubon	91	150
Bluffton	326	500
Brainerd	2,319	6,000
Detroit	554	1,200
Duluth	3,483	10,000
Moorhead	200	4,200
Thomson	251	550
Wadena	307	800
Fergus Falls	1,635	4,000
Elizabeth	75	200
Pelican Rapids	200	500[18]

The two-year gain is nothing short of astounding, but a comparison with figures compiled from the state census of 1885 will indicate that the estimates are probably quite accurate.[19]

Estimates of populations of counties either on or adjacent to the Northern Pacific line in Minnesota indicate the same trend. The increase in these counties, all rural with the exception of St. Louis, is very nearly 100 per cent, as will be noted in the following table:

TABLE XIV
Estimated Populations of Minnesota Counties
1882 Compared with 1880 Census

Town	1880	1882 (Est.)
Aitkin	366	2,000
Becker	5,218	7,827
Carlton	1,230	1,845
Cass	486	1,737
Clay	5,887	9,000
Ottertail	18,675	25,000
Polk	11,433	17,150
St. Louis	4,504	13,000
Todd	6,133	9,200
Wadena	2,080	4,630
Totals	56,012	91,389[20]

The trend was even more marked in North Dakota towns and counties, the increases there running well above 100 per cent.

TABLE XV
Estimated Populations of Dakota Towns
1882 Compared with 1880 Census

Town	1880	1882
Fargo	2,693	7,020
Casselton	361	1,200
Wheatland	147	350
New Buffalo	45	300
Tower City	159	500
Valley City	302	1,500
Jamestown	393	2,000
Bismarck	1,758	3,000
Totals	5,858	15,875[21]

TABLE XVI
Estimated Populations of Dakota Counties
1882 Compared with 1880 Census

County	1880	1882
Barnes	1,585	4,585
Burleigh	3,246	5,000
Cass	8,998	18,566
Kidder	89	2,089
Stutsman	1,007	7,007
Totals	14,925	37,247[22]

The foregoing charts further bear out this writer's contention that population gains in Minnesota and Dakota counties and towns adjacent to the Northern Pacific line took place at times when the railroad was exerting its greatest pressures in those areas. It may be that the agricultural prosperity of this region during these two years would have been sufficient to attract many settlers to the territory without Northern Pacific promotion, but it must be remembered that Northern Pacific promotion informed the country of that prosperity. Again the correlation between heavy Land Department promotion and large population gains is so marked that at least some of the credit for attracting the new settlers must be given to the Northern Pacific.

It would be foolhardy to attempt to prove that railroad promotion alone produced the rapid growth of Minnesota and Dakota. But when the populations of wholly rural counties grew rapidly just at the time that Northern Pacific promotion was at high tide, there is every reason to believe that railroad promotion was one of the important factors that brought about the increases. That being the case, the effectiveness of the work being carried on by the Land Department cannot be disputed.

One further test should be applied before final judgment is passed on the worth of the Northern Pacific promotional campaign. It has already been pointed out that land sales and population boomed when promotion was strongest, subsided when it relaxed. If it can be proved that land buyers and settlers came from the specific areas into which the railroad conducted its promotion, then we should be reasonably certain that Land Department officials were wasting neither time nor money in their promotional endeavors.

The Direction of the Migratory Movement

It is obvious from the foregoing chapters that Northern Pacific policy in respect to the regions in which it sought land buyers shifted from period to period. It will be remembered that during the early seventies the areas of greatest concentration of promotional effort were New England, eastern Canada, and northern Europe.

In the late seventies and early eighties New England and eastern Canada gave way to the Middle Atlantic states and the East North Central group. The European campaign, counter to the general trend of westward movement, was intensified. By the late eighties and early nineties, Europe had been dropped and the largest share of the effort was directed west of the Alleghenies, extending all the way to Wisconsin, Iowa, and southern Minnesota. During the final period almost all effort was concentrated on the states west of Illinois.[23]

It is apparent, too, that Northern Pacific policy in regard to the type of persons it wanted on its lands clarified and crystallized with experience. In 1872 George Hibbard wrote that it was then the policy of the company to encourage settlers from any part of the world, including those from the Southern states.[24] Only six years later the company had decided that it was a sounder policy to seek emigrants only from the United States and to make no appropriations for promotion abroad.[25]

This policy changed in 1880, however, when George Sheppard returned to England to set up the very elaborate system described in a foregoing chapter.[26] Even with Sheppard's extensive organization working in Europe, however, it seems that there was a conflict of opinion as to the worth of the campaign there.

Col. R. M. Newport, who was Land Commissioner at the time, wrote to Oakes in 1881:

> I have observed that the very best class of settlers which we have secured are those who have passed through a frontier experience in the older states and those who know how to adapt themselves to the work of subjugating these prairies and of establishing new homes thereon. I would rather have one settler from Illinois or Wisconsin, who had opened a farm there, than a half dozen emigrants from England or from any other European country. The latter, especially English emigrants, require a good deal of advice and attention when they first come over and have not the power of adaptation to circumstances that settlers from other parts of our own states have. Of course we want to secure all the emigration we can from all quarters but I see no good reason why we should pay large bonuses to secure foreign emigration when we can, by a judicious outlay, largely increase the emigration from other states in the Union.[27]

RESULTS OF THE CAMPAIGNS

Although it would seem inevitable that, with 831 agents in the United Kingdom and 124 on the European continent in 1881 and 1882, a large share of the immigration to the Northern Pacific lands should come directly from Europe, such was evidently not the case. In January, 1884, Charles B. Lamborne, Land Commissioner, wrote that nine tenths and probably more of the settlers on the lands of the company had come from states and territories west of the Allegheny mountains. He added that western New York, Pennsylvania, and West Virginia were also sending a large number of land purchasers.[28]

It would seem apparent that if nine tenths of the settlers on Northern Pacific lands up to January, 1884, had come from states west of the Alleghenies, the railroad's foreign promotion must have been a failure. But such a conclusion is unwarranted. What actually seems to have happened is that many of the European migrants were stopping briefly in states to the east of Minnesota and North Dakota before going on to those states.

Carleton C. Qualey explained the Norwegian migration to North Dakota when he wrote:

> The Norwegian settlement of North Dakota was essentially part of an inter-state migration. This is particularly true of the earlier stages of the settlement period. A writer in the Valley City *Times* in 1882 stated, "But little foreign emigration has reached North Dakota directly from the old country; nearly all have become Americanized through a former settlement in older states." Nevertheless, it was the tremendously increased immigration from Norway in the eighties which was responsible for a large part of the Norwegian population of North Dakota. The emigrants stopped for a brief time in the older settlements in Wisconsin, Iowa, and Minnesota, worked as laborers or tenants there for a time, and then moved on westward where there was plenty of free or cheap land to be had.[29]

That this is essentially true is borne out by several specific cases with which the writer is familiar. The writer's own paternal grandfather migrated from Norway to Wisconsin in the 1870's. After a brief period in which he worked as a laborer in lumber camps there, he moved to Central Minnesota, where he bought land. Several Becker and Clay county, Minnesota, families migrated first to Goodhue and Freeborn counties in Minnesota, which had been settled much earlier, and then, impelled by a desire for big estates of cheap land, moved to the Red River country in the 1880's.[30]

This theory of migration is further substantiated by the fact that several colonies of Becker and Clay county residents of Norwegian birth left their homes in those counties shortly after 1900 and moved to western North Dakota and eastern Montana.[31] The motives were the same: large farms and cheap land. These cases could no doubt be multiplied by scores if it were possible to interview descendants of migrating families.

This trend is in accord with the general theory of American frontier history that the westward migration was accomplished not by long jumps but by a continuous series of short moves.

The significance of these facts here is that, although a large percentage of foreign born will appear on Minnesota and North Dakota census reports, many of those foreign born actually came to the Northern Pacific lands from older and better-established communities in the United States. This further justifies Land Department officials in their decisions to concentrate their promotional efforts on the East North Central and North Central states. It is also probable that many immigrants came to the United States with the ultimate intention of settling in the Northwest but were forced by circumstances to stop for brief intervals en route.

The tendency to concentrate promotion on the states immediately adjacent to Northern Pacific land was much more marked in the 1897-1902 period of activity.[32] Both W. H. Phipps, Land Commissioner, and F. W. Wilsey, Eastern Land Agent, emphasized this policy.

In an interview Phipps said:

> The class of emigrants locating in Minnesota as well as in North Dakota, are chiefly from the central western states; that is to say, Iowa, Nebraska, Kansas, Wisconsin, and northern Illinois, while a considerable number come from the states of Ohio, Indiana, and Kentucky... But that

which strikes me best of all is the fact that nearly all the new settlers are men who have been successful farmers in the older states, and, having sold their farms there at high valuations, bring with them into this new country ample means to insure a good and safe start.[33]

A story in the *Homestead* magazine quoted Wilsey as saying that a large part of his purchasers during the past two years (1897 and 1898) had been Iowa farmers, mostly from the northern part of the state although every Iowa county was represented.[34]

It is evident from the foregoing that most of the settlers on Northern Pacific lands were coming from the regions in which the company was concentrating its promotion. After 1880 most of the promotional efforts were directed to areas west of the Alleghenies. After that year most of the land buyers, according to company officials, came from the North Central states.

The situation in respect to foreign immigration is considerably more complex, but it is evident, as has been pointed out, that many Europeans migrated to the United States and arrived on the Northern Pacific lands after one or more stops en route, which is as the officials of the Land Department desired.

Further evidence to support the belief that migrants were coming from regions in which Northern Pacific promotion was the heaviest may be found in census reports breaking down the populations of the Northwest states according to state, territory, or country of birth. These statistics are inadequate in that they fail to distinguish between those who moved directly from their home areas to the Northwest and those who made stops between, but they are sufficient to indicate the general direction of the movement.

TABLE XVII
Population According to State, Territory, or Country of Birth

1890	Total	New England	North Atlantic	North South Atlantic	South South Atlantic
MN	1,301,867	35,949	67,169	4,575	841
ND	182,719	3,536	10,307	691	99
MT	132,159	4,581	11,790	2,123	676
WA	349,390	12,990	28,494	4,541	2,239
1900					
MN	1,751,394	30,089	63,008	4,703	1,040
ND	319,146	3,326	10,877	1,734	202
MT	243,329	5,716	15,917	2,447	950
WA	518,103	13,888	33,364	6,114	3,003

1890	East North Central	West North Central	East South Central	West South Central	West	Ireland
MN	124,970	584,877	4,174	900	1,155	28,011
ND	22,102	62,911	1,475	151	285	2,967
MT	19,820	17,153	2,463	844	26,573	6,648
WA	60,680	51,585	7,251	4,324	80,108	7,799
1900						
MN	167,025	963,499	4,912	1,181	3,563	22,428
ND	35,022	151,116	769	321	1,160	2,670
MT	33,689	35,961	3,660	1,903	74,073	9,436
WA	80,413	76,122	8,927	5,548	171,163	7,262

1890	England	Scotland	Denmark	Norway	Sweden
MN	14,730	5,315	14,133	101,169	99,913
ND	3,309	1,788	2,860	25,773	5,583
MT	6,480	1,585	683	1,957	3,771
WA	9,854	3,514	2,807	8,334	10,272
1900					
MN	12,022	4,810	16,299	104,895	115,476
ND	2,909	1,800	3,953	30,206	8,419
MT	8,077	2,422	1,041	3,354	5,346
WA	10,481	3,623	3,626	19,891	12,737

1890	Germany	Austria	Bohemia	Russia	Poland	Total Foreign
MN	116,995	5,168	9,655	7,233	7,503	467,356
ND	8,943	300	1,129	4,098	237	81,461
MT	5,609	939	98	719	16	43,096
WA	15,399	1,110	239	2,118	209	90,005
1900						
MN	117,007	8,872	11,147	5,907	9,985	505,318
ND	11,546	1,131	1,145	14,979	1,054	113,091
MT	7,162	3,575	177	394	213	67,067
WA	16,686	2,343	396	2,426	508	111,364[35]

An investigation of the Minnesota column for 1890 discloses that, as would be expected, most of the settlers came from the East North Central states. The second greatest number of migrants came from the North Atlantic region, and the third greatest from New England. By subtracting the number of Minnesota-born from the total for the West North Central states we find that migrants from that area ranked in fourth place.[36]

The statistics on foreign countries show only the place of birth and not the most recent place of residence before moving to the New Northwest. We are unable, therefore, to determine how many of these persons may have lived temporarily in Illinois, Wisconsin, or Iowa before moving on to Minnesota. It is evident, however, that Minnesota was getting the settlers whom the Northern Pacific considered the most desirable and on whom it worked the hardest. Germans made up the largest total, Norwegians the second largest, Swedes the third largest, and English ranked far down the list. These results coincide with the often-expressed opinions of Land Department officials concerning the desirability of immigrants of these nationalities.

A comparison between 1890 and 1900 reveals even more significant facts. It will be noted that the total numbers born in New England and the North Atlantic states declined, indicating that very few persons were coming from these sections during the later periods of migration. At the same time there was a marked increase in the number coming from the East North Central area and an even greater degree of increase in the number coming from the West North Central states, including Minnesota.

In 1900 Minnesota's population included 81,292 Wisconsin-born persons, 42,096 Iowa-born, and 36,112 Illinois-born. A reversal of the East-to-West migration trend is noted in the fact that there were 7,264 South Dakota-born, 9,094 North Dakota-born, 3,622 Nebraska-born, and 2,201 Kansas-born residents recorded in the Minnesota census total.[37]

While migration to Minnesota from the North Central states had increased markedly by 1900, that from Northern Europe had leveled off. Again, it is almost certain that, if the table indicated the place of most recent residence before migration to Minnesota, the foreign totals would be much less and the North Central totals would register even stronger gains.

Statistics for North Dakota lead to the same general conclusions. In 1890 the East North Central states had supplied more North Dakota residents than any other section of the United States. The West North Central states, excluding North Dakota, were second, and the North Atlantic area third. Norway led the foreign born, with Germany second and Sweden third.

RESULTS OF THE CAMPAIGNS   151

A comparison with 1900 shows that the West North Central states, again excluding North Dakota, had passed the East North Central district, with the other regions maintaining their same positions. Minnesota had become the leading state in supplying settlers to North Dakota. Wisconsin was second.[38] Germans, Swedes, and Norwegians all increased their totals slightly while Irish and English totals fell. Russians rose from 4,098 to 14,979, probably because of a movement of Russian-Germans to North Dakota lands in the early nineties.

The records for Montana show trends strikingly similar to those for North Dakota and Minnesota. In 1890 the East North Central states ranked first, the West North Central second, and the North Atlantic third. By 1900 the West North Central had advanced to first place, East North Central had dropped to second, and the North Atlantic held third. The West, excluding Montana, was fourth.

The 1900 figures record slight increases for Montana from all sections, probably because of the fact that Montana was a newer state than the others and its mining industry was attracting a greater variety of migrant types.

Irish, English, and Germans led the foreign-born in Montana, in that order. The reason for the difference in the nationalities of the leading immigrants between this state and Minnesota and North Dakota probably lies in the fact that agriculture has relatively less importance in Montana in the early history of the state.

The entire table bears out the conclusions expressed heretofore in this chapter. The early migration, when the Northern Pacific was concentrating on attracting land buyers from the North East sections of the United States, came from the East North Central, North Atlantic, and New England states. As the railroad shifted its policies and began to exert its promotional pressures on residents of the areas west of the Alleghenies, the Eastern migration slumped and the greatest numbers came from the regions immediately adjacent to the Northwestern states.

We already have evidence from Northern Pacific officials and students of the immigration movement that many of the foreign migrants also came to the Northwest from states in the North Central area.

All this would seem to indicate that the largest share of the migration into Minnesota and North Dakota came from the areas where Northern Pacific promotion was operating at its strongest.

There is one discordant note in the thesis advanced in this chapter, however. It is a curious fact that English migration is so small as to be hardly discernible when the railroad was seemingly exerting more effort on the United Kingdom than on any other part of Europe. In order to judge adequately the effectiveness of promotion in the United Kingdom, however, it is necessary to add the totals of foreign-born in the Northwest states who came from Ireland, Scotland, and Wales, as well as England. While this composite total does not measure up to the totals of Swedes, Norwegians, and Germans who migrated to the Northwest, it is far more impressive than the figures for the Central and Southern European countries. It is probably true, also, that because of the conflict that was taking place among Land Department officials in regard to the desirability of English migrants, agents in that country were not exerting as much effort in behalf of the company as were those on the continent.

Whatever may have been the situation in regard to England, it is certain that the Europeans whom the Northern Pacific considered the best prospects for land ownership were the ones who came to the United States in the greatest numbers. The Land Department wanted Germans, Norwegians, and Swedes on its lands. While more agents may have been placed in the United Kingdom, officials constantly expressed the opinion that it was the Germans and Scandinavians they wanted. Significantly, Germany, Sweden, and Norway supplied the greatest number of migrants. French were discouraged from coming to the Northwest. There were not enough French migrants to merit a position on the foregoing table.

Conclusions on the Effectiveness of Northern Pacific Promotion

At the time when the Northern Pacific began to organize its promotional campaign in 1870 its task was not as great as it might seem. There was a pronounced dissatisfaction with conditions in the older states of the United States and in Europe. There was a distinct desire for ownership of land, which the Land Department could utilize in its promotional efforts.

The task of the railroad was not to create a demand for land. The demand for land already existed. Its task was to increase the dissatisfaction in the older areas by pointing out that cheap land was available in the Northern Pacific area. That being done, its next task was to direct the flow of migration to the Northwest where it had cheap land to sell.

That the organization of the promotion and the contents of the promotional material were the products of skillful public relations men has already been proved. That the entire promotional effort was successful in directing the flow of migration to the New Northwest is evident from the material presented in this chapter.

The Land Department set out in 1870 with three objectives: to sell bonds, to sell lands, and to fill up the country adjacent to the line of the railroad. The driving of the golden spike in Montana in 1883 is evidence of the successful fulfillment of the first goal. The fact that only a little more than 15,000,000 acres of the total 46,000,000-acre grant remained to be sold in 1903 is proof of the attainment of the second. The growth of population of counties and towns along the railroad's line between 1870 and 1910 is ample proof that the third was realized.

The effectiveness of Northern Pacific promotion in the attainment of these objectives can be questioned on only one score, that other factors which brought about the American frontier movement might have achieved the same results without the mobilization of the railroad's promotional machinery. That possibility has been discounted by evidence that the Land Department was not only able to sell its lands and to people the Northwest but that it was also able to direct the flow of migration as it desired. It is probably more accurate to assume conversely that the Northern Pacific's promotional efforts were among the many factors that motivated the frontier movement.

It is quite probable that the Northwest would ultimately have been settled even without any activity on the part of the Northern Pacific, but it is certain on the basis of the evidence which has been presented in the foregoing pages of this thesis, that the railroad hastened the flow of migration and directed that flow to conform to its own desires.

With these facts established, the effectiveness of the railroad's promotional efforts is indisputable. In the activities of the Land Department and the Bureau of Immigration of the Northern Pacific Railroad we have a valid example of successful commercial propaganda and promotion carried on in the nineteenth century.

Appendix

I. Northern Pacific Promotional Policy

A. Some examples of statements of company officials that illustrate early plans for the Bureau of Emigration are explained in the following excerpt from "Northern Pacific Railroad, Its Route, Resources, Progress and Business":

The Northern Pacific Railroad Company is organizing an emigration bureau in connection with its Land Department... In carrying out the details of this scheme the company will aim: 1, to employ as its land and emigration agents, at home and abroad, only men of the highest character; 2, to permit no representations to be made by its authority which the facts will not fully warrant; 3, to promote, as far as possible, the formation of colonies, both in Europe and in the older states of our own country, so that neighbors in the old home may be neighbors in the new; so that friends may settle near each other, form communities, establish schools, and in short, avoid most of the traditional hardships which have usually attended pioneer life; 4, to exercise over emigrants, en route, whatever supervision their best interests require, seeing to it that transportation charges are the lowest obtainable, that accommodations on ships and cars are comfortable, that their treatment is kind, their protection against compulsion, fraud and abuse of all sorts, complete, and that every dollar of unnecessary expenditure on the way is avoided, and the emigrant enabled to husband his means for the work of starting a homestead... by seeing to it that all the elements of a sound civilization, including education, church, and mail facilities, keep pace with the progress of the road and the growth of the communities.[1]

B. A proposal for a counter propaganda with positive suggestion is made in the following letter:

> I am satisfied that our company has got to adopt unusual measures in order to secure the settlement of its land as rapidly as the best interests of the enterprise demand. Blink at it as we may, the question of climate is a sockdolager, and this obstacle, it seems to me, can only be overcome by convincing people that, in spite of the long and cold winters, they can live comfortable and make money on the line of the Northern Pacific road, east of the Missouri River. Newspaper advertising is valuable, to a certain extent, but unless that is supplemented by more tangible things, I fear we shall, in a great degree, shake the tree without getting any fruit...
>
> Spend a few thousand dollars the coming season in breaking from forty to a hundred acres of sod on a number of quarter sections, judiciously distributed along the line so as to accommodate the tastes of a variety of purchasers. I would do this as an experiment, and if it proved successful, the company could then adopt the policy for the future on a larger scale. My belief is that during next winter and the spring of 1874 every one of these quarter sections on which breaking has been done would be snapped up by a desirable class of settlers, men possessed of some means and desirous of raising a crop without waiting a year on expense for the sod to rot. This plan would appeal to the sensible and cautious business man...
>
> Major Hibbard and I are just now endeavoring to secure the names of twenty to thirty stock and bond holders of the company who will consent to purchase from one to two sections of land each and break up from 300 to 500 acres this year. I have already got my part of the list well started and have not a doubt that it can be put through. This would give a great impetus to farming matters along the line of the road in Minnesota, furnish needed employment to poor settlers with teams, and would give a generally lively appearance to things up there which would greatly

APPENDIX

encourage settlement and strengthen the backbones of the pioneers who are already on the ground.[2]

C. The newspaper advertising and publicity policies for the 1897-1902 period of Northern Pacific promotion are outlined in the following letter:

Mr. George F. Spinney
President

Dear Sir:

I beg to submit the following in response to your favor of the 8th inst.

Prior to January 1, 1897, the date I took charge of this office, the advertising was conducted in the Land Commissioner's office and the datum pertaining to the contracts made in the year 1896 has been gathered from records kept at that time.

I find that during the year 1896 contracts were made with 36 newspapers, 19 of which were in Minnesota and 16 in Iowa. Two were partly payable in transportation. Several of the contracts were based on cash or transportation but the publishers demanded cash except in the two instances mentioned, where both cash and transportation were accepted. Divided, with reference to the fiscal year, it is found that 19 contracts with Minnesota papers and 9 with Iowa papers were made prior to June 30, 1896. Between that date and December 31, seven contracts were made with Iowa papers.

Between the first of January and June 30, 1897, contracts were made with 171 newspapers distributed as follows: Iowa 84, Minnesota 47, South Dakota 16, Nebraska 20, Wisconsin 3, Illinois 1. Of those 145 were payable in cash; 16 in transportation and cash, and 10 in transportation, as follows: [table omitted]

In addition to the contracts described two special ones were made as follows: write up of Aitkin county in Des Moines *Homestead*, $31 in cash; advertisement in German Evangelical report, $19.10 in transportation.

As you will observe the proportion of the contracts based on transportation is very small. This is due partly to the fact that publishers so remote from the line of our road either prefer cash or more transportation than I feel that they earn. It is also due to the inhibition placed upon us by the Interstate Commerce law and the complications that, as I am assured, would ensue to the traffic arrangements. Of this latter point I am not competent to judge.

When I took charge last January and mapped out my advertising plans it was understood that payment might be made in either cash or transportation, and with that in view I prepared a circular letter which was sent to hundreds of publishers soliciting propositions for a double column six inch display advertisement... The fee transportation contracts above described were made in good faith but on the first demand for payment by the publisher it was discovered – or a least remembered – that the Interstate Commerce law stood in the way. The publisher had performed, or was performing, his part of the contract and was entitled to the transportation. I therefore sought to furnish it through the passenger department, but after repeated efforts I found that it was impracticable or else beyond the power of the general passenger agent to assure my obligations.

I desire to state, however, that the general passenger agent very kindly placed at my use some 30 or 40 papers with which he had contracts and even made contracts at my request with two or three papers. But the demand upon his space created by the Klondyke craze had made it necessary for him to use all of his papers so that at present I have but one with which he has a contract.

You ask if any reason suggests itself why transportation contracts cannot be substituted for cash contracts. To this I beg to say that if a plan could be devised whereby this office could have the privilege of extending to publishers a proposition to pay in transportation, I feel sure that much of our new necessary outlay of cash for advertising could be curtailed. I presume that transportation would be liberally bestowed so as to offer the public an opportunity to enjoy a trip to the Yellowstone Park or even the Coast. The contracts could be approximately enlarged or extended, at least in point of time. There is nothing that represents as little value to this company, in discharge of an obligation, as transportation of an occasional passenger over its road; and while the average publisher prefers cash to a limited amount of transportation, he might cheerfully avail himself of the opportunity to exchange advertising space for a pleasurable trip that would otherwise be beyond his means or expectations. There is another point in this connection worthy of consideration; every publisher favored with transportation would undoubtedly record in the columns of his paper the experiences of this trip thereby benefitting the passenger as well as the land department.

This department has millions of acres that it is daily making an effort to sell. My experience teaches me that the best known method of communicating the fact to the proper public is through the country newspapers. If, therefore, we could combine transportation with cash, or use it largely instead, in making contracts we could surely employ many more papers and thereby extend the mediums of giving publicity to the fact that we have lands for sale. I therefore say that if it can be brought about without interfering with traffic arrangements or controverting the Interstate Commerce law, the use of transportation in payment of advertising would be of most substantial benefit to the department.

I estimate that it will require not less than $2,500 to defray the cost of advertising necessary to be done to June 30, 1898. This includes the advertising already done or contracted for since last June.

I have had 35,000 copies of the *Homeseeker* printed. The first lot of 5,000 cost about $25 but this was due to the fact that the composition was done without expense to the company. Subsequent issues have cost $34 for cost of 10,000 copies. It was our intention to issue the *Homeseeker* monthly but it was found desirable to limit the production of new copies to four editions per year. Therefore the issues referred to have been reprints from electros. It is estimated from figures furnished by local printers that it will cost about $55 or $60 per 10,000 copies when new matter will be required to be set.

The Aitkin county pamphlet cost $134.38 including the engravings, for the first 10,000 copies and $75 for the subsequent issue, from electros, of 10,000 copies. Only 20,000 copies have been issued.

In answer to your inquiry I beg to say that there is no correspondence in my files bearing on the subject of the use of transportation in payment of advertising contracts except the various requests that I have made of the general passenger agent to either make contracts for me or to use the space in papers with which he already had contracts. Most, if not all my intercourse with the Passenger Department on the subject has been personal and not through correspondence.

F. W. Wilsey[3]

D. Cooperation between the Land Department and its sales solicitors is illustrated by the following circular sent to all solicitors in 1898:

Dear sir:

In organizing the work for 1898 it is my desire to aid sales solicitors in every way possible and to that end propose to do a liberal amount of advertising in your territory. For the purpose of accomplishing this work in a systematic and satisfactory manner I will be pleased to have you furnish me, at your earliest convenience, the information requested below.

What papers (give name of each and place where published) in your territory will, in your judgment, do you, as sales solicitor, and the company, the most good?

Which do you believe will bring the most returns—a standing display advertisement or frequent, liberal reading notices, or both?

Where, and whom, have you appointed sub-solicitors? Give names and addresses in full that they may be inserted in advertisements in the respective districts.

You are in a position to secure considerable gratuitous advertising in the way of notices from time to time in the various papers for you can assure the publishers that it is through your recommendation that the advertising was placed with them.

As I am desirous of starting the ads as soon as possible I will appreciate an early response, together with any suggestions on the advertising that you may think will be mutual benefit.

                          Yours truly,
                          F. W. Wilsey[4]

II. Some samples of advertisements placed by the Northern Pacific's Land Department:

A. Advertisement sent to fifty-two Iowa newspapers March 16, 1897, for insertion up to April 7, 1897:

NOW IS YOUR OPPORTUNITY TO MOVE TO CENTRAL NORTH DAKOTA

The Northern Pacific Railroad Company will run special excursion trains of free colonist cars from St. Paul on April 1 and April 7.

                St. Paul to Carrington, $2.50

Twenty or more persons purchasing tickets at the same time and place can secure a party rate of 2 cents per mile to St. Paul.

Our colonist sleepers will be left on the track at Carrington until such time as those who go up in them have an opportunity to provide themselves with temporary or permanent accommodations.

Be sure to reach St. Paul in time to leave at 8 p.m. on April 1 or April 7 over the Northern Pacific.

For full particulars as well as for application blanks for tickets and space in the colonist sleepers, write to

Wm. H. Phipps	C. W. Mott
Land Commissioner	General Emigration Agent

With this advertisement was the following reading notice:

When the Northern Pacific runs an excursion it does it in great shape. Besides reducing rates on its North Dakota excursion to the lowest notch, it offers the advantage of free colonist sleepers which will be left on the track for the benefit of its patrons until they can make other arrangements, thus saving them all the expenses for lodging while they are hunting locations. We predict that it will have plenty of passengers on this occasion.[5]

B. The following advertisement was sent to the Banning Advertising Company of St. Paul to be inserted seven times in Chicago *Markets:*

$1.00 Per Acre

IMPORTANT TO STOCK GROWERS

Western North Dakota and Eastern Montana possess the best ranges for sheep and cattle in the United States.

RICHEST GRASSES – PLENTY OF WATER

The Northern Pacific Railway Company has millions of acres that it is offering at from $1.00 to $2.50 per acre on easy terms.

Correspondence solicited. For full particulars address

| Wm. H. Phipps | F. W. Wilsey |
| Land Commissioner | Eastern Land Agent[6] |

C. The following advertisement was sent to the *Age* at Aikin, Minnesota, May 19, 1898, to be run until further notice:

NORTHERN PACIFIC LANDS

Mr. B. M. Hungerford has been appointed sales solicitor for the Northern Pacific Railway Company to succeed the sales of the company in this city. Mr. Hungerford is sup-

APPENDIX 163

plied with maps of all the company lands in Aitkin county and is prepared to furnish prices and full information respecting terms of sale, etc. All applications to purchase should be made to him.

F. W. Wilsey[7]

D. Advertisement sent to Dodge County, Minnesota, *Fair Book*, September 13, 1897:

TAKE IN THE FAIR

And then if you can spare the time from your harvesting avail yourself of the opportunity presented by inspecting the fine farming lands offered for sale by the Northern Pacific Railway Company at reduced rates.

THESE LANDS

Are situated in the central and western part of Minnesota and are among the choicest in the state. They have fine soil, splendid water, and are close to railroad stations, churches, schools and the best markets of the West.

LOW PRICES

And 10 years time in which to pay for the land are the inducements held out to actual settlers. The lands range from $2.50 to $8.00 per acre and no place in the United States offers so much encouragement to the man of limited means as the section of the Northwest traversed by the Northern Pacific Railway Company.

These lands are diversified in character and embrace timbered lands, partly timbered, prairie, and natural meadows with endless numbers of beautiful lakes and streams.

HOMESEEKER EXCURSION

Tickets good for 21 days, with stop-over privileges west of Staples, Minnesota, will be on sale September 21 for one fare plus $2.00. No such opportunity is elsewhere offered for acquiring a home where there are good lands at low prices and on long time in communities that are settled by a thrifty and industrious people.

The following reading notice was sent with the advertisement:

The Northern Pacific Railway Company is anxious to secure actual settlers and with that end in view, has placed a low price on its lands and sells them on a long time. It is directing special attention to its lands in Aitkin, Crow Wing, Cass, Mille Lacs, and Itasca counties, where one can secure a home almost at his own price and his own terms. These counties abound in beautiful lakes, belts of forests, prairies, and natural meadows.[8]

E. Advertisement submitted for general distribution April 1, 1897:

$3.00 PER ACRE

And 10 years in which to pay for it. Of course, you can't buy improved farms for that, but the Northern Pacific Railway Company has hundreds of thousands of acres of

FINE FARMING LANDS

in Central Minnesota, which it is selling to actual settlers at from $2.50 to $3.50 per acre, on 10 years time.
- - - - - - - - - - - -
The prices are cheap, but lands are good.
- - - - - - - - - - - -
Fine soil, splendid water, best of markets, and near churches, schools, and railroad stations.
- - - - - - - - - - - -
The famous Red River Valley lands at $4 to $8 per acre.
- - - - - - - - - - - -
Buy a Home! Stop Paying Rent! Be Independent!
For maps, prices and terms of sale, call upon
F. W. Wilsey
Eastern Land Agent

APPENDIX 165

The reading notice to accompany this advertisement was as follows:

Three dollars per acre is pretty cheap for good lands, and yet the Northern Pacific Railway company has hundreds of thousands of acres in Central Minnesota that it is selling to actual settlers at this price, and even lower, on ten years time. The lands are not sandy wastes or rocky hills but first class farming lands having good soil, fine water, and plenty of timber, in counties that abound in beautiful lakes, belts of forests, prairies and natural meadows. See the company's ad in another column.[9]

F. Advertisement submitted for general distribution during 1897:

IF YOU ARE GOING TO MOVE
WHY NOT MAKE A
CAREFUL SELECTION

WHY DON'T YOU STOP PAYING RENT?

The yearly payment on land bought from the Land Department of the Northern Pacific Railway Company would be less than your present rent, and in 10 years the farm would be yours.

WHY DON'T YOU MOVE WHERE YOU CAN GET LOW PRICED LAND FOR YOUR CHILDREN?

You may own your own farm, but you cannot afford to settle your boys and girls near you at the price you would have to pay in your present locality.

For maps, prices, and terms of sale, write to
F. W. Wilsey
Eastern Land Agent[10]

G. Advertisement submitted for general distribution September 2, 1897:

Do You Want A
FARM AND HOME?

Where you can engage in diversified farming and not be dependent on any one particular crop,
Where the climate is free from malaria and perfectly healthy,
Where there is sure and dependable rainfall,
Where the soil does not need to be fertilized,
Where your children will have the best of schools,
Where your family can enjoy church privileges,
Where stock raising is assured by good pastures covered with nutritious grasses and watered by spring fed streams and lakes,
Where fuel can be had for the labor of cutting it,
Where you will have a ready market for your stock, field, garden, and dairy products,
Where you can buy land at from $3.00 to $8.00 per acre, on ten years time at 6 per cent interest?
If you do
The Northern Pacific Railway Company
Has Lands in

Central Minnesota
That Will Make Both Farms and Homes

The reading notice to accompany the advertisement was as follows:

The excellent crops this year have given an impetus to farming that has not been experienced for some time. Central Minnesota has felt the effects as much or more than any other section of the Northwest and hundreds of farmers have taken advantage of the opportunity to secure some of the low priced but splendid lands being offered for sale by the Northern Pacific Railway Company. See ad in another column.[11]

APPENDIX 167

H. Advertisement printed in the Orange City (Iowa) *Herald* and the Lake Mills (Iowa) *Graphic* August 11, 1898:

The small fruits of Minnesota are noted for their size, firmness and delicious flavor and in no part of the commonwealth are they produced in greater abundance and excellence than in the central part of the state.

Strawberries, raspberries, blackberries, currants, gooseberries, and many kinds of apples are sure crops and always command the highest prices.

But fruit is not the only product of this prolific section. Splendid harvests are annually yielded of wheat, corn, oats, rye, buckwheat, barley, etc. and the hay and root crops are famous.

The best markets of the West, excellent railroad facilities, the telegraph, fine stores, splendid schools and churches, pure water, rich soil, and the healthiest climate on earth are a few of the conditions that combine to make Central Minnesota the ideal spot for diversified farming.

The Northern Pacific Railway Company has hundreds of thousands of acres in that favored section that it is offering to actual settlers at from $2.00 to $4.00 per acre on 10 years time at 6 per cent interest.

Maps and full particulars sent free by
F. W. Wilsey[12]

I. Copy for Advertisement for the Bowling Green (Missouri) *Times* handed to a Mr. Pfaff of that publication August 9, 1898:

Another
BIG WHEAT CROP

The famous wheat producing lands of North Dakota have placed one more enormous crop of Number 1 hard to their credit, and every acre in the state is consequently enhanced in value.

These lands are in well settled communities with railroads, telegraph, schools, churches, and other facilities and privileges and are speedily being settled by the best of people.

The Northern Pacific Railway Company has hundreds of thousands of acres of land in that favored section that it is offering to actual settlers at from $2.00 to $4.00 per acre on 10 years time at 6 per cent interest.

Maps and full particulars sent free by
F. W. Wilsey[13]

J. Advertisement submitted to Blue Earth (Minnesota) *Post* August 23, 1897:

LAND IS CHEAP

In Central Minnesota—the Garden Spot of America—but it is good and every man who is thinking of building a home for himself and family should pay that section a visit before buying.

A COUNTRY HOME

Is admitted by everyone to be the best place to live and raise your children. In this section of the state land is so high priced that the man of limited means cannot afford to buy a farm. It is not so in Central Minnesota. The Northern Pacific Railway Company has hundreds of thousands of acres of fine farming lands that it is selling at from $2.50 to $4.00 per acre on ten years time at 6 per cent interest.

Fine soil, splendid water, best markets, and near churches, schools, and railroad stations.

Famous Red River Valley lands at from $4.00 to $8.00 per acre.

For maps, prices, and terms of sale call upon F. P. Barnes, local sales solicitor, Blue Earth City, or write to
F. W. Wilsey[14]

K. Two column, full length advertisement published in the St. Paul *Pioneer Press* during 1898:

A LAND OF

    Prosperous Homes
Is found in Minnesota and North Dakota which are in the belt of progress stretching westward through these two great states.

IT IS HERE
That are found the most prosperous farming regions of the Northwest. It is here that thousands have come and found a land which has richly rewarded their efforts with comfortable homes, fields of grain yearly bearing an increase of from 20 to 60 fold and where cattle, horses, sheep, and swine come to their

HIGHEST PERFECTION
IN
MINNESOTA

    The Northern Pacific Railway Company has 500,000 acres of meadow, prairie, and timber lands for sale, principally in the counties of Wadena, Todd, Cass, Crow Wing, and Morrison. The soil is a rich, black loam which produces abundantly of all crops...

NORTH DAKOTA

    has received thousands of homeseekers this year and there is room for thousands more. Its prairies, black with the richest soil, annually raises crops of tens of millions of bushels of wheat, oats, rye, flax, barley, and other grains. While the yearly gain in cattle, sheep, horses, and swine is so rapid that it is rapidly becoming one of the great livestock states in the union. We have nearly 2,000,000 acres of land in the counties of Stutsman, Dawson, McLean, Burleigh, Emmons, McIntosh, Logan, and other counties to choose from... [15]

L. Advertisement printed in *Good Health* magazine August 3, 1898:

GOOD HEALTH

Is only to be found in regions favored with pure water and the purest air. Crops will grow and people exist after a fashion in malaria infested sections but real happiness and prosperity only join hands where the climate and water combine to bring nature's greatest blessing – Good Health . . .

TO THE FARMER

Who seeks a location where annually assured abundant harvest are an adjunct to the best and most beautiful climate on earth – who really desires to enjoy good health without money and without price – Central Minnesota offers a most inviting field for investigation.

IN CENTRAL MINNESOTA

The bracing atmosphere, the purest water – and lots of it in spring fed streams and lakes – a most productive soil, hardwood timber for buildings, fences, and fuel, the best markets in the West – St. Paul, Minneapolis, Duluth, and Superior – without easy access, all combine to make it the ideal location for the husbandman whether he be rich or of moderate means.

The Northern Pacific Railway Company has hundreds of thousands of acres of land in that favored section that it is offering to actual settlers at from $2.00 to $4.00 per acre on 10 years time at 6 per cent interest.

Maps and full particulars sent free by
F. W. Wilsey[16]

M. One column by two inch advertisement run for six months, beginning in December 1881, in the weekly editions of the best papers in Boston, Portland, Rochester, New York City, Philadelphia, Cleveland, Cincinnati, Columbus, Indianapolis, Detroit, and the best papers printing this advertisement was 73 and the cost to the company, $7,000:

APPENDIX 171

Best Wheat
Grazing Lands are Found On

The NORTHERN PACIFIC

In Minnesota, Dakota, and Montana

BIG CROP AGAIN IN 1881

Low prices, long time, rebate for improvements,
Reduced fare and freight to settlers.

For full information address
R. M. Newport, General Land
Agent
St. Paul, Minn.

Mention this paper.[17]

III. Samples of reading notices, in addition to those quoted in the preceding section, which accompanied paid advertisements:[18]

A. Five reading notices, typewritten on one sheet, which were evidently prepared at one time and held for submitting with advertisements:

1. In another column will be found an interesting suggestion from the Northern Pacific Railway Company Land Department. A spirit of unrest seems to be influencing the destiny of many a man just now, and if he cannot be satisfied with his present location he should not at least be led astray by distorted pictures of unhealthful localities. The great Northwest offers wonderful opportunities and abundant health and those who are seeking a new home would do well to read the advertisement.

2. There are few sections of the country that possess such resources and such diversified opportunities for the average man as that traversed by the Northern Pacific Railway. The Land Department has an advertisement in

another column, calling attention to the company's enormous grant and those who may think of seeking a new location or want to invest in cheap lands will be repaid by reading it.

3. The Northern Pacific Land Department has an advertisement in another column calling attention to the fertile and low priced lands which it is offering to settlers on favorable terms. Those who are seeking to find new locations will do well to inquire into the opportunities offered by this company.

4. In another column will be found an advertisement of the Northern Pacific Railway Land Department, calling attention to its immense and diversified land grant. Probably no section of the country is so resourceful or offers so many advantages to the poor man as that through which the Northern Pacific runs.

5. In an advertisement in another column the Northern Pacific Railway Land Department directs attention to the choice and low priced lands it is offering for sale. The company's grant embraces about 36,000,000 acres, and of course, is so diversified in character that it includes prairie, timber grazing, and forest lands.[19]

B. Reading notice sent to the *Park Region* at Frazee, Minnesota, to be run for the duration of the advertising contract with that newspaper:

IT IS A FACT

That less than 15 years ago lands in Southern Minnesota were selling at from $7.00 to $8.00 per acre. Today those same lands are worth, and sell readily at, from $20 to $40 per acre. What has been true in that section of the state is just as sure to be true in the Park Region and there will never be a time when the beautiful lands around Frazee can be bought so cheaply as at present. The Northern Pacific is offering its choice lands at low prices and on ten years time to actual settlers. Write to F. W. Wilsey, Eastern Land Agent at St. Paul, Minnesota, for full particulars.[20]

APPENDIX 173

IV. Some excerpts from news publicity stories submitted to or printed in newspapers during the 1897 to 1902 period of promotional activity:

A. Story in Grand Forks (North Dakota) *Herald,* January 2, 1898:

Carrington, – William H. Phipps, the Land Commissioner of the Northern Pacific Railway Company, about three years ago inaugurated a movement looking toward the settlement of these lands by new people who were being crowded out of the older states by high prices of land and high rents. Mr. Phipps wisely decided to place a very low valuation on these lands and to give terms of payment that cannot be equaled anywhere for easiness...

... the man who buys on 10 years time buys just as cheaply as does the man who pays all cash, thus giving the poor man an equal show with the man who is in a better condition in life. Every care has been taken to keep these lands out of the hands of speculators and to sell only to legitimate tillers of the soil.

When this movement was started men were sent into the older states to work up the immigration and Mr. F. M. Vangergent was placed at Carrington... Since the month of April (1897) there have been 41,000 acres of land disposed of to actual settlers in Foster, Wells, and Eddy counties and all sold to settlers who will go on to the lands in the spring and begin improvements... People have come here during the summer from almost every state in the Union...

There has been a large number of Dunkards settled in the three counties who make a most desirable class of settlers. A large Dunkard church has been erected in Carrington where Elder D. H. Miccum holds regular services each Sabbath. Elder Miccum was formerly from Flora, Indiana... Carrington has almost doubled in size in the past two years, while thousands of acres of wild land has been placed under a good state of cultivation. Iowa is furnishing the largest portion of new settlers... [21]

B. Story sent to the Primghar (Iowa) *Democrat* August 5, 1898:

... There are forests so vast that man might spend a lifetime grubbing and still not build a farm, and there are others that offer but little opposition to the cultivation of the soil. It is of these latter that this article speaks. These are not timbered lands in the strict use of the term for the growth is so light that it may easily and cheaply be removed, yet the timber is sufficiently large to be of value for building purposes, fences, and fuel.

... Counties of Becker, Ottertail, Wadena, Hubbard, Cass, Crow Wing, Morrison, and Aitkin.

These lands are especially adapted to diversified farming on a small scale...

... The soil, according to Prof. W. M. Hays of the Minnesota State Experimental Farm, is among the first that the homeseeker should select. It will absorb much water and is open enough to let excess drain out, yet it will, by capillary power, hold a large supply to be used by plants in times of draught... It is rarely... too dry for crops.

... There is no place in the Northwest where more bountiful results are annually obtained. All kinds of grasses grow wild, luxuriously, and wherever seed is sown crops of astounding proportions are the result.

One of the chief beauties of this part of Minnesota is the numerous lakes and streams. The lakes number several hundred and range up in size from one-half an acre. They all contain the purest water and are plentifully stocked with fish of all kinds.

The climate is the finest on earth. The residents of Central Minnesota have no fears of the rigors of winter for they know from experience that they are far preferable to the same season "back east" or farther north. In summer cool nights follow the warmest days and the absolute absence of malaria makes good health an assured fact.

The Northern Pacific Railway Company has several hundred thousand acres in this region which it is offering to actual settlers at from $2.00 to $4.00 per acre, one-tenth

APPENDIX   175

down payment, ten years to pay, at only six per cent interest.²²

C. Letter from W. E. Stephens of Churdan, Iowa, printed in the Churdan *Reporter* September 24, 1897:

I have traveled through a great many states and investigated their surroundings, and in all my travels, never have I seen as contented, well dressed, sociable, intelligent, and prosperous people as I found in North Dakota... The railroad has placed Mr. F. M. Vanbergen at Carrington, North Dakota, to make sale of these lands a gentleman in every respect, a man with whom I would place implicit confidence.

... I must say that it is the pleasantest outing that I have ever taken. We had a tourist car, slept and ate on the car all the time we were gone. When we arrived at Carrington Mr. Vanbergen had arranged to have four double seated buggies to drive us in the country at the expense of the railroad company. We drove from 25 to 50 miles a day, and looked at the most beautiful prairie country I have ever laid my eyes on. The soil is black loam with yellowish clay sub-soil, which makes it the garden spot of the world for wheat, oats, rye, flax, barley, and vegetables. Wheat will average, I would think, from 15 to 20 bushels per acre, and the farmers are getting 82 cents per bushel... They have plenty of good water, as good as I ever drank, and they get it at from 18 to 30 feet.

... A great many people who had moved from Iowa, Kansas, Indiana, Illinois, and other states... told me that they would rather winter in North Dakota than in any of these other states.

W. E. Stephens

Reading notice accompanying foregoing letter:

Elsewhere in today's *Reporter* may be found a very interesting letter from the pen of W. E. Stephens, our popular townsman and enterprising general merchant. Mr. Stephens returned last Friday from a visit to North Dakota. He was much delighted and very favorably impressed with the country.[23]

V. A sample of a monthly expense account of a land solicitor:

J. VanderLas January, 1901
Salary – $90.00
Expenses

January	1 – Post Office Box Rent at Dickinson	.50
	9 – Hotel bill at Taylor	1.50
	10 – Hotel bill at Richardton	2.50
	11 – Livery at New Salem	3.00
	12 – Hotel at New Salem	2.00
	15 – Hotel at Taylor	1.50
	17 – Richardton	2.50
	19 – Three meals in county Hotel	1.00
	and livery at Hebron	11.50
	23 – Livery at Richardton	2.50
	24 – Hotel at Richardton	3.00
	25 – Hotel at Hebron	6.00
	26 – Livery at New Salem	3.00
	Hotel at New Salem	2.50
	28 – Office rent for December, 1900	9.00
	30 – Hotel at Taylor	2.00
	31 – Hotel at Richardton	7.00
	Use of own team on January 8, 9, 15, 16, and 27; 5 days at $2.00	10.00
	Total	70.50[24]

Notes and References

Foreword

1. Findings of some of these case studies are described in Pringle, Henry F., "Mass Psychologist," *American Mercury*, 19:155 (February, 1930); Flynn, John T., "Edward L. Bernays: The Science of Ballyhoo," *Atlantic Monthly*, 149:562 (May, 1932); Bent, Silas, "Ivy Lee, Minnesinger to Millions," *New Republic*, 60:369 (November 20, 1929); Bernays, Edward L., "Scope and Functions," pp. 1-57, *Crystallizing Public Opinion*, New York, 1923; Lee, Ivy, "The Art of Publicity," in Samuel Crowther, editor, *Book of Business*, 4:78.

2. Public relations activities of business institutions are described in Batchelor, Bronson, *Profitable Public Relations*, New York, 1938; Walker, S. H., and Sklar, Paul, *Business Finds Its Voice*, New York, 1928; and Wright, Milton, *Public Relations for Business*, New York, 1938.

3. "The Colonization Work of the Northern Pacific Railroad," *Mississippi Valley Historical Review*, 13:311 (September, 1926); "Promotion of Immigration to the Pacific Northwest," *Mississippi Valley Historical Review*, 15:183 (September, 1928); and *Henry Villard and the Railways of the Northwest*, New Haven, 1930.

4. *Railroads and the Colonization of Minnesota, 1862-1880.* This thesis was submitted in May, 1927.

Chapter I

1. Eugene V. Smalley, *History of the Northern Pacific Railroad*, New York, 1883, 116.
2. *Ibid.*, 117.
3. "Northern Pacific Railroad, Its Route, Resources, Progress, and Business," Number 37, in the *Northern Pacific*

Railroad Pamphlets, II, 4. This volume may be found in the Minnesota Historical Library in St. Paul.

4. *Annual Report of the President of the Board of Directors*, 1892, 50.

5. Smalley, "The Story of the Northern Pacific," *Northwest*, October, 1892, 8.

6. Robert E. Riegel, *The Story of the Western Railroads*, New York, 1926, 131.

7. Cooke to Billings, December 23, 1872, *Letters, Jay Cooke & Co.*, I.

8. Smalley, *History of the Northern Pacific Railroad*, 164.

9. *Ibid.*

10. *Ibid.*, 171. These bonds received the name "7-30" from the fact that the interest to be paid on them was to be 7.30 per cent.

11. *Ibid.*

12. Barney to Nettleton, September 25, 1872, No. 94, in *Nettleton Letters*, II. All of the volumes and boxes of letters to which reference is made in this thesis are located in the archives of the Northern Pacific Railway Company in St. Paul. The boxes are stuffed with both originals and duplicates, arranged in no particular order. The books are bound volumes of duplicates, arranged in chronological order. The writer saw every volume and every box to which reference is made.

13. For a complete discussion of railroad building in the Western states, see Riegel, *op. cit.*

14. Early railroad building in Minnesota, which includes the construction of feeder lines and extensions into South Dakota, is adequately described in Harold Fern Peterson, *Railroads and the Settlement of Minnesota* (Master's Thesis), 21 to 28. Copies of this thesis are available both in the University of Minnesota library and library of the Minnesota Historical Society.

15. For the exact population of this area and its minor political divisions, see Tables in Chapter VIII.

16. Riegel, *op. cit.*, 283.

17. See Chapter VIII, page 145. Carlton Qualey, "Pioneer Norwegian Settlement in North Dakota," *North Dakota Historical Quarterly*, 12:247 (October, 1930), includes a detailed

NOTES AND REFERENCES 179

discussion of the routes followed by the Norwegians, many of whom stopped in New York, Illinois, Wisconsin, northern Iowa, Minnesota, and Dakota. The statement is repeatedly made in Northern Pacific correspondence that the railroad much preferred migrants who had already been through a frontier experience to those who would come directly from Europe to the Northern Pacific lands. They often further explained that fully nine-tenths of their settlers came from other sections of the United States.

18. Stephenson, *A History of American Immigration*, Boston, 1926, 11.

19. *Ibid.*, 29.

20. *Ibid.*, 31.

21. For a complete discussion of the frontier movement in American history, see Paxson, *History of the American Frontier*, or a number of other works by Paxson or Frederick Jackson Turner.

22. Harold E. Briggs, "The Great Dakota Boom, 1879 to 1886," *North Dakota Historical Quarterly* 4:80 (January, 1930).

23. An excellent account of the correlation between state and railroad agencies may be found on page 29 of Harold Peterson's thesis, *Railroads and the Settlement of Minnesota*. For an earlier period see Livia Appel and Theodore C. Blegen, "Official Encouragement to Minnesota During the Territorial Period," in *Minnesota History Bulletin*, 5:167-203 (August, 1923). The work of the Bureau of Immigration of Dakota Territory is discussed briefly in Carleton Qualey, "Pioneer Norwegian Settlement in North Dakota," in *North Dakota Historical Quarterly*, 5:14-38, (October, 1930).

24. For a more detailed account of Mattson's activities see Hans Mattson, *Reminiscences of an Emigrant*.

25. Stephenson, *op. cit.*, 140.

26. *Ibid.* For a discussion of the use of this publication by the Northern Pacific as a promotional medium, see page 91.

Chapter II

1. Excellent accounts of the early organization of the Land Committee and the Bureau of Immigration may be found in

James B. Hedges, "The Colonization Work of the Northern Pacific Railroad," in *Mississippi Valley Historical Review*, 13:309 et ff. (December, 1926), and in Harold Peterson's thesis, which has been cited previously, on p. 22 et ff. An account of activities which date back to 1866 may be found in W. Milnor Roberts, *Special Report of a Reconnaissance of the Route for the Northern Pacific Railroad Between Lake Superior and Puget Sound, 1869*. This report is No. 9 in *Northern Pacific Railroad Pamphlets*, II, in the Minnesota Historical Library.

2. A detailed statement of this plan may be found in the Northern Pacific archives, Letter of John S. Loomis to Fredrick Billings, Chairman of the Land Committee, February 20, 1871, *Recommending a Plan for the Organization and Operation of the Land Department, Including Plans for Promoting Migration and Land Settlement*. The essence of the letter is found in both the works of Mr. Peterson and Dr. Hedges, cited previously.

3. "Northern Pacific Railroad, Its Route, Resources, Progress, and Business," Number 37 in *Northern Pacific Railroad Pamphlets*, II, 14.

4. Hedges, *op. cit.*, 319.

5. *Ibid.*, 321.

6. *Ibid.*

7. Peterson, *op. cit.*, 56.

8. Nettleton to Billings, March 27, 1871, in *Nettleton Letters*, I.

9. Peterson, *op. cit.*, 39.

10. *Northern Pacific Railroad, Its Route, Resources, Progress and Business*, No. 37, in *Northern Pacific Railroad Pamphlets*, II. Contents of this publication are described in Chapter VII.

11. Turner to Loomis, August 30, 1871, in *Letters, Jay Cooke & Co.*, I. It will be noted that all four of these persons were influential newspapermen with wide followings. Taylor had been a very popular writer for Horace Greeley's New York *Tribune*; Dana had worked on the staff of the *Tribune* and was, at this time, editor of the New York *Sun*: Bowles was the editor of the Springfield *Republican*, and Bryan a staff member.

12. Riegel, *op. cit.*, 125.

13. This conclusion is based on several letters from Hibbard to interested individuals found in *Letters, Hibbard, Superintendent of Emigration*, 5.

14. Nettleton to Billings, October 7, 1871, in *Nettleton Letters*, II.

15. Schroeder to Loomis September 28, 1871, No. 58 in *Advertising Letters*, I.

16. Nettleton to Dudley, November 25, 1871, in *Nettleton Letters*, I.

17. Nettleton to Billings, October 27, 1871, in *Nettleton Letters*, I.

18. Dudley to Nettleton, January 3, 1872, No. 4, in *Land Commissioner's Letters*, March 28, 1871, to . . . .

19. Nettleton to Dudley, May 23, 1872, in *Nettleton Letters*, I.

20. Sears to Dudley, July 5, 1872, in *Nettleton Letters*, I.

21. Nettleton to Dudley, November 2, 1872, in *Nettleton Letters*, II.

22. Nettleton to Dudley, October 10, 1872, No. 78, in *Nettleton Letters*, II.

23. Hibbard to Nettleton, November 13, 1872, No. 242, in *Letters, Hibbard, Superintendent of Emigration*, V.

24. Nettleton to Billings, July 19, 1872, in *Nettleton Letters*, I.

25. Whitman to Loomis, October 24, 1871, No. 51, in *Foreign Emigration*, I.

26. Marvin to Hibbard, August 20, 1872, No. 63, in *Letters, Hibbard, Superintendent of Emigration*, and Marvin to Hibbard, July 8, 1872, No. 32, in the same volume.

27. Wales to Billings, January 18, 1872, No. 86, in *Advertising Letters*, I.

28. Coffin to Hibbard, April 11, 1873, No. 170, in *Advertising Letters*, I. There is much correspondence throughout the 1870-74 period concerning the activities of Coffin.

29. Nettleton to Dudley, October 2, 1872, No. 22, in *Nettleton Letters*, II. Two of the brief reading notes that Abbott was sending to the New York press were included with a letter from Sears to Dudley, June 24, 1872, in *Nettleton Letters*, I. The paragraphs, each of which deals with prospective excursions, follow:

A New Pleasure Trip

The Northern Pacific Railroad Company are organizing a series of first class excursions to the Red River country and the park region of Minnesota. The trip will be made one way at least over the Great Lakes and will reach many places of interest beside the objective points. The intention is to extend the arrangements for these excursions throughout the later summer and early autumn.

Summer Excursion

From Buffalo, Erie or Cleveland to Duluth by the splendid steamers now running the Great Lakes, is a charming sail. From Duluth across Minnesota to the working end of the Northern Pacific in North Dakota ought to be an interesting journey. Over this route the Northern Pacific proposes to send out first class excursion parties, at such reduced rates of transportation with, at the same time, such perfected arrangements for comfort as will no doubt turn a considerable tide of summer travel toward the area.

30. Bryan to Hibbard, January 29, 1872, No. 18, in *Hibbard Letters*, and Bryan to Sears, August 21, 1871, No. 46, in *Advertising Letters*, I. See page 11 et ff.

31. Sears to Hibbard, August 10, 1872, No. 65, in *Hibbard Letters*.

32. Nettleton to Hibbard, March 8, 1873, in *Nettleton Letters*, II.

33. The outstanding example of this form of promotion used by the Northern Pacific is the mammoth excursion to western Montana for the driving of the golden spike in 1883 (see page 42). There are many other occasions when newspapermen were taken on expense-paid tours by the railroad. One trip, to Yellowstone Park, is described on page 42, others on page 51 et eff.

34. Allusions to stories in these papers are numerous in *Advertising Letters*, I, *Hibbard Letters*, and *Nettleton Letters*,

NOTES AND REFERENCES 183

I. In almost all cases the stories mentioned are of longer type, the officials not seeing fit to mention the reading notices which probably were printed in a good share of the many papers to which they were sent. Usually the railroad asked for copies of the issue in which the publicity story was printed and then used the story in preparation of printed publicity matter.

35. Woolston to Loomis, January 9, 1872, No 87, in *Advertising Letters*, I.

36. Riegel, *The Story of the Western Railroads*, 282.

37. Coffin to Dudley, November 8, 1871, No. 72, in *Advertising Letters*, I, explains that Coffin was booked for a considerable length of time in New England in the fall of 1871, and after finishing there he was to go west. Williams to Hibbard, April 4, 1873, No. 169, in *Advertising Letters*, I, describes a rousing meeting in Boston at which Coffin and Barrows spoke. Williams suggested bringing the same pair to New York for a similar meeting.

38. The newspapermen's excursion is mentioned on page 11 and again on page 15. Samples of the reading notices used to advertise the big drive of the autumn of 1872 may be found in footnote 30 of Chapter II.

39. The entire story of the machinations of the bogus lord is told in Folwell, *History of Minnesota*, St. Paul, 1921-1930, Volume III, 364.

40. Nettleton to Dudley, July 3, 1872, in *Nettleton Letters*, I.

41. These topics are discussed fully by Mr. Peterson on page 63 of *Railroads and the Settlement of Minnesota.*

42. Nettleton to Billings, July 3, 1872, in *Nettleton Letters*, I. In this letter Nettleton also argues that climate is one of the greatest obstacles that must be overcome. He maintains that people must be convinced that, in spite of the cold winters, they can live comfortably in Minnesota, and in the part of North Dakota east of the Missouri River, and while living comfortably they can make money. He also suggested breaking some land in scattered sections so that persons coming to the land in the spring would not have to wait a year before raising a crop. This policy, Nettleton maintained, would also provide an income for some of the persons then on the land, and would

cost the Northern Pacific nothing because the price of the land could be raised in proportion to the amount expended.

43. Nettleton to Dudley, June 12, 1872, in *Nettleton Letters*, I.

44. Nettleton to Dudley, November 8, 1872, in *Nettleton Letters*, I.

45. Pettengill to Dudley, October 17, 1872, No. 145, in *Advertising Letters*, I. For a complete story of the Pettengill agency, see Frank Presbrey, *The History and Development of Advertising*, Gordon City, 1929.

46. Nettleton to Dudley, June 12, 1872, in *Nettleton Letters*, I.

47. A complete list of these newspapers may be found on pp. 200-210 in *Hibbard Letters*, V.

48. Whitman to Loomis, October 24, 1871, in *Letters, Foreign Emigration*, I.

49. Reference to Hibbard's contract with the *Farmers' Union* was found in a letter from Hibbard to Nettleton, November 13, 1872, No. 240, in *Hibbard Letters*, V; and in Hibbard to Wright, November 16, 1872, No. 248, in the same volume. The remainder of the information, with the exception of that which is specifically documented, was gleaned from scattered letters in the *Hibbard Letters, Nettleton Letters*, II, and *Advertising Letters*, I.

50. Nettleton to Dudley, October 16, 1872, No. 83, in *Nettleton Letters*, II.

51. Joseph H. Mills, Publisher to A. Wackerhagen, December 23, 1872, No. 157, in *Advertising Letter, I.*

52. Coffin to Dudley, July 10, 1872, No. 112, in *Advertising Letters*, I.

53. Nettleton to Dudley, September 24, 1872, No. 65, *Nettleton Letters*, II.

54. Nettleton to Dudley, September 27, 1872, No. 66, in *Nettleton Letters*, II.

55. Extract from the official report of the examining committee appointed by the state Agriculture Society of the Maryland State Fair, No. 84, in *Nettleton Letters*, II.

56. Kindred to Hibbard, October 7, 1873, in *Hibbard Letters*. With his letter Kindred enclosed a clipping from the

Chicago *Tribune* of October 2, 1873, which indicates the attitude of that paper toward the Northern Pacific. The story included the paragraph, "Something new has appeared in the shape of a circular about the Northern Pacific railroad and containing extracts from various papers laudatory of that myth. The road is called a 'great work' and undoubtedly it is a 'great work' to build it; and then there is advice to intending colonists in the 'valley route to the Pacific.' According to all accounts, it is more likely the valley route to the valley of the shadow of death. A curious omission from this circular is any reference to Jay Cooke and his late financial exploits. In the present state of the public mind it is hardly possible that Mr. Cooke's railroad will meet with favor."

57. Nettleton to Wackerhagen, December 3, 1872, No. 112, in *Nettleton Letters*, II.

58. Sears to Hibbard, March 4, 1873, in *Nettleton Letters*, I.

59. The best available discussion of Northern Pacific colonization activities is found in Peterson, op. cit., 67 to 89. Mr. Peterson describes the New England Military and Naval Bureau of Migration Colony at Detroit Lake, the Red River colony at Glyndon, the Yeovil colony at Hawley, and the Furness colony at Wadena. He discusses the organization work, the leadership, the process of establishing new homes, and the results. It is apparent that most of the promotional work was done by persons not directly connected with company, but who were working on a commission basis. The New England Military and Naval Bureau did its preliminary organization work in cooperation with the Northern Pacific's Bureau of Immigration for Soldiers and Sailors. The firm of Tenney and Company signed a contract with the Northern Pacific and took full responsibility for the Red River colony. Both the Yeovil and Furness groups were from England, the Yeovil colony being an idea of the Rev. George Rodgers. Rodgers was paid a moderate salary for his efforts. The Furness movement seemed to have been solely a private venture.

Dr. Hedges also described colonizing efforts in his monograph in the *Mississippi Valley Historical Review*, 13:311 (September, 1926).

60. Loomis to Ross, February 22, 1871, in *Land Commissioner*, Letters, from March 28, 1871, to . . . , IV.

61. Loomis to Haskell, January 6, 1872, in *ibid*.

62. Loomis to Seeger, February 24, 1872, in *ibid*.

63. Loomis to Ross, February 22, 1871, in *ibid*.

64. It will be noted that each of the letters to prospective colonists that has been listed here has been addressed to Illinois or Ohio. This is a good indication that the Northern Pacific had already started to throw its publicity into the older Middle Western states and that there was a considerable urge to move in those states.

65. Loomis to Stewart, February 1, 1871, in *Land Commissioner*, Letters, from March 28, 1871 to . . . , IV.

66. The correspondence concerning Governor Potts' appointment includes two letters. Nettleton wrote to Potts August 24, 1872, in a letter that is No. 52 in *Nettleton Letters*, II, that "Mr. Billings agrees that there should be someone in the territory empowered to represent the land interests of the company, give advice to settlers and to answer questions. At my suggestion, Mr. Billings requests me to say that if you are willing to form a quasi-connection with the company during your official term as governor, with merely a nominal compensation for the present, the company will be glad to have you act as its representative in connection with land matters in Montana. You must be your own judge as to whether this will be inconsistent with your public position and duties. At this distance I cannot see that it would be. The duties you would have to discharge in behalf of the road for a year to come would be extremely light and that of a figurehead [sic]. But if this partial and temporary connection with the road should lead to something more permanent and desirable of the same nature you would probably have no objections."

That Governor Potts accepted is indicated in a letter from Nettleton to Billings, September 14, 1872, No. 53, in the same volume: "You will note that he accepts to the position of semi-representative of our land interests in the Montana Territory and is prepared to do whatever is desired of him." Evidence of the fact that Potts actually did work for the company was discovered in the fact that the Northern Pacific published a

NOTES AND REFERENCES 187

pamphlet in 1874 written by Benjamin J. Wade and B. F. Potts. The title of the pamphlet was *A Brief Statement Concerning the Proposed Legislation to Secure Early Completion of the Northern Pacific Railroad*. This pamphlet is No. 47 in *Northern Pacific Railroad Pamphlets*.

Chapter III

1. George Gray to Nicholas Zareton, October 3, 1876, No. 66 in *Gray Letters*. The middle seventies are the period of the so-called "bonanza" farming. Holders of large blocks of bonds were exchanging those bonds for lands with the intention of holding the lands for the speculative purposes. This practice led to the establishment of many large farms in North Dakota which were called "bonanza farms." The practice is described in detail by Dr. Hedges in the article previously cited in the *Mississippi Valley Historical Review*, 13:311 (September, 1926).

2. Power to Stark, January 5, 1877, No. 9 in *Land Department Letters, New Series*, I.

3. Power to Stark, June 6, 1877, No. 59 in *ibid*.

4. *Annual Report*, 1880, 24.

5. Hedges, *Henry Villard and the Railways of the Northwest*, 173. In this volume Hedges presents a detailed description of the promotion activities of the Oregon Steamship Company.

6. Billings to Power, August 4, 1880, No. 19a in *Land Department Letters, New Series*, IV.

7. *Annual Report*, 1881, 14.

8. Hedges, "The Colonization Work of the Northern Pacific Railroad," *Mississippi Valley Historical Review*, 13:329 (September, 1926).

9. Newport to Williams, March 21, 1881, in Unnamed book of letters, *March 1881 to November 1881*.

10. Newport to Barney, June 27, 1881, in *ibid*.

11. Kidder to Gray, August 5, 1881, No. 3 in *Letters, July 1881 to November 1883, Impression Book*.

12. Newport to Billings, March 14, 1881, in Unnamed book of letters, *March 1881 to November 1881*.

13. Kidder to Villard, June 27, 1882, No. 227 in *Letters, March 1881 to November 1883, Impression Book.*

14. Winser to Lamborne, August 10, 1882, No. 141 in *Letters, 1882, Impression Book.* It is important to bear in mind while reading of this period of Northern Pacific promotion that Villard had for many years been a widely known newspaperman. At this time he was the publisher of the New York *Post* and *The Nation,* having bought the two publications in 1881. Previously he had reported the Lincoln-Douglas debates, written special articles for the Cincinnati *Commercial* and the Chicago *Tribune,* and had established a reputation as a war correspondent by covering the Civil War for the New York *Herald* and the Austro-Prussian War for the New York *Tribune.*

15. *Annual Report,* 1883, 57.

16. Oakes to Lamborne, October 18, 1883, No. 647 in *Letters, July 1881 to November 1883, Impression Book.*

17. Kidder to Schulze, February 2, 1885, No. 241 in *Letters, 1883-1885, Impression Book.*

18. Lamborne to Barney and Bullitt, December 4, 1883, No. 50 in *Land Department Letters, New Series,* VII.

19. *Annual Report,* 1884, 63.

20. *Federal Census Reports* for Minnesota, North Dakota and Montana, included in Chapter VIII of this thesis, show that populations almost doubled between 1880 and 1885. From 1885 to 1890 there was an increase, but that increase was by no means as great as that of the preceding five years.

21. Power to Stark, June 14, 1878, No. 72 in *New Series Letters, Land Department,* II. If the Northern Pacific had any financial agreement with the *Times,* it must have been wholly sub rosa. Pettengill's *Newspaper Directory and Advertiser's Handbook for 1887,* published in New York by S. M. Pettengill and Co., lists E. B. Chambers as publisher of the Fargo *Times.* It describes the *Times* as a weekly paper published on Saturdays, as Republican, with a circulation of 625, and "the largest paper on the line of the Northern Pacific Railroad." *N. W. Ayer and Sons' American Newspaper Annual for 1880* lists the same publisher for the *Times* and records that its publication day has changed to Thursday and that its circulation had climbed to 1,488. It is almost certain, however, that Chambers must

NOTES AND REFERENCES 189

have either been partly financed by or subsidized by the Northern Pacific. A letter from Kidder to Power, dated November 26, 1878, and found on page 258 of the *George Gray Letters* volume, speaks of the use of some cuts of Northern Pacific territory owned by the *New Northwest*. Kidder suggests: "It strikes me that in putting out a new edition of the Fargo *Times* you could not do better than use these illustrations." If Power were privileged to put out an edition and to use the material he saw fit in that edition, it certainly must have been true that the railroad had some authority in the *Times'* editorial policies.

22. Kidder to Power, September 25, 1879, No. 379 in *Gray Letters*.

23. Kidder to Creamer, September 27, 1879, No. 379 in *Gray Letters*. This letter and the one mentioned in the preceding footnote each occupied one half a page on page 379.

24. Kidder to Sprague, July 1, 1880, No. 453 in *Gray Letters*.

25. Kidder to Sheppard, May 3, 1881, No. 545 in *Gray Letters*.

26. "The Golden Northwest," an editorial on page 5 of the *Golden Northwest*, April 1, 1880. Whether the strong claims for accuracy made by the publication are justified may be determined by a study of abstracts from some of the articles, included in Chapter VII of this thesis.

27. Winser to Lamborne, August 10, 1882, No. 141 in *Letters, 1882, Impression Book*.

28. Barnes to Oakes, January 22, 1882, in *Letters, New Series, Land Department*, V.

29. *Annual Report*, 1883, 39.

30. Lamborne to Barney and Bullitt, November 19, 1883, No. 27 in *New Series Letters, Land Department*, VII. Actual work in the preparation of this record of previous orders and recommendations for the future ones was done by P. B. Groat, General Emigration Agent.

31. Winser to Oakes, October 11, 1883, No. 221 in *Letters, 1883-1885, Impression Book*.

32. Stark to Ralston, December 29, 1877, No. 157 in *Gray Letters*.

33. Land Committee to Board of Directors, January 3, 1878, No. 170, in *ibid*.

34. Stark to Hoyt, January 5, 1878, No. 160 in *ibid*.

35. Stark to Power, April 4, 1878, No. 196 in *ibid*.

36. Kidder to Sheppard, May 13, 1880, No. 429 in *ibid*.

37. For a previous case of the employment of a photographer to make photographs of company lands see page 13.

38. Power to Stark, October 12, 1878, No. 136 in *New Series Letters, Land Department*, II.

39. Power to Stark, October 30, 1878, No. 142 in *ibid*.

40. Winser to Haynes, January 30, 1883, No. 14 in *Letters, 1883-1885, Impression Book*.

41. Winser to Oakes, August 22, 1882, No. 246 in *Letters, 1882, Impression Book*.

42. Complete files of the *Northwest* may be found in the office of the Northern Pacific Land Department or in the Minnesota Historical Society.

43. Smalley to Oakes, October 15, 1883, No. 141 in *New Series Letters, Land Department*, VI.

44. *Ibid*. This letter included both Smalley's acceptance of the terms as they had previously been outlined to him and his further proposal of the subsidy.

45. Lamborne to Oakes, October 25, 1883, No. 146 in *New Series Letters, Land Department*, VI.

46. Oakes to Barney and Bullitt, November 5, 1883, No. 153 in *ibid*.

47. Kidder to Oakes, November 10, 1883, No. 679 in *Letters, July 1881 to November 1883, Impression Book*.

48. Barker to Barney, February 20, 1884, No. 90 in *New Series Letters, Land Department*, VII.

49. Smalley to the president and Land Committee, February 13, 1884, No. 88 in *ibid*.

50. Kidder to Barker, February 23, 1884, No. 107 in *Letters, 1883-1884, Impression Book*.

51. Villard, *Memoirs of Henry Villard*, 309. The title of Smalley's volume is *History of the Northern Pacific Railroad*. It was published in New York by G. P. Putnam's Sons in 1883. The celebration itself is discussed on page 42.

52. Newport to Oakes, November 16, 1881, in Unnamed book of letters, *March 1881 to November 1881*.

53. *Ibid*. It is also of interest that advertising done by the Land Department was kept separate from that done by the passenger department. The copy for the advertisement mentioned above was as follows: "Best Wheat Grazing Lands are found on the Northern Pacific in Minnesota, Dakota, and Montana. Big Crop again in 1881. Low prices, long time; rebate for improvement; reduced freight and fare to settlers. For full information address R. M. Newport, general land agent, St. Paul, Minnesota. Mention this paper." "Best wheat" was set in large type at the top of the two-inch ad, and the lines "The Northern Pacific" and "Big Crop again in 1881" were also given prominent display.

54. *Annual Report*, 1883, 38.

55. Lamborne to Barney and Bullitt, December 5, 1883, No. 33 in *New Series Letters, Land Department*, VII.

56. *Ibid*.

57. Lamborne to Kidder, January 31, 1884, No. 84 in *New Series Letters, Land Department*, VII.

58. *Ibid*.

59. Stark to Power, March 21, 1879, No. 318 in *Gray Letters*.

60. Winser to Newport, March 6, 1882, No. 3 in *Winser Letter*, 1882. See footnote 14 page 29 above for a discussion of Villard's newspaper connections.

61. For an analysis of the reader notice technique used in the later period see in Chapter V the sections devoted to newspaper advertising and to newspaper publicity. Several examples of the types of "readers" used are reprinted there.

62. Correspondence in regard to the use of these stories in the Chicago *Tribune* may be found in letters from Winser to Raymond, March 21, 1882, No. 19 in *Winser Letter, 1882*; April 25, 1882, No. 25 in *ibid.*, and Winser to Smalley, March 30, 1882, No. 25 in *ibid*.

63. Winser to Halsted, July 31, 1882, No. 102 in *ibid*.

64. Winser to Smalley, March 30, 1882, No. 25 in *ibid*.

65. *Annual Report*, 1883, 39.

66. Taylor to Wemyss, May 21, 1884, No. 130 in *New Series Letters, Land Department*, VII.

67. Lamborne to Oakes, December 29, 1883, No. 43 in *ibid*.
68. Winser to Halsted, July 21, 1882, No. 102 in *Letters, 1882, Impression Book*.
69. This entire account is taken from two sources, *Memoirs of Henry Villard*, 309-312, and *Annual Report*, 1883, 7-8.
70. *Annual Report*, 1883, 7.
71. *Annual Report*, 1881, 17.
72. Newport to Oakes, October 18, 1881, in Unnamed book of letters, *March 1881 to November 1881*.
73. Wemyss to Lamborne, November 19, 1883, No. 40 in *New Series Letters, Land Department*, VII.
74. Lamborne to Oakes, January 25, 1884, No. 82 in *ibid*.
75. Circular letter to district agents of the Land Department included with the above letter in *ibid*.

Chapter IV

1. *Annual Report*, 1885, 39.
2. *Ibid.*, 1887, 48.
3. *Ibid.*, 21.
4. *Ibid.*, 1888, 49.
5. *Ibid.*, 1889, 49.
6. Briggs, op. cit., 99.
7. *Annual Report*, 1891, 48.
8. *Ibid.*, 1892, 37.
9. *Ibid.*, 52.
10. *Ibid.*, 1892, 52.
11. *Ibid.*, 1886, 16. Hedges, in his monograph "The Colonization Work of the Northern Pacific Railroad," uses this transfer of land as a convenient point at which to conclude his discussion, evidently feeling that it would mark the end of strenuous promotion efforts in the Minnesota-Dakota area. Such is not the case, however, as will be noted from the evidence presented in Chapter V. It will be seen that a good share of the railroad's promotion from 1897 to 1902 was concerned with selling lands in the vicinity of Carrington, east of the Missouri but on a branch line running north from Jamestown, and in the timbered areas of Northern Minnesota.

NOTES AND REFERENCES 193

12. *Ibid.*, 1888, 49. A study of land sales charts through this period, found in Chapter VIII, will show that sales remained rather uniform each year from 1886 on, indicating that the land must have been transferred in small parcels over a rather long period of time.

13. *Ibid.*, 1891, 49.

14. *Ibid.*, 188, 55. There are no figures available for 1877, but there is a statement on page 64 of the *Annual Report* for that year to the effect that large expenditures were made in connection with Land Department advertising and the employment of district agents throughout the East and South.

15. *Ibid.*, 1889, 58.

16. *Ibid.*, 1890, 60.

17. *Ibid.*, 1891, 53.

18. *Ibid.*, 1892, 60.

19. Circular sent out by P. B. Groat, General Emigration Agent, from St. Paul, October 24, 1889, in *Scrapbook of the Old Printed Letters and Circulars.*

20. *Ibid.*

21. Anonymous article in the *Northwest*, (March, 1890), 29, col. 2.

22. Kidder to Martindale, October 10, 1893, No. 414 in *Land Department Letters*, No. 4, *Impression Book.*

Chapter V

1. Wilsey to Spinney, November 10, 1897, in *Newspaper Advertising Contract*, Book 25. *Newspaper Advertising Contracts* includes four books, one entitled "Book 25," one was termed merely "Number 1" and the other two were listed according to their dates, "February 10, 1897, to January 18, 1898," and "January 18, 1898, to August 31, 1898."

2. *Ibid.*

3. *Ibid.*

4. Spinney to Wilsey, December 11, 1897, in *Box 112, Advertising Contracts, Appointment of Solicitors.*

5. Fee to Wilsey, December 15, 1897, in *ibid.*

6. Loose circular found in *Newspaper Advertising Contracts, No. 1* under general heading, "Newspaper Contracts."

7. The writer discovered many letters from Wilsey and Willis Drummond, his assistant, to publishers and from the publishers to Wilsey and Drummond concerning details of the transportation-advertising contracts. In almost all cases the publisher was allowed no more on his ticket than the actual amount due him for advertising on the basis of the contracted rates. An example of the functioning of this plan is found in a letter from Wilsey to Scammon and Gillrup, publishers of the *Worth County Index* at Northwood, Iowa, in which Wilsey wrote that he would furnish one first class passage from St. Paul to Cinnabar, Mont., worth $35.55, in exchange for a two column by six inch advertisement run for six months with ten lines of reading notice each issue. The letter was written February 27, 1897, and is in *Newspaper Advertising Contracts, Book 25*.

8. Wilsey to Spinney, November 10, 1897, in *ibid*.

9. *Ibid*.

10. These statistics were compiled from duplicate copies of contracts with advertisers filed in *Newspaper Advertising Contracts, Number 1*. There is one discrepancy in totals between Wilsey's figures and the contracts. Wilsey reports that advertisements were contracted for with sixteen newspapers in South Dakota during the first six months of 1897. The contract book lists only fifteen for the entire year.

11. *Ibid*.

12. Wilsey to Shervin and Foss March 2, 1897, No. 152 in *Newspaper Advertising Contracts, Book 25*.

13. *Ibid*.

14. Wilsey to Meachem and Company, December 28, 1897, No. 971 in *Newspaper Advertising Contracts, February 10, 1897 to January 1, 1898*.

15. Memorandum Agreement with David R. McGinnis, December 1, 1898, in *Land Department, Box 112; Advertising Contracts; Appointment of Solicitors*.

16. *Ibid*.

17. *Ibid*.

18. *Ibid*.

19. Wilsey to Dow, March 1, 1897, No. 149 in *Newspaper Advertising Contracts, Book 25*.

NOTES AND REFERENCES 195

20. Wilsey to Fee, May 3, 1898, No. 139 in *ibid.*
21. Wilsey to Haupt, August 19, 1898, No. 199 in *Newspaper Advertising Contracts, January 1, 1898, to August 31, 1898.*
22. Wilsey to Winn Powers, March 1, 1898, No. 147 in *Newspaper Advertising Contracts, Book 25.*
23. Wilsey to Craft, March 26, 1898, No. 81 in *Newspaper Advertising Contracts, January 18, 1898, to August 31, 1898.*
24. Wilsey to Robie, March 21, 1898, No. 77 in *ibid.*
25. Wilsey to Cuches, March 28, 1898, No. 83 in *Newspaper Advertising Contracts, Book 25.*
26. Wilsey to Spinney, December 20, 1897, in *Box 112, Land Department, Advertising Contracts; Appointments of Solicitors.*
27. *Ibid.*, December 16, 1897. In this same communication Wilsey observed that a display ad together with frequent readers would accomplish the best results.
28. Circular letter sent by Wilsey to all solicitors of the Northern Pacific Land Department in 1898 in *Newspaper Advertising Contracts, Clipping Book.*
29. These facts are extracted from duplicate copies of all advertising contracts lent by the company in 1898 found in *Newspaper Advertising Contracts, January 18, 1898 to August 31, 1898.*

A copy of the contract signed with LeMars, Iowa *Post* follows:

"I enclose herewith copy for a double column 6-inch display advertisement, and a local reading notice, which you are authorized to print and publish in each and every weekly issue of the LeMars (Iowa) *Post* for a period of thirteen (13) consecutive issues from the date of your acceptance of this proposition; for which the Northern Pacific Railroad Company agrees to pay you eight and 50-100 dollars ($8.50) at the expiration of the period named, subject to the conditions below stated which are made a part of this agreement.

The said display advertisement shall be inserted next to reading matter on a local page and the reading notice shall be inserted in the local columns of the newspaper named.

The right is reserved by the Eastern Land Agent below named to cancel this agreement upon giving 30 days notice in writing, in which case the printing and publishing done shall be paid for pro rate.

You will be required and hereby agree to mail a copy of each and every issue of your paper, during the life of this contract, to F. W. Wilsey, Eastern Land Agent of the Northern Pacific Railroad Company, St. Paul, Minn., free charge."

F. W. Wilsey

30. Several of these reading notices may be found in *Newspaper Advertising Contracts, Clipping Book.*

31. All of the clippings mentioned in this section are filed in *Newspaper Advertising Contracts, Clipping Book.*

32. For a more complete discussion of this contract see page 55.

33. Garfield's *Climates* is referred to many times in Chapter II. It was widely used during the earlier periods for distribution in both the United States and Europe.

34. Garfield, "Climates of the Northwest," No. 41 in *Northern Pacific Railroad Pamphlets*, II, 18.

35. Clipping in *Newspaper Advertising Contracts, Clipping Book*. The fact that this letter was clipped and the clipping placed in this particular volume is additional evidence that some official of the Land Department wrote it.

36. *Ibid.*

37. This clipping was found with the "Hometaker" article mentioned above. It was impossible to determine where it had been published. However, it was set in a different typeface, indicating that it must have come from another newspaper.

38. The four clippings were all found in *Newspaper Advertising Contracts, Clipping Book.*

39. *Ibid.*

40. *Ibid.*

41. *Ibid.* The *Homestead* story, a paid advertisement, was discussed on page 58.

42. *Ibid.*

43. *Ibid.*

44. Drummond to Kirby Thomas, November 26, 1897, No. 432 in *Newspaper Advertising Contracts, Book 25.*

45. Wilsey (Drummond's "D" was signed below Wilsey's name) to H. B. Waite, August 5, 1898, No. 191 in *Newspaper Advertising Contracts, January 19, 1898, to August 3, 1898.*

46. Two of these reading notices were discovered in *Newspaper Advertising Contracts, Book 25.* One of them, sent out September 28, 1897, read:

A Cheap Trip

Another of the popular Homeseekers' Excursions to the fine farming lands for sale by the Northern Pacific Railway Company in Central Minnesota will be run on Tuesday, October 5. Tickets for the round trip are one fare plus $2. Stopovers allowed going or returning west of Staples, Minnesota. For full information call upon _____, local sales solicitor at _____, or write F. W. Wilsey, Eastern Land Agent, St. Paul, Minn.

A reader which was printed in the Cottonwood, Minn., *Current* Oct. 25, 1897, read:

Do You Want a Home?

If you do, join the excursion on November 16 to the fine, cheap lands in Central Minnesota for sale by the Northern Pacific Railway Company. Ten years time with interest at only 6 per cent. Low railroad fares. Tickets good for 30 days with stopovers, going or returning, west of Staples. For full particulars apply to O. Hanson, Cottonwood, Minn.

More samples of reading notices may be found in the appendix.

47. Circular letter dated February 24, 1897, in *Newspaper Advertising Contracts, Book 25.* The periodical was to consist

of eight eleven-inch by sixteen-inch pages, each page containing four thirteen-em columns, fourteen-inches deep. It was to be profusely illustrated with half-tone engravings of scenes and farms along the road. Fifty thousand copies were to be printed in the first edition. Later this figure was to be increased.

48. *Ibid.*

49. *Ibid.*

50. Clipping of news story printed in Iowa City *Iowa State Press*, February 28, 1899, in *Newspaper Advertising Contracts, Clipping Book*. This article is also illustrative of the news publicity technique used by the Land Department. A by-product of the exhibit car itself was the news stories about it printed in the cities and towns where it stopped. It is doubtful whether it was necessary for the Land Department employees to write these stories as the exhibit car was newsworthy enough in itself to induce newspapers to send staff members to cover the event.

51. *Ibid.*

52. *Ibid.*

53. Advertisement sent to fifty-two Iowa newspapers March 16, 1897, for insertion up to April 7, 1897, in *Newspaper Advertising Contracts, Book 25*. Accompanying this ad was a reading notice for free insertions which read:

"When the Northern Pacific Railway runs a free excursion it does it in great shape. Besides reducing the rates on its North Dakota excursion to the lowest notch, it offers the advantage of free colonist sleepers which will be left on the track for the benefit of patrons until they can make other arrangements, thus saving them all expenses for lodging while they are hunting locations. We predict that we will have plenty of passengers for this occasion."

54. Wilsey to J. Vander Las, Western North Dakota Land Solicitor, January 11, 1901, in *Land Department, No. 13*. Wilsey's letter was in answer to a query from Karl Hoff to Vander Las concerning the possibility of getting free transportation to inspect the land before bringing parties from Parkston and Eureka in South Dakota.

55. *Ibid.*

56. Clipping from Churdan (Iowa) *Reporter* dated October 8, 1897, in *Newspaper Advertising Contracts, Clipping Book*.

NOTES AND REFERENCES 199

This clipping was in the form of a letter written by editor Adrian Cross from Carrington, North Dakota.

57. Memorandum Agreement between Edwin H. McHenry and Frank W. Bigelow, Receivers for the Northern Pacific, and H. C. Dodge of Morris, Minn., May 1, 1897, in *Box 112, Advertising Contracts; Appointment of Solicitors.*

58. *Ibid.*

59. Authorization of Sales Solicitors, John F. Robinson, January 29, 1901, in *Box 112, Advertising Contracts; Appointment of Solicitors.*

60. Authorization of Sales Solicitor, J. M. Rhodes, January 28, 1901, in *ibid.*

61. Contract between Karl Simmon and the Land Department in *Box 112, Advertising Contracts; Appointment of Solicitors.*

62. Expense Account of J. Vander Las for the month of January, 1901, *Box 112, Advertising Contracts; Appointment of Solicitors.*

63. A compilation of contracts and lists of solicitors found in *Box 112, Advertising Contracts; Appointment of Solicitors.* No figures were discovered for 1897. An additional forty-six solicitors were working in Minnesota for the St. Paul and Duluth Railroad which was later incorporated in the Northern Pacific.

64. Clipping from Miles City (Montana) *News*, August 20, 1898, and St. Paul *Globe* of same date in *Newspaper Advertising Contracts; Clipping Book.*

65. Drummond to Wilsey, August 28, 1898, in *Newspaper Advertising Contracts, January 18, 1898, to August 31, 1898.*

66. Vander Las to Wilsey, July 7, 1902, in *Land Department, No. 13, J. Vander Las, 1901-1902.*

Chapter VI

1. No matter how fascinating or how glamorous the European campaign may be, it is necessary to ascribe to it only the importance that it deserves. Land Department officials constantly iterated and reiterated two facts that have been mentioned previously in this thesis: first, that they preferred as

settlers on their lands persons who had gone though previous frontier experience, and secondly, that by far the largest share of the migrants to their lands came from states to the east of Minnesota and Dakota. Many of the Scandinavians and Germans who ultimately settled along the Northern Pacific probably first stopped in states to the east of the Northern Pacific line and were induced from there to move on to the territory adjacent to the railroad.

2. See page 49 et ff.

3. The story of the foreign campaign has been told quite adequately by both Dr. Hedges and Mr. Peterson in works previously cited. Dr. Hedges describes the organization of the Bureau of Emigration in his article in the *Mississippi Valley Historical Review*, 13:311, and an entire chapter of Mr. Peterson's dissertation is devoted to colonization schemes tried by the railroad.

4. Sheppard to Goegg, July 12, 1872, No. 47 in *Foreign Agents*, I.

5. For a more complete delineation of Northern Pacific policy in regard to the source of immigrants after 1884 see Chapters IV and V.

6. Cooke to Billings, April 6, 1872, in *Jay Cooke & Company Letters*, I.

7. Sheppard to Nettleton, April 21, 1873, No. 45 in *Foreign Agents*, III.

8. Sheppard to Billings, July 16, 1872, No. 45 in *Foreign Agents*, I.

9. Hedges, "The Colonization Work of the Northern Pacific Railroad," *Mississippi Valley Historical Review*, 13:317 (September, 1926). For a complete story of Mattson's life see his autobiography. *Reminiscences: The Story of an Emigrant*, St. Paul, 1891.

10. Hedges, *op. cit.*, 317.

11. Nettleton to Dudley, September 17, 1872, No. 55 in *Nettleton Letters*, II.

12. *Ibid.*

13. Sheppard to Goegg, July 12, 1872, No. 47 in *Foreign Agents*, I. It is especially interesting to note the manner in which the Northern Pacific sought to conceal the identity of

NOTES AND REFERENCES 201

the interested party behind the publication of Goegg's bulletin. This policy characterized many publications which were inspired but not directly published by the Land Department. Officials were particularly pleased when they could gain access to an official government publication. That, they felt, lent final authority to their claims.

14. See Chapter I, 7 et ff.
15. Hedges, *op. cit.*, 318, 139.
16. *Ibid.*
17. Nettleton to Hibbard, January 2, 1873, No. 132 in *Nettleton Letters*, II.
18. *Ibid.*
19. *Ibid.*
20. Kidder to Hilliard, February 4, 1880, No. 404 in *George Gray Letters*. Although there is no evidence that the Bureau of Immigration maintained any staff in Europe between 1873 and 1880, European immigrants continued to arrive and to purchase land. This continued migration was probably due to the interest set in motion before the Cooke crash and by the efforts of other interested groups to bring Europeans to the United States. It is possible, too, that efforts to finance the second phase of the construction of the road kept the Northern Pacific in the public attention.
21. Kidder to Barney, Bullitt, and Oakes, December 18, 1883, No. 37 in *Land Department, Letters, New Series*, VII.
22. *Annual Report*, 1882, 35.
23. *Ibid.* The Yellowstone division at that time included the trackage through Montana to Livingston.
24. *Ibid.*
25. *Annual Report*, 1883, 22.
26. *Ibid.*
27. *Ibid.*
28. Anon., *Northwest*, (September, 1883), 20.
29. *Annual Report*, 1883, 22.
30. *Ibid.*
31. Kidder to Barney, Bullitt and Oakes, December 18, 1883, No. 37 in *Letters, Land Department, New Series*, VII.
32. *Ibid.*
33. *Ibid.*

34. Sheppard to Billings, March 18, 1872, No. 3 in *Foreign Agents*, I.
35. *Ibid.*
36. Stevens to Jay Cooke & Co., April 6, 1872, *A. B. Nettleton Letters*, I.
37. Nettleton to Billings April 27, 1872, *A. B. Nettleton Letters*, I. In this letter Nettleton wrote, "Minnesota and Dakota are too cold for these Alsatians, and I only wish that they could be held for a year or so until we are in a condition to plant them on the Pacific coast where the seasons will be more congenial."
38. Sheppard to Hibbard, December 13, 1873, No. 49 in *Foreign Agents*, II.
39. *Ibid.*
40. Power to Howard, April 26, 1873, No. 84 in *Letters, Minnesota District*, VII.
41. Power to Hibbard, May 24, 1873, *Letters, Minnesota District*, VII.
42. *Ibid.*
43. *Ibid.*
44. *Ibid.*
45. Nettleton to Billings, May 13, 1872, in *Nettleton Letters*, I.
46. Sheppard to Billings, May 17, 1872, No. 25 in *Foreign Agents*, I.
47. *Ibid.*
48. Sheppard to Billings, May 13, 1872, No. 24 in *Foreign Agents*, I.
49. For a more complete description of these pamphlets see the sections devoted to printed publicity on page 11 et ff. of Chapter II and page 31 et ff. of Chapter III. For an analysis of the contents see Chapter VII.
50. Kidder to Sheppard, March 3, 1880. No. 411 in *George Gray Letters*. The Helena *Herald* was an independently owned newspaper published in Helena, Montana, and had no financial ties with the Northern Pacific as far as could be ascertained. For a discussion of the Fargo *Times* see page 31.
51. Oakes to the Land Committee, November 16, 1883, No. 50 in *Letters, New Series, Land Department*, VII.

NOTES AND REFERENCES   203

52. Mattson to Nettleton, April 10, 1872, in *Nettleton Letters*, I.
53. Nettleton to Dudley, June 17, 1872, in *Nettleton Letters*, I.
54. Nettleton to Dudley, July 17, 1872, in *Nettleton Letters*, II.
55. Advertisement inserted following No. 48 in *Letters, New Series, Land Department*, VII. The advertisement is a 9 1/2 "by 15" folder printed for the Northern Pacific, the Oregon Railway and Navigation Company, the Oregon and California Railway, and the Pacific Coast Steamship Company.
56. Roedelheimer to Oakes, October 27, 1883, No. 48 in *Letters, New Series, Land Department*, VII.
57. Nettleton to Dudley, July 24, 1872, in *Nettleton Letters*, I.
58. *Ibid.* The writer was unable to discover any information that would indicate whether the Northern Pacific was able to obtain these addresses.
59. For the specific amounts spent on newspaper advertising in the London and Berlin offices during 1882 and 1883 see page 81.
60. Sheppard to Billings, March 16, 1872, No. 1 in *Foreign Agents*, I.
61. Sheppard to Billings, June 12, 1872, No. 38 in *Foreign Agents*, I.
62. Lindau to Sheppard, November 28, 1872, No. 44 in *Foreign Agents*, II.
63. Sheppard to Billings, June 1, 1872, No. 32 in *Foreign Agents*, I.
64. Lindau to Sheppard, *op. cit.*
65. Charles Meyer and Company to Dudley, September 4, 1872, No. 135 in *Letters, Advertising*, I.
66. Johnson to Williams, March 25, 1881, in Unnamed book of letters, *March 1881 to November 1881*. This communication, however, may refer to publicity stories and not to paid advertising.
67. Dudley to Linsley, October 22, 1872, No. 2 in *Letters, Superintendent of Emigration, Miscellaneous*, 5.
68. *Ibid.*

69. Hibbard to M. Biard and Co., December 10, 1872, No. 5 in *Letters, Superintendent of Emigration*, 5.

70. Hibbard to C. W. Mead, General Manager, Brainerd Office, December 12, 1872, No. 8 in *Letters, Superintendent of Emigration*, 5.

71. Hibbard to Lyman Bridges, March 28, 1873, No. 37 in *Letters, Superintendent of Emigration*, 5.

72. Dudley to Gen. T. B. Van Buren, United States Commissioner to the International Exposition at Vienna, October 17, 1872, No. 1 in *Letters, Superintendent of Emigration*, 5.

73. Sheppard to Nettleton, April 17, 1873, in *Foreign Agents*, III.

74. Sheppard to Billings, December 2, 1872, No. 45 in *Foreign Agents*, II.

75. *Annual Report, 1877*, 21.

76. Stark to Power, June 14, 1878, No. 25 in *George Gray Letters*.

77. Sheppard to Hibbard, February 1, 1872, No. 68 in *Foreign Agents*, II.

78. John Swanson to Loomis, March 11, 1872, No. 117 in *Foreign Emigration Letters*, I.

Chapter VII

1. For a complete analysis of the factors influencing migration and emigration see Chapter I, page 5 et ff. The conclusion expressed there is that low land prices and the desirability of Northern Pacific land should constitute the major appeals in the railroad's promotional program.

2. For a more thorough discussion of these factors see page 82 et ff.

3. This study was made of clippings of published advertisements and copy for advertisements to be published found in three volumes: *Newspaper Advertising Contracts, Clipping Book; Newspaper Advertising Contracts, Book 25*; and *Foreign Agents*, II. Nine of the ads were in the clipping book, two in Book 25 and one in *Foreign Agents*, II. Copies of these advertisements may be found in the Appendix.

NOTES AND REFERENCES   205

4. "Northern Pacific Railroad, Its Route, Resources, Progress and Business, The New Northern Pacific and Its Great Thoroughfare," in *Northern Pacific Railroad Pamphlets*, IV, 7.

5. Garfield, "Climates of the Northwest," No. 41 in *Northern Pacific Railroad Pamphlets*, II, 18. For a discussion of Garfield's theory of the climate of the Northwest see Chapter V, 61. For a discussion of the use of the pamphlet for distribution throughout the United States and Europe see Chapter II.

6. "Statement of the Northern Pacific Railroad in Response to Inquires of the Senate Committee on Railroads," No. 49 in *Northern Pacific Railroad Pamphlets*, IV, 19.

7. News story sent to Primghar (Iowa) *Democrat*, August 5, 1898 in *Newspaper Advertising Contracts, January 19, 1898, to August 31, 1898*.

8. News story on the future development of Superior, Wisconsin, printed in the *Superior Evening Telegraph*, November 20, 1897, in *Newspaper Advertising Contracts, Book 25*.

9. *Golden Northwest*, 1:1 (April, 1880).

10. *Ibid.*, 4. Professor Sadtler's analysis of the soil of the Red River Valley follows:

	A (sub-soil)	B (top-soil)
hygroscopic moisture	2.92	4.15
chemically combined water and humus	7.56	14.80
oxide of iron	3.38	2.48
oxide of magna	.41	.18
lime	5.59	.80
magnesia	.05	trace
alkalies	.36	.53
carbonic acid	12.67	.88
chlorine	none	trace
sulphuric acid	.08	trace
phosphoric acid	.20	.15
soluble silica	5.89	4.65
insoluble silica and silicates	55.51	67.05
	100.00	100.00

Whether this chemical combination makes for good or bad soil Professor Sadtler fails to explain, but the theory of the Northern Pacific evidently was that a farmer couldn't fail to be impressed by the scientific diction.

11. *Ibid.*, 1.
12. *Ibid.*
13. *Ibid.*
14. A six-inch-by-eight-inch circular distributed by J. H. Richard, Land Solicitor at Webster City, Iowa, in *Newspaper Advertising Contracts, Clipping Book.*
15. *Ibid.*
16. Letter from Hometaker to the editor, Mower County *Transcript,* Austin, Minn., printed in the *Transcript,* December 28, 1898. This letter is discussed on page 62, where the conclusion is drawn that F. W. Wilsey, Eastern Land Agent, or his assistant Willis Drummund, is "Hometaker."
17. "The National Highway," *Golden Northwest,* 1:5 (April, 1880).
18. *Ibid.*
19. "Climate," *Golden Northwest,* 1:6 (April, 1880).
20. Section of map circular on page 138 1/2 in *Letters, New Series, Land Department,* V.
21. "Guide to the Lands of the Northern Pacific Railroad in Minnesota," No. 44 in *Northern Pacific Railroad Pamphlets,* II, 8.
22. *Golden Northwest,* 1:1 (April, 1880).
23. Section of map circular on page 138 1/2 in *Letters, New Series, Land Department,* V.
24. This pamphlet is No. 41 in *Northern Pacific Railroad Pamphlets,* II. For further references to "Climates of the Northwest" see pages 61 and 100.
25. Nettleton to Billings, February 12, 1873, in *Nettleton Letters,* I.
26. *Op. cit.,* 3.
27. *Ibid.,* 18.
28. News story sent to the Primghar (Iowa) *Democrat* during 1898. Duplicate copy in *Newspaper Advertising Contracts, January 18, 1898, to August 31, 1898.*

29. "Statement of the Northern Pacific Railroad Company in Response to Inquires of the Senate Committee on Railroads," No. 49 in *Northern Pacific Railroad Pamphlets*, II, 19.

30. *Golden Northwest*, 1:6 (April, 1880).

31. Garfield, *op. cit.*, 14. "Montana and Western Dakota assimilate in average temperature to New York and Connecticut but the valleys of Montana have very little snow, and cattle there require neither winter feeding nor shelter."

32. Nettleton to Billings, July 19, 1872, in *Nettleton Letters*, I.

33. See page 41 for a more complete discussion of this practice.

34. "Information for Emigrants" circular inserted following page 27 in *Foreign Agents*, II.

35. The copy for this advertisement, sent out September 13, 1897, was found in *Newspaper Advertising Contracts, Clipping Book*.

36. "Northern Pacific Railroad, Its Route, Its Connections, Its Lands," *Golden Northwest* 1:1 (April, 1880).

37. *Ibid.*, 2.

38. News story sent to the Primghar (Iowa) *Democrat*, August 5, 1898, in *Newspaper Advertising Contracts, January 19, 1898, to August 21, 1898*.

39. *Ibid.* This news story on northern Minnesota illustrates the point that beauty and recreation are subordinate to profit-making potentialities, but the generalization is just as true of every story on that section.

40. "Guide to the Lands of the Northern Pacific Railroad in Minnesota," No. 44 in *Northern Pacific Railroad Pamphlets*, II. Both volumes of the *Northern Pacific Railroad Pamphlets* may be found in the library of the Minnesota Historical Society in St. Paul. Volume I includes pamphlets published before 1868 and Volume II includes those published after that date.

41. This issue of *Golden Northwest* may be found in the Minnesota State Historical Library. This issue is Volume I, Number I. The writer was unable to discover any further issues and it may be that no more were published.

42. For a complete listing of census reports, see Chapter VIII.

43. See page 205 (note 10).

44. A quotation from this editorial may be found on page 104.

45. See sections on printed promotional matter in Chapters II, III, IV, V, and VI. Samples of advertisements placed by the company may be found in the Appendix.

Chapter VIII

1. This figure was arrived at by adding yearly sales, the records which were found in the *Annual Reports* from 1882 to 1904. Totals of annual sales before 1882 were found in a letter from Kidder to Barker, February 2, 1882, No. 108 in *Letters, July 1881, to November 1883, Impression Book.* It is probable that sales of large areas to land companies are not included in this total. The total grant to the Northern Pacific as recorded in the *Annual Report* for 1892, page 50, was 46,824,960 acres. All that remained to be sold June 30, 1903, was 15,532,494 acres, according to *Annual Report* issued June 30, 1904, page 55. This would indicate that sales during this period totaled 31,292,466.

2. The raw material for these totals was found in the sources indicated in the preceding footnote. The 1870 to 1874 totals include the first nine months of 1875 and is only approximate as there seems to be no accurate record of sales during that period.

3. For a discussion of business conditions see the *Annual Reports*, 1882 to 1907.

4. Anon., "A New Immigration Movement," *Northwest*, October, 1897, 36: "We have learned from experience that people do not migrate in times of depression. No matter how clearly it can be pointed out to them that they can improve their conditions, they will not move when business is dull, property hard to sell and labor in small demand." This theory of migration is also emphasized by students of frontier history.

5. Figures previous to 1882 are taken from a letter from Kidder to Barder, February 2, 1882, No. 108 in *Letters, July 1881, to November 1883, Impression Book.* Others are from *Annual Reports.*

NOTES AND REFERENCES 209

6. The exchange of depreciated bonds for lands is thoroughly discussed in Dr. Hedges' article in the *Mississippi Valley Historical Review*, 13:311 (September, 1926). It is mentioned in chapters two and three of this thesis.

7. Figures taken from *Annual Reports*.

8. *Ibid.* For a discussion of the rise and fall of promotional efforts during the 1885 to 1893 period see Chapter IV.

9. Compilation of statistics from *Annual Reports*.

10. Compilation of data from *Abstract of the Fourteenth Census*, 1920; *Abstract of Twelfth Census*, 1900: and *Abstract of Eleventh Census*, 1890.

11. *Minnesota Census Reports*, 1870 through 1905.

12. A compilation of figures from Walker, *A Compendium of the Ninth Census; Abstract of the Twelfth Census*; and *Abstract of the Fourteenth Census*. The *Fifteenth Census*, 1930, shows one additional county, Golden Valley, on the Northern Pacific line west of Billings. There was no record of this county in the census reports studied, however.

13. *Ibid.*

14. See Chapter V, page 67 et ff.

15. See Chapter III, page 31 et ff.

16. *Abstract of the Eleventh Census, Abstract of the Twelfth Census*, and *Abstract of the Fourteenth Census*.

17. *Annual Report*, 1882, 23.

18. Winser to Oakes, August 12, 1882, No. 170 in *Letters, 1882, Impression Book*.

19. For a comparison with some of these cities in the 1885 census see Table XI, 137.

20. Winser to Oakes, August 12, 1882, No. 170 in *Letters, 1882, Impression Book*.

21. *Ibid.*

22. *Ibid.*

23. For a more complete discussion of the areas into which the railroad threw its promotion during these four periods of Land Department activity, see Chapters II, III, IV, and V. Placement of newspaper advertising is a good criterion for judging the sections from which the company desired to entice land buyers as are the placement of solicitors and the routing of lecturers and exhibit cars.

24. Hibbard to P. E. Bacon, November 18, 1872, No. 260 in *Hibbard Letters,* V.

25. Stark to Reidel, February 27, 1878, No. 187, in *George Gray Letters.*

26. See Chapter VI for a description of the company's European organization.

27. Newport to Oakes, October 18, 1881, in Unnamed book of letters, *March 1881 to November 1881.*

28. Lamborne to Kidder, January 31, 1884, No. 84 in *Letters, New Series, Land Department,* VII.

29. Qualey, "Pioneer Norwegian Settlement in North Dakota," *North Dakota Historical Quarterly,* October 1930, 16.

30. Mrs. Harriet Mickelson to the writer, February 20, 1939.

31. Mrs. Harriet Mickelson to the writer, February 5, 1939.

32. For further evidence to substantiate this conclusion see Table II, on page 54, and Tables III, on page 55.

33. Anon., "Flattering Prospects for the Northwest," interview with W. H. Phipps, *Northwest,* December, 1897, 15.

34. Copy of news story sent to *Homestead* for publication in July, 1898, in *Box 112, Advertising Contracts; Appointment of Solicitors.*

35. A compilation of figures from *Twelfth Census, Supplementary Reports,* 860-869. The state groupings include the following states:

New England: Connecticut, Rhode Island, Massachusetts, Vermont, New Hampshire, Maine
North Atlantic: New York, Pennsylvania, New Jersey
North South Atlantic: Delaware, Maryland, District of Columbia, Virginia, West Virginia
South South Atlantic: North Carolina, South Carolina, Georgia, Florida
East North Central: Ohio, Indiana, Illinois, Michigan, Wisconsin
East South Central: Kentucky, Tennessee, Alabama, Mississippi
West North Central: Minnesota, Iowa, Missouri, North Dakota, South Dakota, Nebraska, Kansas
West South Central: Louisiana, Arkansas, Indian Territory, Oklahoma, Texas

Western: Montana, Idaho, Wyoming, Colorado, New Mexico, Arizona, Utah, Nevada, Washington, Oregon California

36. *Ibid.*
37. *Ibid.*
38. *Ibid.*

Appendix

1. Page 14. This pamphlet, now incorporated as No. 37 in *Northern Pacific Railroad Pamphlets*, II, was published by Jay Cooke & Co. in 1871.

2. Nettleton to Billings, February 12, 1873, in *Nettleton Letters*, I.

3. Wilsey to Spinney, November 10, 1897, No. 925 in *Newspaper Advertising Contracts, Book 25*.

4. Printer circular inserted in *Newspaper Advertising Contracts, Clipping Book*.

5. *Newspaper Advertising Contracts, Book 25*, 262 1/2.

6. *Ibid.*, 408.

7. *Newspaper Advertising Contracts*, January 19, 1898, to August 31, 1898, 153. This advertisement was also sent to Aitkin *Republican*.

8. Loose sheet in *Newspaper Advertising Contracts, Clipping Book*.

9. *Ibid.*
10. *Ibid.*
11. *Ibid.*
12. *Ibid.* Although there is no record of it, it is very probable that this advertisement, too, was submitted for general distribution.
13. *Ibid.*
14. *Newspaper Advertising Contracts, Book 15*, 734.
15. Loose clipping in *Newspaper Advertising Contracts, Clipping Book*.
16. *Ibid.*

17. Enclosed with letter, Newport to Oakes, November 16, 1881, in Unnamed book of letters, *March 1881 to November 1881.*

18. Samples of reading notices submitted with advertisements during the earliest period of Northern Pacific promotion are located in a footnote on page 181 of this thesis.

19. *Newspaper Advertising Contracts, Clipping Book.*

20. *Newspaper Advertising Contracts, Book 25,* 661.

21. *Newspaper Advertising Contracts, Clipping Book.*

22. *Newspaper Advertising Contracts,* January 19, 1898, to August 21, 1898, 191.

23. *Newspaper Advertising Contracts, Clipping Book.*

24. *Box 112, Advertising Contracts; Appointment of Solicitors.*

Bibliography

1. Bound volumes and boxes of typewritten and handwritten letters, in the Northern Pacific storage building, St. Paul:

Foreign Agents, I, II, III, IV, V.
Lands and Colonies, I, II, III, IV.
Minnesota Agents, I, II.
Soldiers' Colonies, I.
Foreign Emigration, I.
Yeovil Colony.
Red River Colony.
Detroit Lake Colony.
Letters, New Series, Land Department, I, II, IV, V, VI, VII, VIII.
Letters, Replies to Circulars Asking Information.
Scrap Book, Miscellaneous Lands and Colonies Circulars.
Letters, Land Department, George B. Hibbard, Superintendent of Emigration.
A. B. Nettleton Letters, I, II.
Letters, Jay Cooke & Co., I.
Letters, Advertising, I.
Letters, Minnesota District, VII.
Unnamed book of letters, *March 2, 1881, to November 28, 1881.*
Newspaper Advertising Contracts, Clipping Book.
Newspaper Advertising Contracts, Book 25.
Newspaper Advertising Contracts, January 10, 1897, to January 18, 1898.
Newspaper Advertising Contracts, January 19, 1898, to August 31, 1898.
H. J. Winser, 1882.
Scrap Book of Old Printed Letters and Circulars.
Letters, Land Commissioner, March 28, 1871, to _____.
Impression Book, Letters, IV, *January 5, 1891, to August 18, 1896.*

Impression Book, Letters, Land Commissioner, IV.
Impression Book, Letters, 1882, March 6, 1882, to December 31, 1882.
Impression Book, January 19, 1883, to March 16, 1885.
Impression Book, Miscellaneous, Superintendent of Emigration, 1872.
Impression Book, George Gray Letters.
Impression Book, George B. Hibbard, Superintendent of Emigration.
Impression Book, Letters, October 10, 1886, to December 31, 1890.
Impression Book, Letters, 1883, 1884.
Impression Book, Letters, July, 1881, to November, 1883.
Box IV (1884), Miscellaneous Letters Received, (Broken Files, 1871 to 1903).
Box 112, Advertising Contracts and Appointment of Solicitors.
Land Department, Box Number 13, J. Vander Las, 1901, 1902.

2. Pamphlets and Printed Reports published by the Northern Pacific Railroad and allied organizations:

Northern Pacific Railroad Pamphlets, 2 vols.

These volumes are in the library of the Minnesota Historical Society in St. Paul. Volume one includes pamphlets published before 1868 and volume two those published after that date. Following is a partial list of those included in volume two:

No. 23, *Northern Pacific Railroad, Memorial of the Board of Directors of the Company, with communications from Lieutenant General Grant and Others,* 40th Congress, 2d session, Miscellaneous Document No. 9.

No. 24, *Northern Pacific Railroad, Statement of Its Resources and Merits as Presented to the Pacific Railroad Committee of Congress,* 1868.

No. 25, Ritz, Philip, *Letter Upon the Agricultural and Mineral Resources of the Northwest Territories on the Routes of the Northern Pacific Railroad,* 1868.

BIBLIOGRAPHY 215

No. 26, *The Northern Pacific Railway: Its Effect on the Public Credit, Speech of Honorable William Windom,* Washington, 1869.

No. 28, *Northern Pacific Railroad, Report of Edwin F. Johnson, Engineer-in-Chief, to the Board of Directors,* Hartford, Conn., 1869.

No. 29, *Wilkeson's Notes on Puget Sound,* 1869. (No place of publication).

No. 30, Roberts, W. Milner, *Special Report of a Reconnaissance of the Route for the Northern Pacific Railroad Between Lake Superior and Puget Sound,* Philadelphia, 1869.

No. 31, *Northern Pacific Railroad, The Charter and Amendments,* Philadelphia, 1869.

No. 32, *Northern Pacific Railroad, Proceedings of a Convention Held at East Saginaw, Michigan on November 23 and 24, 1869,* East Saginaw, 1869.

No. 33, *The Northern Pacific's Land Grant and the Future Business of the Road,* Philadelphia, 1870.

No. 34, *The Land Grant of the Northern Pacific Railroad, As Described in a Debate in the United States Senate,* Cambridge, Mass., 1871.

No. 36, *Speech of Colonel John S. Loomis, Land Commissioner of the Northern Pacific Railroad at Demilt Hall,* New York, New York, 1871.

No. 37, *The Northern Pacific Railroad, Its Route, Resources, Progress and Business, The New Northern Pacific and Its Great Thoroughfare,* Philadelphia, 1871.

No. 38, *The Great Thoroughfare, An Address by Hon. William D. Kelley.*

No. 39, *The Land Department of the Northern Pacific Railroad Company, Bureau of Immigration for Soldiers and Sailors, George B. Hibbard, Superintendent of Immigration,* New York, 1871.

No. 39 (a), *The New 7-30 Loan of the Northern Pacific,* Philadelphia, 1871.

No. 40, *The New Northwest, An Address by Hon. William D. Kelley,* Philadelphia, 1871.

No. 41, Garfield, S., *Climates of the Northwest,* Philadelphia, 1871.

No. 42, *Progress of the Northern Pacific Railroad, Banking House of Jay Cooke & Co.*, Philadelphia, 1871.

No. 43, *The New Northwest and Its Great Railroad, Jay Cooke & Co., Financial Agents*, Philadelphia, 1871.

No. 44, *Guide to the Lands of the Northern Pacific Railroad in Minnesota*, New York, 1872.

No. 45, *Investing Money, 7-30 Gold; A Railroad Bond and Real Estate Mortgage Combined*, Philadelphia, 1871.

No. 46, *Northern Pacific vs. St. Paul and Pacific*, Washington, 1873.

No. 47, *A Brief Statement Concerning the Proposed Legislation to Secure Early Completion of the Northern Pacific Railroad*, 1874. Wade, Benjamin F., and Potts, B.F.

No. 48, *Report of the Chief Engineer on the Unfinished Portion of the Northern Pacific Railroad, Made to the President of the Company April 27, 1874*, New York, 1874.

No. 49, *Statement of the Northern Pacific Railroad Company in Response to Inquires of the Senate Committee on Railroads*, New York, 1874.

Annual Reports, 1876, 1877, 1879-1892, 1897-1904.

The titles of these reports vary. The reports for 1876 and 1877 were entitled *Report of the President and Directors of the Northern Pacific Railroad Company to the Stockholders;* that for 1879, *Annual Report and Proceedings of the Regular Meeting of the Stockholders;* those for 1880 and 1881, *Annual Report and Proceedings of the Stockholders at Their Annual Meeting;* those for 1882 and 1883, *Report of the President to the Stockholders.* From 1884 through 1892 the reports held the title *Report of the Board of Directors to the Stockholders* and after 1897 they were known merely as *Annual Reports.*

Golden Northwest, The, St. Paul, 1880.

This is a magazine published by the Northern Pacific Land Department on April 1, 1880. It was to have been published at irregular intervals, but only this one issue was discovered. It is in the Minnesota Historical Library.

Guide to the Northern Pacific Lands in Minnesota, Boston, 1872.

Letter of John S. Loomis to Frederick Billings, Chairman of the Land Committee, February 20, 1871, Recommending a

BIBLIOGRAPHY 217

Plan for the Organization and Operation of a Land Department, Including Plans for Promoting Emigration and Land Settlement, New York, 1871.

Life of Thomas Hawley Canfield, His Connection with the Early History of the Northern Pacific Railroad, from the History of the Red River Valley, North Dakota and the Park Region of Minnesota, Burlington, Vermont, 1889.

Northern Pacific, The, Number, 1 January, 1872, Philadelphia, 1872.

Northern Pacific Business Directory for 1883 and 1884, Minneapolis, 1883.

Northern Pacific Railroad, Its Land Grant, Resources, Traffic and Tributary Country, Valley Route to the Pacific, Philadelphia, 1873.

Members of the Chicago Press, *Northern Pacific Railroad, Sketch of Its History and Descriptions of the Regions Traversed by It,* Chicago, 1882.

Official Northern Pacific Railway Guide for the Use of Tourists and Travelers over the Lines of the Northern Pacific Railway and Its Branches, St. Paul, 1889.

Opening Excursion, List of Guests, Portland, Oregon, 1883.

Opportunities, Openings for Business Locations on the Line of the Northern Pacific Railway, St. Paul, 1899.

The Pacific Northwest, New York, 1882.

Red River Country and Northwest Minnesota, Letters to the New York Times, Chicago Tribune, and Springfield Republican from Distinguished Journalist Descriptive of the Climate, Soil, Resources and Prospects of the Country Traversed by the Northern Pacific Railroad, Philadelphia, 1871.

Red River Gazette, New York, 1873.

Statement of Advantages Offered to Settlers, New York, 1871.

Villard, Henry, *Statement of Mr. Henry Villard to the Stockholders of the Northern Pacific Railroad Company,* New York, 1884.

Winser, Henry Jacob, *The Great Northwest, A Guide Book and Itinerary for the Use of Tourists and Travelers over the Lines of the Northern Pacific Railway, the Oregon Railway*

and *Navigation Company, and the Oregon and California Railway,* St. Paul, 1883.
Wonderland, A Description of the Country Traversed by the Northern Pacific, Chicago, 1888.
Wonderland Route to the Pacific Coast, The, St. Paul, 1885.

3. Periodicals:

The Bismarck Tribune.
    Files of copies published from July 11, 1873, to February 27, 1885, are in the Minnesota Historical Library.
The Minneapolis Journal.
The Minneapolis Tribune.
The Northwest, published by E. V. Smalley, St. Paul.
    Volumes 1 through 20 of this magazine are invaluable to a study of Northern Pacific Railroad promotion. *The Northwest* was subsidized by the Northern Pacific and used extensively as a promotional medium. Bound volumes may be found in the Minnesota Historical Library or in the archives of the Northern Pacific Railway Company in St. Paul.
Red River Star, Moorhead.
    Publication of this newspaper began in 1872. In 1877 the name was changed to the *Advocate* and in 1881 changed again to the *Argonaut.* Complete files are in the Minnesota Historical Library.
The St. Paul Pioneer Press.

4. Federal and State Documents:

Abstract of the Eleventh Census of the United States, 1890, Washington, 1894.
Abstract of the Twelfth Census of the United States, 1910, Washington, 1902.
Abstract of the Fourteenth Census of the United States, 1920, Washington, 1923.
Census of the State of Minnesota, June 1, 1870, St. Paul, 1871.
Census of the State of Minnesota, May 1, 1875, St. Paul, 1876.

BIBLIOGRAPHY   219

Census of the State of Minnesota, May 1, 1885, St. Paul, 1885.
Fourth Decennial Census of the State of Minnesota, June 1, 1895, St. Paul, 1895.
Fifth Decennial Census of the State of Minnesota, June 1, 1905, St. Paul, 1905.
Twelfth Census of the United States, 1900, Supplementary Analysis and Derivative Tables, Washington, 1906.
Compendium of the Ninth Census, 1870, Washington, 1872.
Compendium of the Tenth Census, 1880, 2 v., Washington, 1883.

5. **Directories and Theses:**

Ayer, N. W., *American Newspaper Annual,* 1880, Philadelphia, 1880.
Peterson, Harold Fern, *Railroads and the Settlement of Minnesota, 1862 to 1880,* Master's Thesis, University of Minnesota, 1927.
Pettengill's Newspaper Directory and Advertiser's Handbook for 1877, New York, 1877.
Read, Donald Edward, *The Development of a Northern Route to the Pacific,* Master's Thesis, University of Minnesota, Minneapolis, 1931.
Rowell, George P. and Co., *American Newspaper Directory, 1880,* New York, 1880.

6. **Books:**

Albig, William, *Public Opinion,* New York, 1939.
Andreas, A. T., *Historical Atlas of Dakota,* Chicago, 1884.
Andrews, Christopher Columbus, *The Grand Celebration of the Completion of the Northern Pacific Railroad, with St. Paul as the Eastern Terminus,* Syracuse, 1890.
Babcock, Kendrick C., *The Scandinavian Element in the United States,* Urbana, 1914.
Bailey, A., *Minnesota Railroad and River Guide for 1867, 1868,* St. Paul, 1867.
Batchelor, Bronson, *Profitable Public Relations,* New York, 1938.

Bernays, Edward L., *Crystallizing Public Opinion*, New York, 1923.
Bernays, Edward L., *Propaganda*, New York, 1928.
Blegen, Theodore C., *Norwegian Migration to America*, Northfield, 1931.
Castle, Henry Anson, *Minnesota, Its Story and Biography*, Chicago, 1915.
Childs, Harwood L., *An Introduction to Public Opinion*, New York, 1940.
Cleveland, F. A., and Powell, F. W., *Railroad Promotion and Capitalization in the United States*, New York, 1909.
Crawford, Lewis Ferandus, *History of North Dakota. North Dakota Biography by a Separate Staff of Special Writers*, Chicago, 1931.
Davenport, James, Pub., *Minnesota Tourist's and Traveler's Guide*, St. Paul, 1872.
Doob, Leonard E., *Propaganda, Its Psychology and Technique*, New York, 1935.
Emery, Grace and Rhoda J., *The Story of Minnesota*, Rochester, 1916.
Faust, Albert B., *The German Element in the United States*, Boston, 1909.
Folwell, William Watts, *History of Minnesota*, 4 v., St. Paul, 1921-1930.
Folwell, William Watts, *Minnesota, The North Star State*, Boston, 1908.
Haney, Lewis Henry, *Congressional History of Railroads in the United States, 1850-1887*, 2 v., Madison, 1908.
Hanson, Joseph H., *Grand Opening of the Northern Pacific Railway*, St. Paul, 1883.
Hedges, James Blaine, *Henry Villard and the Railways of the Northwest*, New Haven, 1930.
Hill, James J., *Highways of Progress*, New York, 1910.
Hillman, George N., *Driving the Golden Spike, The Story of a Great Achievement*, St. Paul, 1932.
History of the Red River Valley, Past and Present, Including An Account of the Counties, Cities and Villages of the Valley from the Time of Their First Settlement and Formation, by various writers, Grand Forks, 1909.

Jenks, J. W., and Lauck, W. Jett, *The Immigration Problem*, New York, 1917.
Lee, Ivy, *Publicity*, New York, 1925.
Lumley, F. E., *The Propaganda Menace*, New York, 1933.
Mattson, Hans, *Reminiscences: The Story of an Emigrant*, St. Paul, 1891.
Mayo-Smith, Richmond, *Emigration and Immigration*, New York, 1890.
McClung, John W., *Minnesota As It Is in 1870*, St. Paul, 1870.
Moody, John, *The Railroad Builders*, New Haven, 1919.
Moody, John, *The Romance of the Railways, The Northern Pacific System*, New York, 1908.
Oberholtzer, Ellis Paxson, *Jay Cooke, Financier of the Civil War*, 2 v., Philadelphia, 1907.
Orfield, Matthias Nordberg, *Federal Land Grants to the States with Special Reference to Minnesota in the University of Minnesota Studies in Social Sciences*, v. 2, Minneapolis, 1915.
Parson, E. Dudley, *The Story of Minnesota*, New York, 1913.
Paxson, Frederick L., *The History of the American Frontier*, Boston 1924.
Paxson, Frederick L., *The Last American Frontier*, New York 1910.
Presbrey, Frank, *The History and Development of American Advertising*, Garden City, 1929.
Poor, Henry Varnum, *Manual of Railroads, 1868-1920*, New York, 1868 to 1920.
Pyle, Joseph Gilpin, *The Life of James J. Hill*, New York, 1917.
Quiett, Glenn C., *They Built the West*, New York, 1934.
Riegel, Robert Edgar, *The Story of the Western Railroads*, New York, 1926.
Ringwalt, J. L., *Development of Transportation Systems*, Philadelphia, 1888.
Robinson, Edward Van Slyke, *Early Economic Conditions and the Development of Agriculture in Minnesota*, Minneapolis, 1918.
Saby, Rasmus S., *Railroad Legislation in Minnesota, 1849-1875*, St. Paul, 1912.
Sanborn, John B., *Congressional Grants of Land in the Aid of Railways in University of Wisconsin Bulletin Number*

30, Economics, Political Science, and History Series, v. 2, no. 3, Madison, 1899.
Smalley, Eugene Virgil, *History of the Northern Pacific Railroad,* New York, 1933.
Spearman, Frank Hamilton, *Strategy of Great Railroads,* New York 1904.
Stephenson, George M., *A History of American Immigration,* Boston, 1926.
Stephenson, George M., *Political History of Public Lands,* Boston, 1917.
Strand, Algot E., *A History of Swedish-Americans in Minnesota,* Chicago, 1910.
Thompson, Slason, *A Short History of American Railways,* Chicago, 1955.
Villard, Henry, *Memoirs of Henry Villard, Journalist and Financier,* Boston, 1924.
Walker, S. H., and Sklar, Paul, *Business Finds Its Voice,* New York, 1938.
Wellington, A. M., *Economic Theory of Location of Railways,* New York, 1887.
Wright, Milton, *Public Relations for Business,* New York, 1939.

7. Articles:

Appel, Livia, and Blegen, Theodore C., "Official Encouragement of Immigration to Minnesota During the Territorial Period," *Minnesota History Bulletin,* 5:167 (August, 1923).
Baker, James Heaton, "Transportation in Minnesota," *Minnesota Historical Society Collections,* 9:1 (1901).
Bent, Siles, "Ivy Lee, Minnesinger to Millions," *New Republic,* 60:369 (November 20, 1929).
Blegen, Theodore C., "The Competition of the Northwestern States for Immigrants," *Wisconsin Magazine of History,* 3:3 (September, 1919).
Blegen, Theodore C., "The Minnesota Campaign for Immigrants," *Year Book of the Swedish Historical Society of America,* 11:3 (1918).

Briggs, Harold E., "The Great Dakota Boom," *North Dakota Historical Quarterly*, 4:78 (January, 1930).

Briggs, Harold E., "The Settlement and Development of the Territory of Dakota, 1860-1870," *North Dakota Historical Quarterly*, 7:114 (1933).

Briggs, Harold E., "The Settlement and Economic Development of the Territory of Dakota," in *Abstracts from Dissertations. Graduate College State University of Iowa*, 1922-1930, pp. 89-104 (1931).

Casey, Ralph D., "The Press and Propaganda," in Mott, Frank L., and Casey R. D., eds., *Interpretations of Journalism*, New York, 1937.

Christensen, Thomas P., "Danish Settlements in Minnesota," *Minnesota History*, 8:363 (December, 1927).

Delwig, Jacob, "From Hungary to North Dakota," *North Dakota Historical Quarterly*, 3:204 (April, 1929).

Dun, Finlay, "A British Agricultural Expert in the Red River Valley, 1879," *North Dakota Historical Quarterly*, 7:94 (January, 1933).

Egan, Howard Easton, "Irish Immigration to Minnesota," *Mid-America*, 12:223 (January, 1930).

Egan, Howard Easton, "Irish Immigration to Minnesota, 1865-1890," *Mid-America*, 12:133 (October 1929).

Encyclopedia of Social Sciences, "Communication," "Propaganda."

Hanson, Marcus L., "Official Encouragement of Immigration to Iowa," *Iowa Journal of History and Politics*, 19:159 (April, 1921).

Hartsough, Mildred, "Transportation and the Twin Cities," *Minnesota History*, 7:218 (September, 1926).

Hazen, General W. B., "The Great Middle Region of the United States and Its Limited Space of Arable Land," *North American Review*, 120:21 (January, 1875).

Hedges, James B., "The Colonization Work of the Northern Pacific Railroad," *Mississippi Valley Historical Review*, 13:311 (September, 1926).

Hedges, James B., "Promotion of Immigration to the Pacific Northwest by Railroads," *Mississippi Valley Historical Review*, 15:183 (September, 1928).

Jerabek, Esther, "The Transition of a New World Bohemia," *Minnesota History*, 15:26 (March, 1934).

Lasswell, Harold D., "The Practice of Propaganda," introduction to Lasswell, H. D.; Casey, R. D.; and Smith, B. L., *Propaganda and Promotional Activities*, Minneapolis, 1935.

Larsen, Arthur J., "Early Dakota Newspapers," *Minnesota History*, 15:200 (1934).

Lee Ivy, "The Art of Publicity," in Samuel Crowther, *Book of Business*, 4:78-86.

Nute, Grace Lee, "New Light on Red River Valley History," *Minnesota History Bulletin*, 5:561 (1924).

Peterson, Harold Fern, "Some Colonization Projects of the Northern Pacific Railroad," *Minnesota History*, 10:2 (June, 1992).

Paxson, Frederick L., "The Pacific Railroads and the Disappearance of the Frontier in America," *American Historical Association Report*, 1:107 (1907).

Power, James B., "Bits of History Connected with the Early Days of the Northern Pacific and the Organization of Its Land Department," *Collections of the State Historical Society of North Dakota*, 3:337 (1910).

Pringle, Henry F., "Mass Psychologist," *American Mercury*, 19:155 (February, 1930).

Qualey, Carlton C., "Pioneer Norwegian Settlements in Minnesota," *Minnesota History*, 12:247 (September, 1931).

Qualey, Carlton C., "Pioneer Norwegian Settlements in North Dakota," *North Dakota Historical Quarterly*, 1:14 (October, 1930).

Shippee, Lester B., "The First Railroad Between the Mississippi and Lake Superior," *Mississippi Valley Historical Review*, 5:121 (September, 1918).

Smalley Eugene V., "The Story of the Northern Pacific," *Northwest*, 15:8 (October, 1897).

Smith, Alice E., "The Sweetman Irish Colony," *Minnesota History*, 9:331 (December, 1928).

Stephenson, George M., "When America Was the Land of Canaan," *Minnesota History*, 10:237 (1929).

"Settlers at Detroit Lakes Complain about Climate and Land," St. Paul *Pioneer Press*, April 16, 1872.

Upham, Warren, "The Settlement and Development of the Red River Valley," *Minnesota Historical Collections,* 8:11 (1898).

Watt, Robert, "A Danish Visitor of the Seventies," *Minnesota History,* 10:155, 309, 409 (June-December, 1929).

Acknowledgments

The Center for Western Studies acknowledges with gratitude the individuals and agencies who made possible the publication of *The Northern Pacific Railroad and the Selling of the West.*

The Augustana College Research and Artists Fund committee generously provided a student-mentor grant to support a summer of editorial work on the project by Marlene Olson and Professor Arthur R. Huseboe, and the Burlington Northern Railroad was kind enough to invite the two editors to take a promotional tour on the line from Sioux Falls to Garretson, a trip faintly reminiscent of the railroad's far-flung promotional efforts a century earlier.

Dr. Don L. Hofsommer, who provided the foreword to the book, assisted as well by reading the manuscript and identifying the photographs printed in the text.

Funding from the Sheldon Reese Foundation for an internship program at the Center for Western Studies permitted graduate intern Deborah Lyon to assist managing editor Harry F. Thompson in bringing this book to publication.

A special word of gratitude is owing to the South Dakota Humanities Council for a grant to help to inaugurate the Center's Prairie Plains Series of essential but limited-market titles at moderate prices.

Index

A
Abbott, 15, 19
Aberdeen (DT), 55
Adel (IA), 58, 59, 60
Aitkin (MN), 101, 138, 139, 140
Aitkin County (MN), 54, 63, 64, 111, 133, 134, 141
Allegheny Mountains, 74, 144, 145, 151
Allen line, 77
Alsace-Lorraine, 76, 83
American Exibition, 92
Anoka (MN), 138, 139
Anoka County (MN), 133, 134
Arthur, President, 42
Altantic Ocean, xi, 76, 85
Audubon, 140
Austin (MN), 62
Austria 75, 149

B
Baltimore, xi
Baltimore & Ohio, xi
Baptist, 75
Barnes County (DT), 111, 136, 142
Barney, A. H., 28
Barney, W. J., 4
Barrows, 17
Becker County (MN), 102, 111, 133, 134, 135, 141, 146
Belfield (DT), 30
Belgium, 1
Belt Mountains, xvi, 2, 137
Belleville (IL), 22
Benton County (MN), 133, 134
Berlin, 89, 90
Berra, 120
Billings (MT), 69, 74, 75
Billings County (DT), 136
Billings, Frederick, 9, 18, 26, 83, 87, 89, 106, 108
Bismarck (DT), 31, 70, 118, 142
Blatchford, 118
Bluffton (MN), 136
Bohemia, 149

Boone (IA), 56
Boseman (MT), 2
Boston, xii, 10, 15, 16, 17, 19, 28, 32, 39, 95
Bowles, Samuel, 11, 25
Brainerd (MN), 10, 14, 18, 28, 70, 105, 109, 111, 116, 138, 139, 140
Breckenridge (MN), 70
Briggs, Harold, 6
British Empire, 87
Bryan, Clark M., 11, 15, 25
Buffalo (NY), 39
Burleigh County (DT), 55, 112, 136, 142
Butte (MT), 2

C
Canada, 19, 39, 87, 142
Canada Pacific, 59
Carbon County (MT), 137
Cardo (IA), 59, 60
Carlton County (MN), 108, 133, 134, 141
Carrington (DT) 30, 58, 59, 60, 64, 66, 67
Casey, Ralph D., xix
Cass, Cheney, 35
Cass County (DT), 111, 133, 134, 136, 141, 142
Cass, George W., 35
Casselton (DT), 142
Castle Garden (NY), 77, 78
Catholic, 85
Central Pacific, xii
Charles Meyer and Co., 90
Cheyenne River, 29
Chicago, xii, 21, 27, 32, 33, 40, 41, 42, 55, 95
Chicago Exposition, 21
Chicago, Milwaukee & St. Paul, 4
Chisago County (MN), 133, 134
Christiania, 90
Church of Sweden, 75
Churdan (IA), 60, 67
Cincinnati, 33, 39
Civil War, xii, xv, 3, 10, 15, 16
Clay County (MN), 133, 134, 135, 141, 146

Cleveland, 39
Coffin, Charles Carleton, 15, 16, 17, 20, 25
Colfax (WA), 28
Colorado, 106
Columbia River, xii
Columbus (OH), 39
Commercial Club Cycle, 70
Como (MN), 122
Congregational Church, 108
Congress, xii
Cooke, Jay, xiii, 2, 3, 74, 115
Council Bluffs (IA), xii
Corvin, von, 74, 76
Creamer, Joseph, 32
Cross, Adrian, 67
Crow Indians, 43
Crow Wing County (MN) 111, 133, 134, 135
Cunard line, 77
Custer County (MT), 137

D
Dakota Territory, 1, 2, 5, 7, 29, 40, 41, 44, 46, 47, 61, 62, 83, 91, 97, 101, 102, 111, 131, 136, 140, 142
Dana, Charles A., 11, 25
Dawson County (MT), 137
Deer Lodge (MT), 20
Denmark, 33, 34, 39, 73, 75, 79, 80, 86, 149
Des Moines (IA), 54, 55, 64
Detroit, 13, 39, 109, 138, 139, 140
Detroit Lakes (MN), 109
Devils Lake (DT), 58
Dickinson (DT), 30, 69, 70
Dodge, H. C., 68
Dodge County (MN), 108
Drummond, Willis, 55, 64, 71, 72
Dudley, James G., 13, 15, 17, 20, 21, 86, 88, 91
Duluth, 10, 15, 16, 18, 77, 138, 139, 140
Duluth/Superior, xii

E
Elizabeth (MN), 140
England, 6, 28, 33, 34, 39, 42, 74, 75, 79, 83, 85, 92, 108, 144, 149, 150, 151, 152

F
Fargo (DT), 29, 31, 32, 35, 70, 85, 111, 140, 142
Fergus Falls (MN), 140
Finland, 33, 73
Foster County (DT), 136

Foster County (IA), 58
France, 83, 84, 152
Franco-Prussian War, 74, 83
Frankfurt, 74, 81, 89
Freeborn County (MN), 146

G
Garfield, 13, 26, 100, 101, 106, 107, 112, 113
Garfield, S., 61, 62
Gattschald, A. M., xix
Germany, xiii, 6, 9, 12, 33, 35, 39, 42, 72, 74, 75, 76, 79, 80, 85, 86, 89, 90, 149, 150, 151, 152
Gladstone (DT), 30
Glen Ullin (DT), 30
Glydon, 10, 18, 138, 139
Georgetown (ND), 102
Goegg, Armand, 76
Goerdeler, R. 81
Goodhue County (MN), 94, 146
Gordon, Lord Gordon, 17
Grand Army of the Republic (G.A.R.), 10
Grand Forks (ND), 64
Grant, U. S., 42
Great Britain, 77, 79, 80, 86
Great Northern, xiv, 59, 60
Great Plains, xiii
Gudgel, J. T., 59

H
H. P. Hall Advertising Agency, 55
Halsted, Murat, 40
Haskell, F. N., 22
Haynes, F. Jay, 35
Hays, W. M. 101
Heaton, George, 59, 60, 67
Hedges, James B., xvi, xvii, xviii
Helena (MT), 2, 69, 86
Hendry, Joseph, 41
Hennepin County (MN), 133, 134
Hibbard, George B., xix, 9, 10, 11, 14, 19, 20, 22, 23, 73, 77, 84, 91, 144
Hofsommer, Don L., xiv
Hogue, H. A., 67
Holland, 1, 9, 33, 80, 85, 86
Hunt, Walter, xix

I
Idaho Territory, 1, 2, 29, 49
Illinois, 54, 55, 61, 63, 70, 144, 146, 150
Indiana 1, 61, 146
Indianapolis, 7, 39, 55

INDEX 229

Indians, 2, 91
Inman line, 77
International Exposition, 90, 91, 92
Iowa, xi, xiii, 4, 35, 51, 52, 53, 54, 55, 56, 57, 58, 61, 64, 66, 69, 70, 101, 102, 103, 144, 145, 146, 147, 150
Iowa City, 66
Ireland, 5, 79, 84, 148, 151, 152

J

Jaeger, C., 81
James River, 29, 111
Jamestown (ND), 70, 142
Jay Cooke & Co., xv, xvi, 1, 2, 4, 9, 11, 14, 15, 19, 21, 25, 27, 74, 78, 100
Jenkins, J. H., 22
Jenkins, Joseph J., 49
Johnson, O. J., 90

K

Kansas, 4, 25, 61, 104, 146, 150
Kansas City, 55
Kansas Pacific, 4
Kansas Pacific Land Company, 4
Kelley, 13
Kentucky, 146
Kidder County (DT), 55, 112, 136, 142
Kidder, L. R., 29, 32, 81
Kindred, C. F., 22

L

LaMoure (DT), 30, 31
Lake Michigan, xi
Lake Superior, 1, 2, 30, 42, 75, 101, 111
Lake Superior & Mississippi Railroad, 75, 76
Lamborne, 30, 33, 34, 37, 39, 145
Las, J. Vander, 69, 71
Lesneski, J. J., xix
Lincoln, Abraham, xii, 1
Lindau, Leopold, 89
Linsley, D. C., 91
Lisbon (DT), 30
Little Falls (MN), 138, 139, 140
Little Rock & Fort Smith, 4
Liverpool, 9, 80, 81
Livingston (MT), 41
London, 9, 16, 74, 79, 92, 104
Loomis, John S., 9, 12, 17, 22, 23

M

Madelia (MN), 63
Madison (WI), 55

Mankato (MN), 108
Marvin, Luke, 15
Maryland, 21
Massachusetts, 105
Mattson, Hans, 7, 75, 76, 86
McGinnis, David R., 55, 56, 61, 62
McLean County (ND), 55
Mecklenburg, 85
Mellen, President, 52
Memphis, xii
Mennonite, 85
Mexican War, xii
Michigan, 35, 75
Mickelson, Sig, xiv
Middle States, xii
Middle Atlantic States, 143
Miles City (MT), 69
Miller, John, 94
Milwaukee, xii
Milwaukee Road, xiv
Minneapolis, 16, 20, 41, 42, 47, 55, 108, 138, 139, 140
Minnesota, xvi, 1, 2, 4, 5, 7, 11, 12, 17, 20, 21, 23, 27, 29, 44, 46, 47, 50, 51, 52, 53, 54, 55, 56, 58, 60, 63, 64, 66, 68, 69, 70, 71, 73, 76, 77, 78, 83, 93, 94, 97, 101, 102, 104, 105, 107, 108, 109, 110, 111, 116, 122, 130, 131, 132, 133, 138, 139, 140, 141, 142, 144, 145, 148, 149, 150, 151, 152
Minnesota Historical Society, xiv, xviii
Minnesota State Fair, 63
Minnesota State Experimental Farm, 101
Minnesota, University of, xvi, xix, 101, 112
Mississippi River, xi, xiv, 106
Missouri, 4, 105
Missouri River, xii, 28, 29, 44, 46, 47, 61, 111, 112, 118, 136, 140
Montague, F., 16
Montana, xiii, xvi, 1, 2, 5, 13, 24, 30, 33, 34, 38, 40, 43, 46, 47, 49, 61, 62, 69, 70, 74, 75, 91, 100, 106, 119, 121, 132, 137, 138, 146, 148, 149, 151, 153
Moorhead (MN), 70, 140
Morris (MN), 68
Morrison County (MN) 133, 134
Morton County (DT), 136

N

N. W. Ayer and Son, 39
Nafziger, Ralph O., xix
Nash, William, 59

National Line, 77
National Editorial Association, 89
Nebraska, 4, 25, 51, 53, 54, 55, 70, 105, 146, 150
Netherlands, 6
Nettleton, A. B., xix, 4, 12, 13, 14, 15, 17, 18, 21, 22, 26, 77, 78, 87, 88, 92, 106, 108
New Buffalo (DT), 142
New Brunswick, 15, 19
New England, xii, xiii, 1, 10, 11, 19, 35, 108, 125, 142, 148, 150, 151
New Orleans, xii
New Salem (DT), 30
New York, 10, 11, 15, 19, 20, 21, 28, 33, 39, 41, 54, 74, 77, 108, 145
New York Central, xi
New York City, 77, 90, 95, 104
Newport, R. M., 28, 29, 39, 40, 43, 144
Nillsson, Alex, 86, 87
North Atlantic, 149, 150, 151
North Central, 148, 149, 150, 151, 152
North Dakota, 6, 29, 30, 35, 44, 46, 47, 49, 50, 55, 56, 57, 58, 61, 63, 64, 66, 68, 69, 70, 71, 73, 100, 102, 103, 106, 111, 117, 118, 120, 130, 131, 132, 135, 138, 139, 141, 142, 145, 146, 148, 149, 150, 151
North Dakota Badlands, 35
Northfield (MN), 108
Northwest, xiv, xvii, 5, 11, 20, 25, 27, 31, 83, 87, 90, 91, 92, 98, 101, 102, 104, 105, 106, 107, 108, 109, 110, 113, 146, 152, 153, 154
Norway, xiii, 33, 34, 39, 73, 75, 79, 80, 85, 86, 93, 145, 149, 150, 151, 152
Nova Scotia, 15, 19

O

Oakes, Thomas F. 30, 37, 43, 86, 144
Ohio, 1, 146
Ohio River, xi
Omaha, xii, 55
Ontario, xii
Oregon, 1, 13, 34, 38
Oregon Railway and Navigation Co., 81
Oregon Steamship Company, 28, 34
Osgood, Ernest S., xix
Ottertail County (MN), 133, 134, 141
Ottertail Lake, 14

P

Pacific Northwest, xvi
Pacific Ocean, xii, xiv, 1, 30, 61, 106

Panic of 1873, xiii
Paris, 83
Park (MT), 137
Parker, A. D., 60
Parker, A. W., 66
Park Region (MN), 109
Pelican Rapids (MN), 140
Pennsylvania, 35, 145
Pennsylvania, The, xi
Perrin, L. L., xix
Perry (IA), 58, 59
Peterson, Harold F., xvi, xvii, xviii
Pettengill, S. M., 19
Philadelphia, 11, 15, 16, 28, 32, 36, 39, 95
Phipps, William H., 64; 65, 146
Pine County (MN), 133, 134
Pittsburgh, 16, 55
Poland, 149
Polk County (MN), 141
Pomerania, 85
Portland, xii, 28, 39, 95
Posen, 85
Potts, B. F., 24
Power, James B., 21, 28, 32, 35, 84, 110
Prairie County (MT), 137
Primghar (IA), 64, 101
Protestants, 85
Prussia, 85
Pudget Sound, xii, 1, 2

Q

Qualey, Carlton C., 145
Quebec, xii
Quigg, L. E., 49
Quincy (IL), 23

R

Ramsey County (MN), 133, 134
Raymond, Henry W., 40
Red River Valley, xiii, 11, 29, 64, 101, 111, 112, 136, 146
Red Water (MT), 71
Redpath, James, 17
Richard, J. H., 102
Richardton (DT), 30
Rhodes, J. M., 69
Riegel, 16
Robinson, John F., 68
Rochester (NY), 39
Rocky Mountains, 13, 106
Roedelheimer, A., 78, 81, 87
Rogers, 108
Rosebud County (MT), 137

INDEX 231

Russia, 85, 149, 151
Russian-Germans, 151

S

Sacramento, xii
Sadtler, Samuel P., 101, 112
St. Cloud (MN), 138, 139, 140
St. John (New Brunswick), 15
St. Louis, xii, 41, 141
St. Louis County (MN), 111, 133, 134
St. Paul, xviii, 9, 17, 20, 21, 27, 28, 33, 35, 37, 42, 49, 52, 53, 55, 59, 61, 62, 64, 65, 67, 70, 77, 95, 138, 139, 140
St. Paul & Pacific, 4
San Francisco, xi, xii, 20
Santa Fe, 4
Sauk Rapids (MN), 140
Sault Ste. Marie, xii
Scandinavia, 6, 7, 9, 32, 75, 76, 79, 90
Schilling, Baron von, 35
Schleswig-Holstein, 85
Schroeder, John, 12
Schwarm, L. L, xix
Scotland, 75, 79, 84, 149, 152
Sears, John W., 14, 22, 78
Seattle, xii
Seeger, Charles, 23
Sheppard, George, xix, 9, 16, 20, 28, 73, 74, 75, 76, 78, 79, 83, 85, 87, 89, 90, 92, 144
Sherburne County (MN), 133, 134
Shippe, Lester B., xix
Simmon, Karl, 69
Sly, 86
Smalley, Eugene V., 3, 31, 36, 37, 38, 40, 41
Smithfield (London), 92
Snyder, Bertram, 15
Soldier's Colony, 13, 17
Soo Railway, 59
South Atlantic, 148
South Central, 148
South Dakota, 4, 51, 53, 54, 55, 70, 150
Spinney, Goerge W., 51, 57
Sprague, J. W., 34
Springfield, 15, 16
Stark, 32, 35
Stark County (DT), 136
Stearns County (MN), 133, 134
Steele (ND), 61, 68
Stephens, W. E., 60
Stephenson, George M. 5, 6
Stewart, C. A., 23

Stewart, D. M., 66
Stillwater County (MT), 137
Stutsman County (DT), 111, 136, 142
Superior, xii, 64
Sweden, xiii, 33, 34, 39, 73, 75, 79, 80, 85, 86, 93, 94, 149, 150, 151, 152
Switzerland, 76, 79, 80

T

Tacoma, ii
Taylor, Bayard, 11, 25
Taylorville (IL), 63
Texas, 105
Thomson (MN), 140
Todd County (MN), 133, 134, 141
Tower City (DT), 142
Treasure County (MT), 137
Tustin, J. P., 75
Twin Bridges (MT), 121

U

Union Pacific, xii, 4
United Kingdom, xiii, 84, 145, 152
Utica, 22

V

Valley City (DT), 117, 142
Vanbergen, 60, 67
Vermont, 16
Vicksburg, xii
Vienna, 90, 92
Villard, Henry, xvi, 28, 29, 33, 34, 38, 40, 41, 42, 43, 45, 81, 114

W

Wackerhagen, 22
Wakeman (OH), 23
Wadena (MN), 70, 111, 133, 134, 138, 139, 140, 141
Wahpeton (DT), 70
Wales, 75, 79, 152
Wales, William, 15
Washington County (MN), 133, 134
Washington Territory, 1, 2, 13, 28, 34, 40, 46, 47, 49, 61, 100, 101, 131, 148, 149
Webster City (IA), 102
Wemyss, R. J., 44
West, 148, 151
West Virginia, 145
Weyerhauser, Frederick, 47
Wheatland (DT), 142
Whitman, James, 19
Whitman, John W., 14

Whitney, Asa, xii
Wibaux County (MT), 137
Wilkeson, Samuel, 20
Williams, James B., 90
Willis, Harvey, 58, 59
Wilsey, F. W., xix, 51, 52, 53, 55, 56, 57, 58, 59, 60, 61, 62, 63, 64, 65, 67, 71, 72, 146, 147
Winona (MN), 61, 108
Winser, H. J., 29, 30, 33, 35, 36, 40, 41, 42, 43

Wisconsin, xiii, 34, 35, 70, 144, 145, 146, 150
World War I, xv
World's Fair, 65
Wright, George, 41
Wyoming, 106

Y

Yellowstone National Park, 35, 42, 49, 52, 79
Young, Edward, 7, 84, 86